FORGING LINKS

Recent Titles in
Praeger Series in Applied Psychology

Family and Peers: Linking Two Social Worlds
Kathryn A. Kerns, Josefina M. Contreras, and Angela M. Neal-Barnett, editors

FORGING LINKS

African American Children
Clinical Developmental Perspectives

Edited by Angela M. Neal-Barnett,
Josefina M. Contreras, and Kathryn A. Kerns

Foreword by Bertha Garrett Holliday

Praeger Series in Applied Psychology
Stevan E. Hobfoll, Series Adviser

Westport, Connecticut
London

Library of Congress Cataloging-in-Publication Data

Forging links: African American children clinical developmental perspectives / edited by Angela M. Neal-Barnett, Josefina M. Contreras, and Kathryn A. Kerns ; foreword by Bertha Garrett Holliday.

p. cm.—(Praeger series in applied psychology)

Includes bibliographical references and index.

ISBN 0–275–96783–2 (alk. paper)

1. Afro-American children—Social conditions. 2. Afro-American children—Psychology. 3. Afro-American children—Race identity. 4. Developmental psychology—United States. 5. Afro-American families. I. Neal-Barnett, Angela M., 1960– II. Contreras, Josefina M., 1960– III. Kerns, Kathryn A., 1961– IV. Series.

E185.86.F66 2001

305.231'089'96073—dc21 00–044591

British Library Cataloguing in Publication Data is available.

Library of Congress Catalog Card Number: 00–044591
ISBN: 0–275–96783–2

First published in 2001

Praeger Publishers, 88 Post Road West, Westport, CT 06881
An imprint of Greenwood Publishing Group, Inc.
www.praeger.com

Printed in the United States of America

The paper used in this book complies with the Permanent Paper Standard issued by the National Information Standards Organization (Z39.48–1984).

10 9 8 7 6 5 4 3 2 1

*To Andrew and Doris Neal and Louise and Edgar Barnett, Sr.,
whose support, encouragement, and prayers made this book a reality*

Contents

Illustrations

FIGURES

TABLES

Foreword

Bertha Garrett Holliday

This is a postmodern book. Its contributors are concerned with the types of issues confronting African American parents and children now, during an era of both unparalleled prosperity, including the entrenchment of the largest African-descent middle class in the world, and simultaneous and continuing patterns of racial inequality and disparities in almost all arenas of human activity. In such a situation (where social structures that support segregation and racism are not readily visible, but instead assume subtle forms) what are the varying values, sensibilities, and resources that African American families and children bring to the tasks of both promoting behaviors that are necessary for successful engagement in the technological and social changes of the twenty-first century, and assuring some continuity in those patterns of adaptive and problem-solving behaviors that are culturally and historically rooted (and therefore, quite often at the center of the group's identity)?

These are the types of questions this book's contributors lay claim to—and they make it clear that the answers are not simple. For example, the book's contributors point out the paucity of research data on the normal developmental and socialization pathways of African American children. They note the array of options and opportunities that are differentially available to varying sectors of African American communities.

The book's contributors also remind us that child development and socialization are shaped not only by biological and family factors, but also by social–economic, historical, ecological, and cultural factors. In the case of African American families and their children, cultural factors often have served as means for promoting continuity within the group and across time and generations. However, social–economic, ecological, and historical factors have tended to be sources of discontinuity and new challenges (Holliday, 1986).

Indeed, challenges confronting today's African American children are to a great extent rooted in this nation's most significant domestic social change associated with the pursuit of twentieth century modernity: the Civil Rights Era. This era began in 1954 when the U.S. Supreme Court issued its decision on *Brown v. Topeka Board of Education* that resulted in dismantling legal racial segregation in the nation's public schools. During the following twenty years, local, state, and federal laws were enacted that assured African Americans voting rights as well as access to the nation's public accommodations (e.g., hotels, restaurants, theaters, and other common-use facilities). In addition, a variety of new federal and state legislation and regulations served to promote nondiscriminatory and equal treatment in a variety of arenas and venues, including housing and employment.

Access to the "new" settings radically changed the contexts of African American child development and socialization. Indeed, in no more than a blink of the historical eye, African American families were expected to not only choose among the growing range of options in a highly informed, strategic, and appropriate manner, but also to make aggressive and effective use of resources found in the new settings whose rules and rituals were at best partially understood. As one would expect, the outcomes of such choice and use were highly variable. Often "success" was related to the psychological, social, and economic resources that were available to individuals prior to their entry into new settings. Consequently, we currently are witnessing an unprecedented social–economic bifurcation of the U.S. African American community.

Two generations of African American children have come of age since the beginning of the Civil Rights Era. And it is the children of these two generations who are the focus of this book. The challenges confronting these children are unique—as are the strengths which must be fostered in support of their optimal development and socialization in the postmodern era of the twenty-first century.

REFERENCE

Holliday, B. G. (1986). African-American families and social change: 1940 to 1980. *Family Perspective Journal, 20* (4), 289–305.

Acknowledgments

Many people helped make this book possible. The forum community participants, including Libert and Madeline Bozelli, Jessica Henderson Daniel, Bertha Holliday, Winston Travis, Pastor Bill and Marsha Mitchell, Minister Herman and Orzella Matherson, Evaughn and Alex Caugle, Jeanette Reuter, and Gloria McCullough, whose insightful comments during the forum helped shape many of these chapters. Thanks also to Margaret Ralston Payne and Bonnie Wojno, whose commitment to development and outreach insured the research was integrated into the community. Edgar Barnett, Jr., who embodies the phrase "supportive spouse" also deserves acknowledgments. Finally, thanks to Kathleen Floody, whose care and attention to the structure of the forum and the structure of this volume allowed the forum participants, editors, and authors to focus on content.

Introduction

Angela M. Neal-Barnett

Several years ago, I interviewed an African American mother and her teenage daughter.[1] The daughter described for me what it was like to be a high-achieving black female in a predominantly white school and how she felt unaccepted by both her black and white peers. Her mother acknowledged that the daughter had told her about the difficulties she was having with the other students. The mother believed that if her daughter simply continued to treat people well, everything would be all right. Upon hearing her mother's assertion, the daughter turned to me and said with a resigned sigh, " My mother doesn't understand what it means to be a Black kid."

I embarked on planning the 1999 Kent Psychology Forum, the think tank that spawned this volume, I found myself reflecting on the words the teenager had spoken two years earlier. Far too many individuals in this society don't understand what it means to be an African American and under 18 at the beginning of the twenty-first century. Thanks to the Civil Rights Movement and affirmative action programs, today's African American child and adolescent have far more opportunities than his or her parents or grandparents. But with new opportunities come new obstacles. Whereas some of the issues faced by African American children and adolescents are similar to past generations, new issues have arisen that warrant investigation.

In examining the existing literature, it is clear that the majority of research on black children fails to consider variables salient to this ethnic group. In this volume, several of the authors address issues examining racial identity (Robert M. Sellers, Program for Research on Black Americans, University of Michigan), racial socialization (Deborah J. Johnson, Institute for Children, Youth, and Families, Michigan State University), and acting white (Angela M. Neal-Barnett, Program For the Study of Anxiety Disorders in African Americans, Kent State University). Furthermore, the child research often fails to take into account variables that apply to all children that may have a different impact for black children. Thus, other authors in this volume examine traditional child variables, such as the effects of teen parenthood on African American males (Waldo E. Johnson, Jr., School of Social Service Administration, University of Chicago), and poverty (Ronald D. Taylor, Department of Psychology and the Center for Research in Human Development and Education, Temple University), violence (Esther J. Jenkins, director of research at the Community Mental Health Council, Inc., and Chicago State University), and sport participation (Robert E. Stadulis, graduate coordinator of the Sport Studies Program in the School of Exercise, Leisure and Sport, Kent State University; Gary Waters, head men's basketball coach, Kent State University; and Angela M. Neal-Barnett) on black adolescents.

In setting the goals for the 1999 forum and this volume, I wanted to make a contribution to increasing our understanding and knowledge of the psychology of African American children and adolescents. Three goals were delineated: (1) to bring together active and dedicated persons interested in understanding the triumphs and challenges of growing up African American, (2) to facilitate interaction between those doing research and individuals from the community who work with African American children and adolescents on a daily basis, and (3) to bring awareness of the research on African American children and awareness to the community.

To achieve these goals, this forum would be different than other scientific workshops. Rather than a think tank consisting of researchers and graduate students only, I wanted to form a microcosm of people who cared about black children and adolescents. Therefore, this forum consisted of researchers, graduate students, parents, grandparents, ministers, counselors–social workers, coaches, educators, and clinic administrators. The entire group, thirty-three strong, converged for three days of virtual seclusion at an Amish country resort. Very quickly, the group began to coalesce. Everyone realized what a rare opportunity we had been afforded: three days to focus exclusively on black children and adolescents. As the first presenter on the first night of the forum, Robert Sellers said, "We are here to talk about Black children, everything else is inconsequential."

For three days and three nights, our conversations centered on African American children and adolescents. By the third day, it was difficult to determine who was a researcher and who was a community representative, because of the open discussion groups that met throughout the forum. Everyone was focused on making sure that what came out of this forum impacted on the lives of black children and adolescents. For example, Waldo Johnson's presentation reconfirmed for agency administrators the need to focus more programming towards adolescent fathers. Several collaborations were formed between scholars and community participants. These collaborations allowed for the integration of the scholar's research into an existing program.

The forum did not end with the conclusion of the think tank. After the van left carrying many of the presenters to the airport, several forum participants returned to Akron, Ohio for a community presentation at the Arlington Church of God. The speaker for that evening was forum participant Jessica Henderson Daniel, who spoke on the "five Ms of preparing African American children for success." An audience of 400 African American men, women, and children listened and took notes as Dr. Daniel spoke about the importance of mentoring, memories, monitoring, mastery, and mantras. More importantly, the audience left the church with information they could use in their own lives and in their interactions with African American children. The community colloquium and its outcome fulfilled the third goal of the forum, to bring awareness of the research to the community.

In the pages that follow, you will read chapters that grew out of the presentations and discussions at the 1999 Kent State Psychology Forum. Some are theoretical, others are empirical; most combine qualitative and quantitative data. The chapters will introduce the reader to recent psychological research and information on African American children and adolescents as well as make the reader think critically about their own research or programs. As senior editor, I am confident that after reading this book, you will have increased your understanding of what it means to be a "black kid."

NOTE

1.Throughout this volume the terms African American and black are used interchangeably.

1

Psychopathology and Assessment in African American Children and Families: A Historical, Ecological, and Strength-Based Perspective

Michael Canute Lambert, Faith Markle, and Valerie François Bellas

Many researchers (e.g., Coll et al., 1996) have voiced concerns regarding the paucity of culturally relevant and coherent theoretical perspectives on children of color (e.g., Gibbs, 1998) and some scholars have (e.g., Cauce, Ryan, & Grove, 1988; Graham, 1992) documented the subsequent absence of culturally relevant, theoretically driven empirical investigations on normal development in children and adolescents of color (McLoyd & Steinberg, 1998). The lack of focus on this group of children and the changing demographics from a white majority to that reflecting people of color (Cauce et al., 1988; McLoyd, 1999) have provided a groundswell in professional ranks for more directed and intense foci on children and adolescents of color (Cauce, Ryan, & Grove, 1988). An example of the response to the critical need to address normal development in children and adolescents of color is the well-noted Society for Research in Child Development 1995 roundtable conference, which focused on developmental issues associated with children of color and its catalytic effect on the recent appearance of volumes focusing exclusively on children and adolescents of color (e.g., Fitzgerald, Lester, & Zuckerman, 1999; McLoyd & Steinberg, 1998). A well-represented theme that runs throughout the volumes, book chapters, and journal articles on children of color is that our understanding of normal development in these children is at best riddled with lacuna and at worst absent (Fabrega, Ulrich, & Loeber, 1996; Cauce, Ryan, & Grove,

1988). We submit that the dearth of clinical, theoretical, and research literature as it pertains to developmental psychopathology and the assessment of strengths and psychopathology in children of color is equally abysmal (Williams & Fenton, 1994).

The recent upsurge of interest in children and adolescents of color is laudable and should be encouraged for the benefit of our population of color and our nation as a whole. We must, nevertheless, begin to move from consistently calling for more culturally relevant theoretical models and culturally sensitive research design in the present literature to beginning to produce and amass a literature base that builds on the foundation of recently espoused theoretical models and generate research that bolsters, modifies, or refutes them. Moreover, the results of our scientific inquiry should begin to inform both policy formulations and intervention decisions regarding children of color. Achieving these goals will move us from treating the critical issues associated with children of color "like the weather," wherein almost everyone talks about it but simultaneously feels powerless to do anything about it (McLoyd & Steinberg, 1998).

This chapter focuses on African American children and adolescents, who are members of the largest minority group in our nation and according to students of this population (e.g., Taylor & Katz, 1996) are members of at least two groups (i.e., minorities and being children or adolescents) who are deemed at risk for the development of psychopathology (American Psychological Society Human Capital Initiative, 1996). First, we briefly focus on the history of African Americans in the United States and how this history and its resulting present-day impact have shaped and continues to shape the development and behavior of African American children. Second, we address the society and culture where African American youth reside, the reality it affords them, and how it influences their developmental process and behavioral outcomes. Third, we examine the strengths that African American children develop from their cultural backgrounds and the societal difficulties they confront. We also discuss psychopathology in African American youth within an ecological and sociocultural framework. Finally, we address problems associated with appropriate measurement of strengths and psychopathology in African American youth and how our own research program is addressing some deficits in this area.

HISTORICAL ISSUES

African American history continues to have an impact on the health and well-being of modern African Americans (McAdoo, 1993). The economy of the United States was dependent for three and a half centuries on the labor of slaves, from whom most modern African Americans descend. Many beliefs, attitudes, practices, and traditions created by the institution of slavery persist to this day. For example, European American culture was founded on a zealous belief in the rights and liberties of all people (Comer, 1995), so to justify slavery, the slaves could not be perceived as people. Race was therefore defined as a genetic characteristic and African Americans as an inferior or subhuman race (Coll et al., 1996; McLoyd & Ceballo, 1998). The notion that there are systematic genetic differences between Caucasian Americans and African Americans endures. This notion is still used to "explain" differences in IQ, academic achievement, physical health, behavior problems, and unemployment rates, and to justify not looking to social causes for these differences (Fischer et al., 1996; Samuda, 1998).

Systemic racism remains an institution by which the white dominant group maintains economic, social, and psychological advantage at the expense of blacks and other minorities who have limited control of economic resources (Comer, 1995). Despite the steps that our nation has made toward desegregation, segregation continues as a way of life for many African American youth. The movement of industry and commerce from cities to suburban areas by white business owners and the subsequent flight of middle class whites from the cities has left a concentration of minority groups in the inner cities with limited economic bases (Fabrega, Ulrich, & Mezzich, 1993). As a result, African American children must cope with not only the normal developmental challenges all children face, but also the additional hurdles imposed by poor living conditions and unsafe neighborhoods (McLoyd & Ceballo, 1998; Steward et al., 1998).

Although middle-class black youth may not face all the challenges their poorer, inner-city peers confront, they still encounter obstacles to optimal development. Their families are generally less well off than their white counterparts, so they must live with the ever-present reality that economic emergencies may push them below the poverty line (McLoyd & Ceballo, 1998). Our recent study of more than 20 focus groups, which surveyed approximately 300 African American youth and parents, teachers, and clinicians of African American children, revealed that worrying about family problems, including economic difficulties, is a major concern for black youth (Lambert, François-Bellas, & Markle, 1999). An additional hurdle for middle-class black youth living in predominantly white neighborhoods and towns is the danger of overidentifying with the white culture and "joining the scapegoating of their own." (Comer, 1995, p. 161). Isolation from other African Americans may deprive these children of the protective effects of strong bonds to an extended family and supportive community.

Despite their socioeconomic status or wealth, all black youth live with the message from the dominant culture that they are inferior, inadequate, evil, and are unworthy of the rights and privileges the U.S. society offers (Comer, 1995). To survive, black families and children must develop specific strategies. Some are adaptive, while others are costly. Some of these strategies are described next.

Behavioral Outcomes of African American Children and Adolescents

Their history and its consequences have a profound effect on the adaptive functioning of black families and children (e.g., McAdoo, 1993). Although systematic research on behavioral outcomes is virtually nonexistent, professionals (e.g., Boyd-Franklin, 1989) theorize that despite the harsh reality in which many black children and their families reside, there are specific strengths within black families that buffer children from the detriment of being born and raised in a racist environment. These strengths have allowed many black youths to survive and often thrive in spite of the odds stacked against them. Boyd-Franklin (1989) listed strong religious–spiritual orientation, emphasis on the value of education, a strong work ethic, the presence of a widely extended family, and the ability to develop and use coping skills (e.g., role flexibility) as major sources of strength within the black family when faced with adversity including economic hardship.

Unfortunately, like other constructs associated with healthy functioning in black children and families, these factors are rarely documented via empirical efforts. Nevertheless, our recent focus group study (Lambert et al., 1999) revealed that when African American adolescents, their parents, teachers, and clinicians were asked about strengths evident in African American youth, spirituality and acceptance of religious teaching, having a sense of humor, getting along with parents and siblings, acknowledgment of and respect for one's family members and particularly one's elders, and strong values regarding education and work were salient strengths mentioned.

These findings were also evident in a recent empirical study of black adolescents living in an urban setting. Their psychological adjustment was closely linked to their sense of humor, social and spiritual support, perceived level of intimacy, and support from their family (Piatt et al., 1993; Steward et al., 1998). Besides these strengths, scholars focusing on black youth have noted that despite normal life challenges and other difficulties that outsiders may consider insurmountable but that are closely linked to their own survival (Steward et al., 1998). Black children are less vulnerable to specific types of problems that plague their white counterparts. Black youths, especially black females are less likely to engage in the consumption of alcohol and are less likely to commit suicide or die in automobile-related accidents than their white counterparts (Gibbs, 1998). They are also less likely to be diagnosed with eating disorders (Fabrega, Ulrich, & Mezzich, 1993). Unfortunately the protective factors that contribute to the strengths and resilience in African American youth are poorly documented, seldom included in assessment measures, and are subsequently misunderstood or neglected.

Also neglected and often misunderstood is the toll that daily survival takes on African American youth. The fact that these youths survive the odds of oppression and poverty, developmentally inhibiting environments such as poor and inadequate health care, culturally insensitive and irrelevant education systems, and unsafe and unhealthy living environments (Coll et al., 1996; Williams & Collins, 1995) has caused some individuals to hold them in the highest esteem. Their strengths and assets are lauded while their deficits and difficulties are minimized (Myres & King, 1983). Similar to theoretical and empirical work that spotlights the deficits of black youth, an emphasis on strengths and simultaneous neglect of deficits gives an inaccurate picture of black children's psychological health. It normalizes all behavior of African American youth and fails to acknowledge that while black youth *are* surviving they are *not* thriving (Myers & King, 1983). This focus fails to acknowledge that to succeed and thrive, black children, like all children, need a supportive and nurturing environment (Coll et al., 1996; Myers & King, 1983). By focusing on psychopathology next, we examine the psychological effects of surviving in a society that inhibits healthy development.

PSYCHOPATHOLOGY AND PROTECTIVE FACTORS

The DSM-IV (American Psychiatric Association, 1994) defines *mental disorder*, with many qualifications and caveats, as "a clinically significant behavioral or psychological syndrome or pattern that occurs in an individual and is associated with present distress (e.g., a painful symptom) or disability (i.e., impairment in one or more important areas of functioning) or with a significantly increased risk of suffering death, pain, disability, or an important loss of freedom" (xxi–xxii). Because children are often unable to report or are unaware of their own distress, however, the association with distress usually refers to the distress of significant adults in these children's lives. The DSM-IV is careful to state that "this syndrome or pattern must not be merely an expectable and culturally sanctioned response to a particular event." In defining, assessing, and treating psychopathology in African American children, one must consider the child's culture and environment.

Recent research suggests that African American children are disproportionately represented among children receiving psychological services. Costello and Janiszewski (1990), for example, found that African American children were more likely than other children to be treated for psychiatric disorders. Children between the ages of 7 and 11 were selected from two different settings—children from a pediatric clinic who were not receiving psychiatric treatment and children from a psychiatric clinic who were. Both groups were considered disturbed according to their mothers' ratings and did not differ significantly on clinician-made diagnoses. African American children were more likely to be receiving treatment, with an inordinate number of African American boys, especially low socioeconomic status (SES) boys, in the treatment group. The children receiving treatment had a higher mean number of behavior problems reported by their homeroom teachers, regardless of level of disturbance. The most reliable indicator of treatment for psychopathology, then, may be whether the child's behavior is causing his or her teachers concern, rather than whether it causes the child distress.

Of course, children may not be distressed by behavior teachers consider problematic. This behavior may, nevertheless, put the child at risk by interfering with academic achievement. In the Costello and Janiszewski (1990) study, however, higher teacher reports of behavior problems was not related to academic failure. They were related to race, sex, and SES. This raises the question of what criteria teachers use to determine whether a child's behavior is problematic. Teachers' expectations of acceptable behavior may be influenced by cultural norms. Thus, a teacher from one culture may report the behavior of a child from another culture as problematic when the child's cultural standards define this behavior as normal or even positive.

Zimmerman, Khoury, Vega, Gil, and Warheit (1995) looked at Hispanic, African American, and non-Hispanic Caucasian adolescent boys and teachers to see if teachers reported more problematic behaviors for children of a different ethnicity than their own. Total problem scores were significantly higher for African American children rated by Caucasian or Hispanic teachers than those rated by African American teachers. No differences were found (i.e., no higher ratings for other children rated by teachers of a different ethnicity from theirs). They also tested for differences between parent and teacher reports. The greatest discrepancy was between African American parents and non-African American teachers, with Hispanic and Caucasian teachers rating African American children considerably higher than their parents rated them. African American children were more than twice as likely as Hispanic or Caucasian children to be rated within clinical case range by their teachers but not their parents. African American teachers reported about equal numbers of problem behaviors for all their students regardless of race, lending some credence to the theory that children's behavior is interpreted through cultural expectations.

Ogbu (1981) contends that minority status has led some groups to form "alternative competencies," that is, social skills which lead to success in the minority culture, but not always in the dominant culture. The previously mentioned focus groups with African American youth, parents, and professionals in several Michigan cities (Lambert et al., 1999) tend to support this argument. When asked to describe a typical, well-adjusted African American child, African American adults mentioned such attributes as "able to stand up for themselves," "able to analyze, see through a situation," "in the teenage years, have a bit of resistance," "not afraid to express their opinions," "have some anger and frustration with the way things are," "be resistant, defiant, showing their own identity, challenging their parents first of all before they go out and challenge the world," "willing to challenge their peer group," and "willing to challenge inconsistency (in adults)." Respect for adults was considered a positive quality, but words such as "obedient" and "compliant" never came up in all the interviews. Strong emphasis was placed on critical thinking, especially in social situations, on being able to size up a situation and keep one's head when provoked, and on maintaining one's integrity. These skills are essential to the psychological well-being of a people who are often treated with contempt and duplicity by the dominant culture, but they can be easily misinterpreted in a school system where compliance and obedience is valued.

Most of the research on psychopathology in African American children has focused on low SES boys. Harris (1995) postulates that African American men who are not able to meet the traditional American standards of masculinity due to marginalization from the broader society redefine masculinity to reflect their experiences. As a result, she states, "Some African American male youth of low-income social status have defined masculinity to emphasize sexual promiscuity, toughness, thrill seeking and the use of violence in interpersonal interactions" (280). While this behavior may provide the adolescent with a sense of self-esteem, it is easily construed as threatening and can be dangerous to the child himself.

Hill and Madhere (1996), in a study of African American fourth and sixth graders, found that children living in violent communities who were willing to retaliate showed significantly less anxiety than children who were not. This suggests that violent behavior may not always be a symptom of mental disorder, but may be a legitimate coping strategy. When assessing the prevalence of psychopathology among African American youth, the children's environment must therefore be taken into account. In violent or dangerous communities, children may develop a "thick skin," may carry a weapon, and may react with suspicion, hostility, and aggression. These behaviors are certainly not conducive to academic success, but may be crucial both for the children's physical safety and for their emotional well-being. While intervention is unquestionably required, it would be unwise and counterproductive to classify defiant or aggressive behavior as pathological in such situations.

Aggressive or hostile behavior may be a natural or understandable response in other contexts as well. Jones (1979) maintains that what appears to be excessively hostile behavior may, in fact, be a displacement of rage resulting from an accumulation of frustration and humiliation in the face of racial discrimination. For example, an African American child raises his hand to ask a question in class and waits for ten minutes while the teacher calls on Caucasian children all around him. When he's finally allowed to ask his question, the teacher admonishes him with, "If you'd been listening, you'd know the answer to that." He throws his book across the room and stomps out the door, cursing at the teacher. The teacher is appalled at what seems to her an extreme reaction to a fairly minor insult, but taken in the context of the child's broader experience of being constantly undermined by teachers, it is an understandable response. Perhaps the finding (Zimmerman et al., 1995) that African American teachers reported fewer problems for their African American pupils than did Caucasian and Hispanic teachers reflects not the African American teachers' greater tolerance for certain behaviors, but the fact that those behaviors do not occur as frequently in these teachers' classrooms. In other words, non-African American teachers could be inadvertently causing behavior problems by disrespectful treatment of their African American students.

Another explanation for these findings is that teachers may interpret the same behavior differently in African American versus non-African American children. In a cross-cultural comparison of African American children and Jamaican children of African descent between the ages of 6 and 11, Puig and colleagues (1998, 1999) and her colleagues found that Jamaican teachers reported fewer behavior problems among their students than did U.S. teachers among their students. A multiethnic team (i.e., African American and Puerto Rican) of observers (with three observers constant over both samples), however, found just the opposite. They rated the Jamaican children as having significantly more problems than the African American children. The Jamaican teachers were all of African descent, whereas the U.S. teachers were predominantly Caucasian. The sample size for teachers was not large enough to determine whether there was a significant difference between teachers of various ethnicity and their reports of children's problems. This study nevertheless raises the question of how much reporting of behavior problems is biased by the informant's racial stereotypes. Teachers may believe, for example, that African American boys are aggressive and disruptive and thus interpret even relatively benign behavior as problematic.

A final explanation for the greater number of behavior problems reported for African American children by their teachers is that these children may be at greater risk for mental disorders because of their minority status. Racial discrimination and the environmental challenges it engenders are substantial causes of stress (Lambert et al., 1999) and young children are especially ill equipped to combat racism from adults. A child looks up to his or her teacher as an authority. When the teacher conveys a message that the child is inferior, it is difficult for the child to resist this message.

Desegregation, while providing African American children with physical access to the same educational resources as Caucasian children, does not yet provide them with practical access. Comer (1995) laments that "desegregation without full, enthusiastic membership in the larger society has made group cohesion and a positive group identity more difficult to achieve." On the one hand, African Americans are being given the message that they have as much opportunity to succeed in life as anyone and that if they aren't as successful as their Caucasian peers, it's their own fault. Discrimination on the basis of race is no longer legal, nor is it considered polite among better educated, liberal Caucasian Americans. On the other hand, racism continues to permeate our society and is such an integral part of the system that it is almost invisible in many of its manifestations. That racism no longer exists is a myth which is just as damaging as overt racial discrimination because it weakens the communities formed by common oppression and forces children into a hostile world before they have developed the ego strength to cope.

It is a wonder that African American children survive at all. Yet, they do. Most African American children grow up to become competent adults and effective parents. Strong support from extended family and community forms a powerful protective factor. A child needs many role models, and among African American children, religion is often considered important (Comer, 1995). In the focus groups in Michigan, for example, one of the qualities frequently mentioned as characterizing a well-adjusted African American child was the child's involvement in religious activities. Religion not only teaches children moral values, but through their interaction with leaders in places of worship, it presents them with positive role models, which can compensate for lack of support among their teachers.

ASSESSMENT OF STRENGTHS AND PSYCHOPATHOLOGY

Much has been written on the importance of cultural relevance in the assessment of black children and families. Like the mainstream (e.g., Nunnally & Bernstein, 1994) literature base, professionals who focus on blacks and other minorities (e.g., Brooks-Gunn, Klebanov, & Duncan, 1996; Jones, 1979) have eloquently discussed the issue of cultural bias and other forms of biases in intelligence, achievement, and aptitude testing. Although the clinical literature (e.g., Jones, 1979) has cautioned us against bias in informal clinical evaluation (e.g., via interviewing, mental status examination), the existing literature on culturally relevant measurement of strengths and psychopathology in African American youth via well-normed instruments is virtually nonexistent. The absence of adequate measures of the behavior and emotional difficulties and strengths African American youth present have contributed to the stagnation in the evolution of a strong empirical literature base on black children and their families (Gibbs, 1998).

Reasons for Absence of Appropriate Assessment Instruments

The nonexistence of appropriate measures designed for and normed on African American children and their families may be attributed to numerous factors. Among them is the "one size fits all" approach to measurement in non-white samples and the use of white middle-class youth as the standard via which all children are measured (Doucette-Gates, Brooks-Gunn, & Chase-Lansdale, 1998). To counteract this problem, funding agencies like those within the National Institutes of Health (NIH) have insisted that researchers who seek research funding from their sources include representative samples of blacks and other minorities in their studies. Some private foundations that fund research on children and adults have followed the lead of NIH in encouraging the inclusion of people of color in projects they fund.

In recent years, test developers (e.g., Conners, 1997; Achenbach, 1991a, 1991b, 1991c) who usually depend heavily on public and private agencies to fund the large scale research projects needed to norm their assessment instruments, have addressed funding agencies' concerns by including what one may consider a representative sample of blacks and other minorities in their samples (Gibbs, 1998). More specifically, they include numbers of blacks and other minorities in their sample to match their representation in the population of the United States. Test developers are thereby reassured that this act makes their measures culturally sensitive and absolves them of responsibility in designing measures that are culturally relevant for children from different ethnic minority groups. Unfortunately, this reflects the broader societal focus on black and minority youth as an afterthought rather than as groups worthy of systematic study in their own sociocultural contests (Doucette-Gates, Brooks-Gunn, & Chase-Landale, 1998; Guerra & Jagers, 1998).

The afterthought of including blacks and other minority youth in assessment standardization samples may be deemed a step in the right direction, yet their representation is usually too inadequate to allow meaningful analyses regarding equivalence of psychometric indices (e.g., equivalent construct validity via confirmatory factor analyses) across socioethnic groups (Knight & Hill, 1998). Moreover, the general population and clinical samples often used in this research do not adequately represent the large numbers of black adolescents from a wide variety of socioeconomic groups. Also, because many test developers (e.g., Conners, 1997; Achenbach, 1991a, 1991b, 1991c, 1991d) obtain clinical samples of children with behavior and emotional problems from "traditional" treatment facilities such as community mental health clinics, child guidance clinics, hospitals, and special education programs, they are likely to miss a large proportion of black youth who are identified as having behavior and emotional disorders but are triaged into more restrictive nontraditional facilities such as those managed by the child welfare and juvenile justice systems.

This practice continues despite our knowledge that blacks and other minorities are overrepresented (all minorities comprise 55%, while blacks represent 32%) in the juvenile justice system (Conley, 1994) and that minority youth with and without mental health problems are more like to be incarcerated than their white counterparts (Taylor & Katz, 1996). We also know that the number of youths with severe behavior and emotional disturbances in juvenile facilities, while higher than the general population for the last several decades (Briscoe, 1996), is dramatically increasing (DeJames, 1997). Nevertheless, researchers seldom focus on this group of children (Forehand et al., 1991; Briscoe, 1996). These children are rarely included in clinical samples used to identify empirically based child psychopathological syndromes or constructs depicting strengths such as social competence.

The absence of children from the juvenile justice system in clinical studies may be an oversight (Forehand et al., 1991). Overt and subtle racism in our nation and its organizations accounts for the overrepresentation of blacks and other minorities in juvenile correction facilities. Furthermore, it contributes to the myopia associated with an intense focus on the nation's middle class majority group at the expense of limited or no focus on blacks and other minorities. The tendency to focus on the white middle class as the ideal standard for everyone and the preponderance of between subjects designs where instruments normed primarily on white children are used to compare black and white youth also exacerbates the problem (Phinney & Landin, 1998).

As in other areas of research, black children and their families are not viewed as worthy of intensive focus in instrument design and in research that establish their norms. Black youth are often compared with white middle-class children, and differences in their scores on measures designed by white researchers for white middle-class children are often viewed as evidence of deficits or deviance (Guerra & Jagers, 1998). Researchers interested in studying development and psychopathology in black youth are therefore forced to use measures that are poorly designed for black youth and are rarely normed on black youth (Gibbs, 1998). Some researchers (see Knight & Hill, 1998) have tried to address the issue of relevance for black youth by testing whether the psychological constructs obtained for white middle-class youth are the same for black children, via sophisticated statistical means including item response analyses and confirmatory factor analyses.

Addressing factor structure equivalence is a step in the right direction. It neglects some of the important tenets associated with instrument design, however, notably that of content validity. Content validity is critical for almost all other forms of validity, especially construct validity (Hanes, Richard, & Kubanay, 1995). Special care must therefore be taken in assuring that the constructs are appropriate for black and other minority youth. Achieving this goal is almost impossible when measures are designed by white middle-class test developers and normed primarily or exclusively on white middle-class youth. More specifically, the content represented in the items of the instrument may fail to include items reflecting critical content for minority youth.

A recent study (Lambert et al., 1999) of the clinic records of 1,605 African American clinic-referred youths ages 4 to 18 throughout a Midwestern state substantiates this view. It revealed that a number of problems African American children's parents reported to clinicians during intake interviews were not represented by the items on widely used assessment instruments such as the Child Behavior Checklist (CBCL) (Achenbach, 1991a, 1991b, 1991c, 1991d). Interestingly, a large number of these non-CBCL problems matched the problems parents of children of African descent in Jamaica reported to clinicians during intake interviews (see Lambert, Lyubansky, & Achenbach, 1998). These findings cast doubt on the validity of efforts that assert psychometric equivalence of instruments used across socioethnic groups yet fail to address whether the items on the measures include content relevant to specific groups of interest.

Another often neglected issue is what Knight and Hill (1998) refer to as subjective judgment bias which suggests that the items on measures are culturally bound, unrelated to the cultural context of blacks and other minorities, or are far removed from the common idiomatic expressions of minority respondents. We are reminded of our own focus group studies of African American adolescents throughout a midwestern state, where the participants noted that many of the assessment instruments to which they had been exposed were obviously authored by "White Men," evidenced by their subsequent difficulty understanding the items from these instruments and their doubt that their responses accurately reflected the information the instruments were designed to extract (Lambert et al., 1999). This finding underscores the erroneous assumption of professionals who design or use measures that the meanings of words are similar across ethnic groups (Wilson & Williams, 1998). Since minority youth may respond differently on these instruments because of item content and language equivalence issues, their response style often results in base rate differences on constructs of instruments designed for and normed on the majority population (Guerra & Jagers, 1989). Base-rate differences across different groups affect the sensitivity and specificity of instruments (MacMahon & Trichopoulos, 1996) and can have profound effects on the classification and diagnostic capabilities of the instrument for any given group.

MACROSYSTEMS

Although we have focused thus far on the responsibilities of individuals or small groups of individuals regarding the present state of affairs, we must address the contributions of macrosystems. These systems include the doctoral training programs where most behavioral scientists receive their training in research methodology and the professional bodies that accredit them. They also include public and private agencies that fund research and the mainstream journals and their editorial boards who act as gatekeepers to the publication of relevant research on minorities and other groups. We believe that these systems have been negligent in their duties to support the development of instruments that are culturally relevant for blacks and other minorities.

Colleges and Universities

Within institutions of higher learning, the absence of programmatic research focusing on diverse populations contributes to the problem of limited research and absence of measures for black youth. A substantial portion of social science research occurs under the roofs of academic institutions. The virtual absence of research on black youth and other youth of color in these institutions perpetuates the dearth in our empirical literature base. A lack of research on diverse samples allows our colleagues to ignore the dilemmas and problems that emerge from the absence of suitable measures for African American youth and other minority youth. More specifically, the ongoing tension between the desire to use appropriate methodology in conducting research on black and other minority youth and the absence of suitable tools to accomplish this task is absent in institutions that do not support or promote research on minority groups. The tension between these two domains that motivate researchers to produce culturally appropriate instruments for blacks and other minorities remains absent in many colleges and universities.

Absence of research on black and other minority youth have far reaching effects as it negatively impacts the potential for future research on these groups. More specifically, most researchers in training obtain a significant portion of their research experience and skills via apprenticeships in ongoing research programs directed by faculty members within institutions of higher learning. The absence of research programs that focus on appropriate measurements for black and other minority youth and on other diversity issues perpetuates a system that ignores black youth and other children of color. Researchers graduating from most colleges and universities do not have the training or the tools they need to conduct research that examines the strengths and pathologies of black and other minority youth (McLoyd & Steinberg, 1998).

Professional Accrediting Boards and Funding Agencies

Accreditation issues have led many training programs in psychology and other social science disciplines to take their own initiative to actively recruit minority students and faculty. Unfortunately, programs often forget that this effort wins only a small portion of the battle. The lack of emphasis on training researchers in conducting research on diverse groups perpetuates the lack of culturally relevant research on black children. Responsibility for this problem does not lie solely with training programs. Whereas accrediting professional organizations have supported inclusion of minority faculty and students, little emphasis has been placed on developing strong research programs on black youth and other minority groups.

Funding agencies' efforts toward making researchers accountable for the inclusion of blacks and other minorities in their research projects, while laudable, remains insufficient. It further reflects the belief that the majority group children, because of their sheer numbers in the

U.S. population, should be the focus of research projects, and that minority youth because of their low numbers and their token representation in research projects are not worthy of study on their own terms, with their own instruments, and within their own ecological contexts (Myers & King, 1983). The statement made by a high-ranking officer in a midwestern foundation is an ever-present reminder of the intolerant and uninformed attitudes some persons continue to hold towards culturally relevant research. At a meeting where we presented a project aimed at standardizing a culturally relevant measure of behavior and emotional problems and strengths for black youth in a midwestern state, the officer stated that "without the inclusion of White youth in the standardization sample, persons like . . . [him] who serve on the boards of funding agencies such as the one . . . [he directed] will prevent research of this nature from being funded."

Peer Review Journals

The editors and editorial boards of mainstream journals need to become more cognizant and become more accountable for their contribution to the lack of research programs on black and other minority children. Several scholars (e.g., Cauce, Ryan, & Grove, 1988; McLoyd & Randolph, 1985) have documented the paucity of studies on blacks and other minority groups in the mainstream journals. Some (e.g., Cauce, Ryan, & Grove, 1988) have alluded to the fact that the institutional racism existing within editorial circles may contribute to the rejection of research papers on minority youth and at the same time the acceptance of papers of comparable quality with research done primarily on white youth.

We also believe that the emphasis on quantitative rigidity these journals embrace makes it difficult to publish studies on black youth. McLoyd (1999) and McLoyd and Ceballo (1998) noted the arduous and slow-paced nature of research on black and other minority youth and the backbreaking groundwork that is necessary to create databases on these children. Others (e.g., Phinney & Landin, 1998) have noted the lack of theoretical and research road maps to guide this research. We believe that if researchers are to build databases on black children and other children of color, the groundwork and the theoretical road maps that are built are an important part of the process and are worthy of publication. A historical review of the literature indicates that the quantitative focus of mainstream journals was built on the foundation of single-case designs and ideographic studies conducted by Piaget, Freud, and other pioneers of developmental and clinical psychology (Wicks-Nelson, 1991).

RECOMMENDATIONS FOR REMEDIATION

Institutions of higher learning must begin to move beyond only actively recruiting minority faculty members and students to also recruiting faculty and graduate students who are interested in programmatic research on blacks and other ethnic minority children. Environments must be created and maintained wherein faculty members and students who conduct research on these populations feel supported. Institutions should provide the resources (e.g., space, release from teaching and administrative duties, internal start-up funds) necessary to furnish a launch pad for new faculty members and students who want to begin establishing their research in this area and for established faculty and other students who want to venture into this type of research. Watchdog groups such as the professional bodies that accredit these institutions should begin holding the institutions responsible for the above recommendations.

Researchers who develop measures for African American and other minority youth should also move beyond the typical test-development tactics wherein "experts" (i.e., they and their colleagues) generate the items for the measures to more vanguard approaches where black and other minority youth who are part of their ecological matrices serve as the experts in content generation and validation. An example is our own instruments designed to measure strengths and psychological problems in African American youth. To generate items we conducted focus groups comprised of African American youth, their parents, teachers, and clinicians throughout a midwestern state and asked them to generate items of strengths and difficulties for the instruments. By combining this with data we derived from the clinical records of 1,605 African American youth, four instruments were designed that measure strengths and difficulties African American children present. While designing the instruments, we not only piloted them on African American youth and their parents and teachers, but we followed Hanes, Richard, and Kubanay's (1995) suggestion of asking another group of African American children, their parents, and teachers, and a group of clinicians who serve black youth to rate the instructions and items on the instrument according to clarity and readability. Besides ratings on the preceding qualities, they were asked to rate each item according to relevance for African American youth. For instructions or items they viewed as lacking in any of these mentioned qualities, we asked for suggestions to improve their quality and incorporated these suggestions in the final drafts.

Agencies that fund instrument standardization research should move beyond requiring token inclusion of blacks and other minorities in instrument development, standardization, and other research, and the occasional request for applications on black and other minority youth, to systematic funding of projects that focus exclusively on clinical and developmental issues associated with these children. These agencies should also examine proposals submitted for development and standardization of instruments for and the study of black and other minority youth based on their own merit, and not necessarily in the context of mainstream research that already has well developed theoretical and empirical road maps.

It is also our belief that mainstream journal editorial boards and editors should begin to provide forums in their journals both for less quantitative foundational work and for the quantitative work on black and other minority youth. This will provide an avenue for lively professional debate that will begin the task of not only developing the theoretical and research models that are desperately needed for developmental and clinical sciences for African American and other minority youth, but give them the same chance that mainstream research models had in the past (and still enjoy) to be refuted, bolstered, modified, or abandoned. Taken together with the other suggested changes, we believe this effort can specifically enhance the knowledge base on measurement and other research-related issues pertaining to minority youth.

SUMMARY AND CONCLUSION

The paucity of culturally relevant theoretical models and empirical research on children and families of color, and black children and families in particular, makes understanding their strengths and difficulties almost impossible. Adequate understanding of these issues is especially critical in light of the history of blacks in the United States and its consequences for black children and families. Knowledge of the strengths within black families and communities and of how these factors buffer the ill effects of racism is critical to interventionists who are charged with the responsibility of assessing distressed children and families.

The absence of measurement procedures that have culturally relevant content means that we have no accurate information about the base rates of strengths and difficulties in black children and families. This leads to dependence on measures designed by and for the white middle class for assessment of black children and families. This can result in misclassification and inappropriate intervention.

Institutions of higher learning, the watchdog professional groups that accredit them, public and private agencies that fund research, and editorial boards that act as gatekeepers to publication of material pertaining to black children and families share the blame for the virtual absence of culturally appropriate and empirically validated measures and for the paucity of published studies on African American children and families. They should be held accountable for their continued neglect of these issues. Despite the essential absence of adequate measures and empirical studies on black children and families, interventionists who assess the difficulties presented by this group should be mindful of, and explore contributing and mediating factors at both the micro and macroecological levels that influence, the problems black children present. These foci seem to be more powerful than those employed by the diagnostic procedures traditional medical model employs. They can simultaneously address the factors that inhibit appropriate development and those that enhance the strength-based qualities necessary for successful outcomes in African American children and families.

NOTE

This chapter was supported by a minority supplement grant HS-08385 to the first author from the Agency for Health Care Policy Research in the National Institutes of Health, from financial support from the David Walker Research Institute, College of Human Medicine, Michigan State University, and from the Kent State University Psychology Forum on "Forging Links: Clinical–Developmental Perspectives on African American Children," which we gratefully acknowledge. We thank Karen Lambert, George Rowan, Beth Kirsch, and Carol Carver for reviewing the manuscript and for their helpful editorial comments.

REFERENCES

Achenbach, T. M. (1991a). *Integrative Guide for the 1991 CBCL/4-18, YSR, and TRF Profiles*. Burlington, VT: University of Vermont, Department of Psychiatry.

Achenbach, T. M. (1991b). *Manual for the Child Behavior Checklist/4-18 and 1991 Profile*. Burlington, VT: University of Vermont, Department of Psychiatry.

Achenbach, T. M. (1991c). *Manual for the Teacher's Report Form and 1991 Profile*. Burlington, VT: University of Vermont, Department of Psychiatry.

Achenbach, T. M. (1991d). *Manual for the Youth Self-Report and 1991 Profile*. Burlington, VT: University of Vermont, Department of Psychiatry.

American Psychiatric Association. (1994). *Diagnostic and statistical manual of mental disorders* (4th ed.). Washington, D.C.: Author.

American Psychological Society Human Capital Initiative. (1996). Reducing mental disorders: A behavioral science research plan for psychopathology [Special issue]. *APS Observer, (3).*

Boyd-Franklin, N. (1989). *Black families in therapy: A multisystems approach*. New York: Guilford.

Briscoe, J. (1996). Treating special needs offenders: Examining juvenile offenders with mental impairments. *Corrections Today, October*, 106–136.

Brooks-Gunn, J., Klebanov, P., & Duncan, G. J. (1996). Ethnic differences in children intelligence test scores: Role of economic deprivation, home environment, and material characteristics. *Child Development, 67,* 396–408.

Cauce, A. M., Ryan, K. D., & Grove, K. (1988). Children and adolescents of color, where are you? Participation, selection, recruitment, and retention in developmental research. In V. C. McLoyd and L. Steinberg (Eds.), *Studying minority adolescents: Conceptual methodological and theoretical issues,* (pp. 147–166). Mahwah, NJ: Erlbaum.

Coll, C. G., Crinic, K., Lamberty, G., Wasick, B. H., Jenkins, R., Garcia, H. V., & McAdoo, H. P. (1996). An integrative model for the study of developmental competencies in minority children. *Child Development, 67,* 1891–1914.

Comer, J. P. (1995). Racism and African American adolescent development. In W.C.V. Rieker, P. P. Kramer, & B. M. Brown (Eds.), *Mental health, racism, and sexism* (pp. 151–170). Pittsburgh and London: University of Pittsburgh Press.

Conley, D. (1994). Adding color to a Black and White picture: Using qualitative data to explain racial disproportionality in the juvenile justice system. *Journal of Research in Crime and Delinquency, 31,* 135–147.

Conners, C. K. (1997). *Manual for Conners' Rating Scales.* North Tonwanda, NY: Multi-Health Systems, Inc.

Costello, E. J., & Janiszewski, S. (1990). Who gets treated? Factors associated with referral in children with psychiatric disorders. *Acta Psychiatrica Scandinavia, 81,* 523–529.

DeJames, J. (1997). Saving youths from themselves: Does your juvenile facility pass the suicide prevention test? *Corrections Today, June,* 72–76.

Doucette-Gates, A., Brooks-Gunn, J., & Chase-Lansdale, P. L. (1998). The role of bias and equivalence in the study of race, class, and ethnicity. In V. C. McLoyd & L. Steinberg (Eds.), *Studying minority adolescents: Conceptual methodological and theoretical issues* (pp. 211–236). Mahwah, NJ: Erlbaum.

Fabrega, H., Ulrich, R., & Loeber, R. (1996). Adolescent psychopathology as a function of informant and risk status. *The Journal of Nervous and Mental Disease, 37,* 102–108.

Fabrega, H., Ulrich, R., & Mezzich, J. E. (1993). Do Caucasian and Black adolescents differ at psychiatric intake? *Journal of the American Academy of Child and Adolescent Psychiatry, 32,* 407–414.

Fischer, C. S., Hout, M., Jankowski, M. S., Lucas, S. R., Swidler, A., & Voss, K. (1996). *Inequality by design: Cracking the bell curve myth.* Princeton, NJ: Princeton University Press.

Fitzgerald, H. E., Lester, B. M., & Zuckerman, B. S. (1999). Preface to *Children of color: Research, health, and policy issues* (pp. ix–xii). New York: Garland.

Forehand, R., Frame, C. L., Wierson, L. A., Armistead, L., & Kemption, T. (1991). Assessment of incarcerated juvenile delinquents: Agreement across raters and approaches to psychopathology. *Journal of Psychopathology and Behavioral Assessment, 13,* 17–25.

Gibbs, J. T. (1998). High-risk behaviors in African American youth: Conceptual and methodological issues in research. In V. C. McLoyd & L. Steinberg (Eds.), *Studying minority adolescents: Conceptual methodological and theoretical issues* (pp. 55–86). Mahwah, NJ: Erlbaum.

Graham, S. (1992). Most of the subjects were white and middle class: Trends in published research on African Americans in selected APA journals 1970–1989. *American Psychologist, 47* (2), 629–639.

Guerra, N. G., & Jagers, R. (1998). The importance of culture in the assessment of children and youth. In V. C. McLoyd & L. Steinberg (Eds.), *Studying minority adolescents: Conceptual methodological and theoretical issues* (pp. 167–181). Mahwah, NJ: Erlbaum.

Hanes, S. N., Richard, D.C.S., & Kubany, E. S. (1995). Content validity in psychological assessment: A functional approach to concepts and methods. *Psychological Assessment, 7*, 238–247.

Harris, S. M. (1995). Psychosocial development and Black male masculinity: Implications for counseling economically disadvantaged African American male adolescents. *Journal of Counseling & Development, 73*, 279–287.

Hill, H. M., & Madhere, S. (1996). Exposure to community violence and African American children: A multidimensional model of risks and resources. *Journal of Community Psychology, 24*, 26–43.

Jones, D. L. (1979). African American clients: Clinical practice issues. *Social Work, 37* 112–118.

Knight G. P., & Hill, N. (1998). Measurement equivalency in research involving minority adolescents. In V. C. McLoyd & L. Steinberg (Eds.), *Studying minority adolescents: Conceptual methodological and theoretical issues* (pp. 183–210). Mahwah, NJ: Erlbaum.

Lambert, M. C., Bellas, V. F., & Markle, F. A. (1999). *Strengths and difficulties in African American youngsters: The voice of adolescents, their parents, teachers and clinicians*. Unpublished manuscript.

Lambert, M. C., Lyubansky, M., & Achenbach, T. M. (1998). Behavior and emotional problems among adolescents of Jamaica and the United States: Parent, teacher, and self reports for ages 12–18. *Journal of Emotional and Behavior Disorders, 6*, 180–187.

Lambert, M. C., Samms-Vaughan, M. E., Lyubansky, M., Poldolski, C. L., McCaslin, S. E., & Rowan, G. T. (1999). Behavior and emotional problems of clinic-referred children of the African diaspora: A cross-national study of African American and Jamaican children ages 4 to 18. *Journal of Black Psychology, 25*, 504–523.

MacMahon, B., & Trichopoulos, D. (1996). *Epidemiology: Principles and methods* (2d ed.). New York: Little, Brown.

McAdoo, H. (1993). The social cultural contexts of ecological developmental family models. In P. G. Boss, W. J. Doherty, R. LaRossa, W. R. Shumm, & S. K. Steinmetz (Eds.), *Sourcebook of family theory and methods: A contextual approach* (pp. 298–301). New York: Plenum.

McLoyd, V. C. (1999). Conceptual and methodological issues in the study of ethnic minority children and adolescents. In H. E. Fitzgerald, B. M. Lester, & B. S. Zuckerman (Eds.), *Children of color: Research, health, and policy issues* (pp. 3–24). New York: Garland.

McLoyd, V. C., & Ceballo, R. (1998). Conceptualizing and assessing economic context: Issues in the study of race and child development. In V. C. McLoyd & L. Steinberg (Eds.), *Studying minority adolescents: Conceptual, methodological, and theoretical issues* (pp. 251–278). Mahwah, NJ: Erlbaum.

McLoyd, V. C., & Randolph, S. (1985). The conduct and publication of research on Afro-American children: A review of child development, 1936–1980. In A. Smutts & J. Hagen, (Eds.), History and research in child development. *Monographs of the Society for Research in Child Development, 50*, (4–5, Serial No. 211).

McLoyd, V. C., & Steinberg, L. (1998). Preface to *Studying minority adolescents: Conceptual methodological and theoretical issues* (pp. vii–x). Mahwah, NJ: Erlbaum.

Myers, H., & King, L. M. (1983). Mental health issues in the development of the black American child. In G. T. Powell, T. Yamamoto, A. Romero, & A. Morares (Eds.), *The psychosocial development of minority group children*. Larchmont, NY: Brunner/Mazel.

Nunnally, J. C., & Bernstein, I. H. (1994). *Psychometric theory* (3d ed.). New York: McGraw-Hill.

Ogbu, J. U. (1981). Origins of human competence: A cultural–ecological perspective. *Child Development, 52*, 413–429.

Piatt, A. L., Ketterson, L., Skita, L. J., Scarbright, H. R., Rogers, B. J., Rutterman, N. A., & Manley, C. M. (1993). The relationship of psychological adjustment to perceived family functioning among African American adolescents. *Adolescence, 28*, 673–684.

Phinney, J. S., & Landin, J. (1998). Research paradigms for studying ethnic minority families within and across groups. In V. C. McLoyd & L. Steinberg (Eds.), *Studying minority adolescents: Conceptual methodological and theoretical issues* (pp. 89–109). Mahwah, NJ: Erlbaum.

Puig, M., Lambert, M. C., Markle, F., François-Bellas, V., Lee, J., Carwell, J., Hannah, S., & Lyubansky, M. (1998, October). *Behavioral and emotional problems among Jamaican and African American children, ages 6 to 11: Teacher reports versus direct observations*. Poster session presented at the Kansas conference in Clinical Child Psychology: Translating Research into Practice, Lawrence, Kansas.

Puig, M., Lambert, M. C., Rowan, G. T., Winfrey, T., Lyubansky, M., Hannah, S. D., & Hill, M. (1999). Behavioral and emotional problems among Jamaican and African American children ages 6 to 11: Teachers reports versus direct observation. *Journal of Emotional and Behavioral Disorders, 4*, 240–250.

Samuda, R. J. (1998). *Psychological testing of American minorities: Issues and consequences* (2d ed.). Thousand Oaks, CA: Sage.

Steward, R. J., Jo, H. I., Murray, D., Fitzgerald, W., Neil, D., Fear, F., & Hill, M. (1998). Psychological adjustment and coping styles of urban high school students. *Journal of Multicultural Counseling and Development, 26*, 71–82.

Taylor, D. A., & Katz, P. A. (1996). Health and related services available to black adolescents. In M. K. Singer (Ed.), *Health issues for minority adolescents* (pp. 62–71). Lincoln: University of Nebraska Press.

Wicks-Nelson, R.I.A. (1991). *Behavior disorders of childhood*. Englewood Cliffs, NJ: Prentice Hall.

Williams, D. R., & Collins, C. (1995). US socioeconomic and racial differences in health: Patterns and explanations. *Annual Review of Sociology, 21*, 349–386.

Williams, D. R., & Fenton, B. (1994). The mental health of African Americans: Findings, questions, and directions. In I. L. Livingston (Ed.), *The mosaic of conditions, issues, and perspectives* (pp. 253–268). Westport, CT: Greenwood Press.

Wilson, L. C., & Williams, D. R. (1998). Issues in the quality of data on minority groups. In V. C. McLoyd & L. Steinberg (Eds.), *Studying minority adolescents: Conceptual, methodological, and theoretical issues* (pp. 237–249). Mahwah, NJ: Erlbaum.

Zimmerman, R. S., Khoury, E. L., Vega, W. A., Gil, A. G., & Warheit, G. J. (1995). Teacher and parent perceptions of behavior problems among a sample of African American, Hispanic, and non-Hispanic white students. *American Journal of Community Psychology, 23*, 181–197.

2

A Multidimensional Approach to Racial Identity: Implications for African American Children

Robert M. Sellers, Laura M. Morgan, and Tony N. Brown

The ways in which African Americans viewed the significance and meaning of race in their lives, their experiences of racial discrimination and their psychological functioning have been historically linked in the psychology research literature. Much of the earliest research on the psychological lives of African Americans was so determined to demonstrate that African Americans suffered from self-hatred as a result of their stigmatized status that the concepts of racial identity, experiences of discrimination, psychological functioning became conflated (Cross, 1991). In fact, measures of racial identity were interpreted as if they were also measures of both stigmatized status and self-esteem. Over the years, researchers have begun to operationalize the constructs of racial identity, experiences of racial discrimination, and psychological functioning distinctly. As a result, several studies have been conducted examining possible direct links between racial identity attitudes and African American psychological well-being (Baldwin, 1984; Carter, 1991; Munford, 1994; Parham & Helms, 1981, 1985; Pyant & Yanico, 1991). The results of these studies have not been conclusive. At the same time, a number of other recent studies have begun to investigate the impact of experiences of racial discrimination on the mental health of African Americans. These studies suggest that racial discrimination is a source of stress that has a deleterious influence on the psychological well-being of African Americans (Billingsley, 1992; Foard, 1991;

Franklin, 1998; Hacker, 1995; Landrine & Klonoff, 1996; Locke, 1992; Outlaw, 1993; Utsey, 1998). Specifically, racial discrimination has been linked with depression, anxiety, obsessive–compulsive disorder, and interpersonal sensitivity (Burke, 1984; Fernando, 1984; Landrine & Klonoff, 1996; Neal & Brown, 1994). It is ironic, given the history of racial identity research, that relatively few studies have investigated the ways in which racial identity and experiences of racial discrimination may interact to impact the psychological well-being of African Americans.

This chapter attempts to address this shortcoming in the literature by delineating proposed relationships between various aspects of African Americans' racial identity and their psychological adjustment and well-being. The recently developed Multidimensional Model of Racial Identity (MMRI) (Sellers, Smith, Shelton, Rowley, & Chavous, 1998) is used as a conceptual framework for understanding African American racial identity. The chapter begins with a review of the existing literature and empirical studies linking racial identity and well-being. Next, the four dimensions of racial identity delineated by the MMRI are introduced. Racial identity's potential role in the relationship between experiences of racial discrimination and psychological well-being is then discussed. A stress and coping paradigm is proposed as a means of systematically examining the complex relationships between racial identity, experiencing racist events, and psychological well-being. Finally, the chapter highlights implications of this research specific to African American children and offers directions for future research on racial identity. It is important to note that many of the proposed relationships in the present chapter are as yet untested empirically. We discuss these relationships not as a crystallized body of knowledge, but instead as a blueprint for future research in the area.

EARLY EXPLORATIONS: RACIAL IDENTITY, MENTAL HEALTH, AND AFRICAN AMERICANS

Many of the earliest social and clinical journals include research and theoretical articles that attempt to articulate the psychological meaning of race in the lives and self-concepts of African Americans (Cross, 1991). (African American children have played an important role in understanding the relationship between racial group identity and psychological well-being. In fact, these early studies of racial identity used primarily African American children as participants.)

Researchers have always assumed that there is an important relationship between psychological attachment to race and psychological well-being among African Americans. Most of the early work linking racial identity and mental health was conducted by white researchers who were interested in understanding the "wretched" lives of an oppressed group. Not surprisingly, these early conceptualizations of the psychological meaning of race in the lives of African Americans took the perspective that African Americans' experiences of discrimination in America resulted in a damaged self-concept (e.g., Kardiner & Ovesey, 1951). This damaged self-concept then took on the form of Negro self-hatred or low self-esteem. The assumption of Negro self-hatred was the driving force behind much of the early research literature on the racial identities of African Americans. The rationale for this perspective was based on the concept of reflected appraisals in which it is hypothesized that individuals' self-concepts are derived in large part from the way in which others view them. Since African Americans were devalued by the rest of American society, logic dictated that African Americans should internalize that devaluation in the form of low self-esteem.

Many of the early researchers studying African American racial issues were so enamored with the concept of Negro self-hatred that they showed little interest in any other racial identity attitudes that African Americans held that were inconsistent with this hypothesis (e.g., Clark & Clark, 1947; Horowitz, 1939). The empirical studies that were designed to demonstrate Negro self-hatred operationalized racial identification and preference as proxies for self-esteem (e.g., Clark & Clark, 1939, 1947; Horowitz & Murphy, 1938). These studies employed a paradigm in which African American children and white children were both given black and white stimuli (e.g., dolls and line drawings) and asked to select the color of the stimuli that was most like them and to select the color of the stimuli that they preferred. Typically in these studies, but not unanimously, African American children were less likely to prefer the same race stimuli than were white children (Cross, 1991). In most instances, the African American child made choices that were not significantly different from what one might expect from chance, while the white children demonstrated a clear ethnocentric bias (Banks, 1976). As a consequence of the pervasive belief in Negro self-hatred, however, the African American children's failure to demonstrate an ethnocentric bias was interpreted as strong evidence of low self-esteem in African American children. As Cross (1991) astutely points out, this early research on Negro self-hatred did not propose that racial identity and self-esteem were related; it assumed that racial identity (as measured by racial identification and racial preference) was synonymous with self-esteem in African Americans.

The assumption of Negro self-hatred persisted in the psychological literature up until the late 1960s and 1970s, when the development of direct measures of self-esteem and the emergence of greater numbers of African American psychologists made the assumption untenable. When researchers finally began to develop direct assessment techniques of self-esteem, they discovered that African Americans' scores on these new scales suggested very positive levels of self-esteem (Rosenberg & Simmons, 1971). Rosenberg and Simmons argued that researchers who assumed self-hatred to be the natural state of the African American self-concept failed to consider that most African American children receive messages about their individual worth from other African Americans who are not likely to stigmatize them because of their race. As a result, African Americans' feelings about themselves are likely to be as varied and as positive as any other group.

During this same time, the opportunities grew for more and more African Americans to earn doctoral degrees and gain access to the intellectual discourse regarding racial identity in African Americans. Many of these new African American scholars were impacted by the political zeitgeist of the civil rights and black power movements. Immersed in this volatile and self-affirming political zeitgeist, African American psychologists in the 1970s began to reframe the discussion of African American racial identity from a stigma-based infirmity to a protective strength in the face of oppression.

In redefining African American racial identity as a positive psychological phenomena that was essential to the mental health of African Americans in an oppressive society, many African American researchers in the 1970s proposed models that attempted to delineate the processes by which African Americans developed optimal racial identities (e.g., Cross, 1971; Milliones, 1980). Cross' model of Nigrescence is the most widely researched and applied model of African American racial identity (Cross, 1971, 1991). The Nigrescence model describes five stages of racial identity development that African Americans experience as they develop a psychologically healthy black identity. In the first stage, *preencounter*, individuals do not believe that race is an important component of their identity. This may include an idealization of the dominant white society or simple placement of more emphasis on another identity component such as gender or religion. Individuals in the second stage, *encounter*, are faced with a profound experience or a collection of events directly linked to their race. This experience encourages individuals to reexamine their current identity and find or further develop their black identity. This experience can be either positive or negative (Cross, 1991). The third stage, *immersion–emersion*, is characterized by extremely pro-black and anti-white attitudes and behaviors. Externally, individuals are obsessed with identifying with black culture, but internally they have not made the commitment to endorse all values and traditions associated with being black. The fourth stage, *internalization*, is characterized by having a feeling of inner security and satisfaction about being black. Moreover, individuals at this stage tend to have a less idealized view regarding the meaning of race. They are able to see both the positive and negative elements of being black or white. *Internalization–commitment*, the final stage, represents those individuals who translate their internalized identities into action.

Parham and Helms (1981) developed the Racial Identity Attitudes Scale (RIAS) to operationalize the Nigrescence model. The RIAS measures attitudes that are representative of attitudes individuals are likely to hold toward oneself, blacks, and whites as they transverse through four stages of Nigrescence. Attitudes are predicted to change from anti-black or low race salience (preencounter); to attitude flux (encounter); to pro-black with reference to anti-white attitudes (immersion–emersion); to pro-black without reference to white attitudes. The RIAS has been used in a number of studies to examine the relationship between racial identity and such varied phenomena as demographic background (Parham & Williams, 1993), attitudes regarding utilizing counseling services (Austin, Carter, & Vaux, 1990; Helms, 1984; Parham & Helms, 1981), self-actualization (Parham & Helms, 1985), and ego functioning (Marriette, 1990).

Cross and other researchers during the 1970s were very interested in capturing the qualitative experiences of being black in America including, but not simply limited to, experiences of stigma. Many of these models emphasize both cultural and political resistance from the mainstream society. Implicit in this approach was the notion of an optimal racial identity for African Americans that was synonymous with positive mental health and functioning. These models, though they vary in a number of ways, tended to assume that a strong identification with being African American as well as a commitment to the overall uplift of black people in general was indicative of an optimal racial identity. In some instances, theorists argued that various racial identity attitudes and beliefs were in and of themselves pathological (e.g., Baldwin or Akbar; i.e., antiself). In their necessary counteroffensive against the pejorative view of the African American as a wretched passive soul that suffers from self-hatred, many African American researchers also implied that racial identity was a proxy measure of psychological well-being and mental health. For example, Baldwin (1984) argued that a strong identification with being black and embracing a definition of black that focuses on a specific African value orientation is a necessary component of a psychologically functioning African American. He argued that any deviation from this identity profile is inherently psychologically unhealthy.

While initial explorations considered racial group attachment and psychological well-being to be one and the same, the research that followed suggested that racial identity has direct and indirect links to psychological well-being. The direct relationship hypothesis supports that racial group attachment predicts mental health, while the indirect hypothesis suggests that identity serves as more of a buffer against racial discrimination (Anderson, 1991; Terrell & Taylor, 1980). Recent research suggests that experiences of racist events may have a deleterious impact on the mental health functioning of African Americans (e.g., Landrine & Klonoff, 1996; Utsey, 1998). Cross, Parham, and Helms argue that a primary function of an internalized racial identity is to buffer against these deleterious mental health consequences. They write that, "an easily perceived but nonetheless essential function of the stabilized Black Identity which the Nigrescence writers address is the protection of the individual from psychological harm that may result from daily existence in a racist society" (1998, p. 11).

Interestingly, the bulk of the empirical research investigating the relationship between racial identity and psychological well-being has focused almost exclusively on the direct relationship hypothesis. Unfortunately, the dearth of studies directly measuring experiences of racism, racial identity, and mental health preclude an explicit examination of the potential buffering functions of racial identity. Nonetheless, a number of studies using regression techniques have found significant relationships between some of the scales of the RIAS and various indicators of mental health. For instance, Parham and Helms (1985) found that scores on the encounter scale were negatively related to the anxiety subscale of the SCL-90 Symptom Checklist. Carter (1991) assessed the relationship between African American college students' scores on the four subscales of the RIAS and the Bell Global Psychopathology Scale. He found only one significant relationship. Preencounter attitudes were positively related to higher symptoms of psychopathology. Pyant and Yanico (1991) investigated the relationship between scores on the RIAS and psychological well-being in a sample of African American female college students. The California Psychological Inventory of Well-Being (CPI), the Rosenberg Self-Esteem Scale (RSES) and the Beck Depression Inventory (BDI) were used as measures of well-being. Preencounter scores were negatively associated with both CPI and RSES scores. Both preencounter and encounter scores were negatively associated with BDI scores. These findings were consistent with Munford (1994), who later examined a mixed-sex sample of African American college students. Munford (1994) found that preencounter, encounter, and immersion–emersion attitudes were associated with higher scores on the BDI and that internalization scores were associated with fewer depressive symptoms. These studies together suggest some direct relationship between scores on the RIAS and indicators of mental health.

However, a number of researchers have expressed concern with the RIAS (Akbar, 1989; Ponterotto & Wise, 1987; Rowley & Sellers, 1998; Stokes, Murray, Chavez, & Peacock, 1998). In particular, Ponterotto and Wise (1987) note the poor internal consistency of the encounter subscale in a number of studies as well as concern regarding the underlying factor structure of the RIAS. Rowley and Sellers (1998) question the face validity of the items in representing the stages Cross describes. The mismatch between the conceptualization and the operationalization of Nigrescence theory extends beyond the properties of the RIAS to the analytical strategies employed with the measure. As a stage theory, Cross's conceptualization of Nigrescence implies that individuals either belong to a single stage or two contiguous stages when the person is in transition from one stage to another. Thus, we should expect empirical investigations of the theory to represent this aspect of the theory as much as possible. In other words, statistical techniques that place individuals within particular groups (such as cluster analysis) should be used to test the internal validity of both the measure and the theory. Individuals should exhibit high scores on one or two contiguous subscales (such as encounter and immersion–emersion) and score very low on the other scales. Such a clustering approach should also be used to investigate the relationship between Nigrescence and other phenomena. Unfortunately, most of the empirical work using the RIAS has used factor analytic and regression techniques. The use of these techniques implicitly assumes that at the time of the assessment each individual has racial identity attitudes and beliefs that correspond to all four stages (e.g., Carter & Helms, 1988; Parham & Helms, 1985; Parham & Williams, 1993; Watts, 1992). Such an assumption is in direct contradiction with stage theory and the way in which the conceptual model is described by Cross (1971, 1991). These growing concerns regarding the RIAS's psychometric properties and the data analysis strategies used to interpret the relationship between the RIAS and mental health makes it difficult to draw any firm conclusions from the results of these previous studies.

Criticism has not been limited to the RIAS. There has also been criticism of the Nigrescence model as a conceptual framework. Stokes, Murray, Chavez, and Peacock (1998) argue that the use of specific developmental stages is too restrictive and should be abandoned for a more experiential model. They also question whether the model is an artifact of the cultural zeitgeist in which it was first proposed (the early 1970s). Other researchers have questioned whether the model is applicable to the experiences of all African Americans (Rowley & Sellers, 1998). Although there are a variety of other models and measures of African American racial identity in the literature (for a review, see Burlew & Smith, 1991; or Marks, Settles, Cooke, Morgan, & Sellers, in press), these models are not without their problems. For instance, Baldwin's model of African Self-Consciousness proposes a number of assumptions that are resistant to empirical investigation (such as a biogenetic predisposition towards a certain identity orientation), making it impossible to verify the model (Sellers, Smith, Shelton, Rowley, & Chavous, 1998). Phinney's (1992) Multigroup Ethnic Identity Measure (MEIM) provides information regarding whether an individual has successfully completed a search for an ethnic identity with little regard for the content and significance of the identity itself. It also does not take into consideration the unique cultural and historical experiences that influence African American racial identity. In general, the racial identity literature is plagued by serious problems. There is little consensus in the way in which racial identity is conceptualized across conceptual models and instruments (Smith, 1989). As a result, there is little consistency in the content of the instruments used to measure racial identity. This has caused a problem regarding the generalizability of results across studies using different models and measures of racial identity. Also, many of the measures lack sufficient evidence of their psychometric utility. As a result, a number of researchers have called for a significant overhaul in the conceptualization and measurement of racial identity (Penn, Gaines, & Phillips, 1993; Phinney, 1992; Rowley & Sellers, 1998; Sellers, 1993; Smith, 1989; Stokes, Murray, Chavez, & Peacock, 1998).

In sum, the studies mentioned provided critical insight into African American's psychological attachment to their racial group and a link between identity and well-being. However, relatively few researchers either from the Negro self-hatred perspective or the racial identity as a protective factor perspective have actually assessed the relationship between racial identity and measures of psychological well-being empirically. The few studies that have directly assessed the relationship are limited by serious methodological errors. Recently, researchers have questioned whether racial identity should have a direct relationship with psychological well-being (Cross, 1991; Sellers, 1993; Penn, Gaines, & Phillips, 1993). There is a critical need for systematic explorations of the link between identity and health among African Americans. The authors of this chapter propose that researchers examine this link by considering the complexity of racial identity, the importance of social context, and the variety of psychological health outcomes. With these goals in mind, we introduce the Multidimensional Model of Racial Identity (MMRI).

THE MULTIDIMENSIONAL MODEL OF RACIAL IDENTITY

The Multidimensional Model of Racial Identity represents a synthesis of ideas from many existing models of African American racial identity (Sellers, Shelton, Cooke, Chavous, Rowley, & Smith, 1998). The MMRI attempts to build on the strengths of these models, providing a conceptual and methodological framework from which to address the aforementioned shortcoming within the identity literature. The MMRI approaches racial identity from an individual difference perspective. As such, it focuses on a description of the status of the different dimensions of individuals' racial identity at a particular point in their lives. The MMRI provides a framework to conceptualize individual differences in the significance and meaning of race in African Americans' beliefs about themselves.

This perspective differs from developmental models (e.g., Cross, 1971, 1991; Milliones, 1980; Phinney, 1992) that attempt to describe the process by which individuals' racial identity attitudes mature across the life span. Built into these models is the idea of change over the life span. The MMRI does not implicitly or explicitly propose a *single* developmental sequence for racial identity. This does not mean, however, that the MMRI is incompatible with a developmental approach to racial identity. The three stable dimensions of the MMRI (centrality, ideology, and regard) are not conceptualized as completely static. Individuals' identities may change as the result of experiencing a negative racist event (Cross, 1971). Individuals may change aspects of their identity as a result of changes in their life circumstances. There may even be systematic changes in the three stable dimensions that occur across the life span. The MMRI provides a framework in which to investigate these propositions. By utilizing longitudinal research designs and measures of individuals' experiences with racist events that are distinct from the measures of racial identity, we can see the influences of both normative influences and racist experiences on racial identity development.

The MMRI defines racial identity as that part of the person's self-concept that is related to her/his membership within a race. As such, the MMRI assumes a phenomenological position in that it focuses on the person's self-perceptions of whether they are race identified (Weiner, 1974). It is concerned with both the *significance* that the individual places on race in defining him/herself and the individual's interpretations of *what it means* to be black. The MMRI proposes four dimensions of racial identity in African Americans (see Figure 2.1). These dimensions consist of identity salience; the centrality of the identity; the ideology associated with the identity; and the regard in which

Figure 2.1
The Four Dimensions of Racial Identity

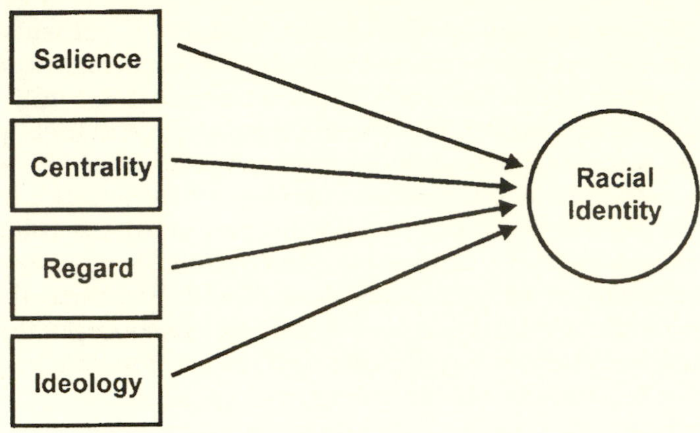

the person holds the group associated with the identity. The first two dimensions address the significance of race in the individual's self-definition. The second two dimensions refer to the qualitative meaning that the individual ascribes to being black.

The first dimension, *salience*, refers to the extent to which a person's race is a relevant part of his or her self-concept at a particular moment in time. Salience is concerned with the particular event as the level of analysis. It is highly sensitive to both the context of the situation as well as the person's proclivity to define himself or herself in terms of race (i.e., centrality). Salience is the dynamic aspect of racial identity, meaning it is the dimension of the MMRI that is subject to frequent and dramatic change based upon situational or contextual influences. It is also the dimension most relevant to predicting proximal behavioral responses to situations. It operates like a self-relevant schema. Salience is the mechanism by which the other three stable dimensions influence the way a person experiences a particular event. When racial identity is made salient, individuals' ideology and regard influences their construal and behavioral response. As such, our conceptualization of salience is consistent with Markus and Nurius's (1986) conceptualization of the working self-concept.

The *centrality* dimension of racial identity refers to the extent to which a person normatively defines her/himself with regard to race. It is a measure of whether race is a core part of an individual's self-concept. Implicit in the conceptualization of centrality is a hierarchical ranking of different identities with regard to their proximity to the individual's core definition of self (Banaji & Prentice, 1994). The dimensions of centrality and salience are related in the sense that the more often race becomes salient to the individual, the more likely the individual is to begin to use race to define him/herself in general (Higgins, 1990; Wyer & Srull, 1981). At the same time, the more central a person's racial identity, the more likely it is to become salient in situations for which there are fewer race relevant cues (Bargh, Bond, Lombardi, & Tota, 1986).

The third dimension of racial identity, *ideology*, is the individual's beliefs, opinions, and attitudes with respect to the way he or she feels that the members of the group should act. This dimension represents the person's philosophy about the ways in which African Americans should live and interact with society. Four ideologies are proposed. These four ideologies are (1) a *nationalist* philosophy, characterized by a viewpoint that emphasizes the uniqueness of being of African descent; (2) an oppressed *minority* philosophy, characterized by a viewpoint that emphasizes the similarities between African Americans and other oppressed groups; (3) an *assimilation* philosophy, characterized by a viewpoint that emphasizes the similarities between African Americans and the rest of American society; and (4) a *humanist* philosophy, characterized by a viewpoint that emphasizes the commonalities of all humans. Although people in general can be categorized as possessing one ideology predominantly, it is likely that most people hold a variety of ideologies that often vary across areas of functioning. For example, a person could believe that African Americans should primarily patronize African American-owned businesses (nationalist) and at the same time feel that blacks should be integrated into white institutions (assimilation). A number of existing models of black identity have focused on ideology—generally placing a nationalist ideology at one end of the continuum (usually the most desirable) and an assimilation ideology at the other end (usually the least desirable) (e.g., Cross, 1971; Baldwin & Bell, 1985; Terrell & Terrell, 1981). The contribution of the MMRI, however, is that it conceptualizes ideology as a distinct dimension of racial identity as opposed to other models that have implicitly conceptualized it as being synonymous with racial identity.

The fourth dimension, *regard*, refers to a person's affective and evaluative judgment of their race. The regard dimension is based heavily on Luhtanen and Crocker's work on collective self-esteem (Crocker & Luhtanen, 1990; Crocker, Luhtanen, Blaine, & Broadnax, 1994; Luhtanen & Crocker, 1992). Like their model of collective self-esteem, the regard dimension consists of both a private and a public component. Private regard refers to the extent to which individuals feel positively or negatively towards African Americans and their membership in that group. Private regard is consistent with the concept of psychological closeness and racial pride in other models (e.g., Demo & Hughes, 1990; Hughes & Demo, 1989). On the other hand, public regard refers to the extent to which individuals feel that others view African Americans positively or negatively.

Sellers and colleagues developed the Multidimensional Inventory of Black Identity (MIBI) to operationalize the MMRI. The MIBI is a 56-item measure developed to assess the three stable dimensions of the MMRI (centrality, ideology, and regard) in African Americans (Sellers, Rowley, Chavous, Shelton, & Smith, 1997). As such, it is comprised of three scales that measure the centrality, ideology and regard dimensions. The ideology scale also consists of four subscales (nationalist, assimilation, minority, and humanist), and the regard scale consists of two subscales (private regard and public regard). There is empirical evidence that the MIBI is a valid and reliable measure of the MMRI (Sellers et. al., 1997).

Figure 2.2 provides a pictorial representation of the dimensions and subdimensions of the MMRI.

STUDIES INVESTIGATING THE MMRI AND WELL-BEING

In recognizing that there are individual differences in the qualitative nature of the meaning individuals ascribe to being a member of the black racial group, the MMRI makes no value judgment as to what constitutes a healthy versus unhealthy racial identity. In order to ask whether a particular identity is either good or bad, one must first de-

Figure 2.2
The Multidimensional Model of Racial Identity

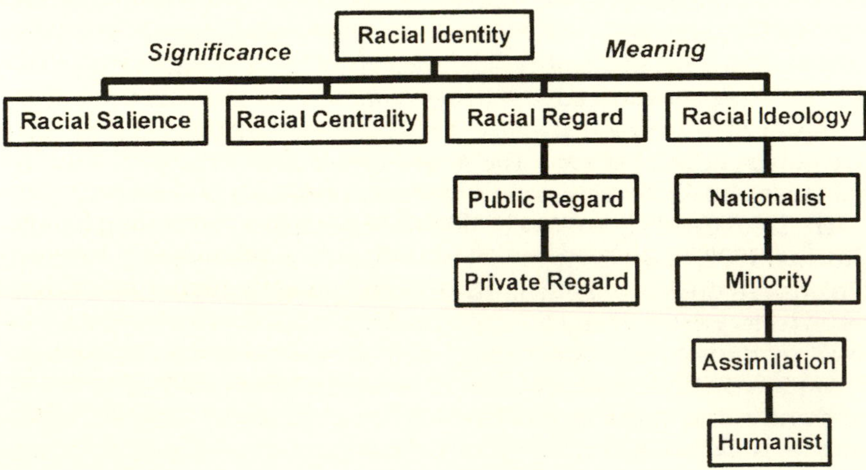

cide what criteria are to be used as the bases of one's evaluation. In addition, any evaluation of the optimality of a particular identity profile can only be conducted after the particular ecological context of the relationship between racial identity and the outcome of interest are taken into consideration. It is very likely that the relationship between racial identity and a given outcome is likely to vary as a function of the context in which the relationship occurs. Thus, the optimality of any particular identity profile is a function of both the environment and the criteria used to evaluate optimality. Because the MMRI does not define a priori what constitutes an optimal racial identity, it avoids the problem of confounding identity and psychological well-being in its conceptualization of racial identity. As such, it is an appropriate model in which to empirically test the relationship between racial identity and well-being. In addition, the delineation of the salience dimension provides a process by which racial identity works at the level of the specific event, allowing researchers to examine both short-term and long-term outcomes.

To date only two studies have used the MMRI to examine issues of psychological well-being. Both studies measured racial identity using the Multidimensional Inventory of Black Identity (MIBI). The first study, conducted by Rowley, Sellers, Chavous, and Smith (1998), examined personal self-esteem among 74 African American high school and 173 African American college students. Findings revealed that, in both the high school and college samples, the relationship between private regard and self-esteem was moderated by racial centrality. That is, positive feelings about one's racial group membership (private regard) were positively related to self-esteem only for African Americans who considered their racial group membership to be an important component of their self-concept. Private regard attitudes were not related to personal self-esteem for those individuals for whom race was not a central identity. Another study in which alcohol use was used as a measure of psychological functioning reported similar findings (Sellers, Caldwell, Zimmerman, & Hilkene, 1999). This study investigated whether private regard, racial centrality, and parental support were predictive of alcohol use in a sample of 434 African American high school students. Private regard, mother's support, and father's support were negatively related to alcohol usage when controlling for age, sex, SES, and mother's level of education. The relationship between private regard and alcohol usage was significantly higher for African Americans who were high race central than for African Americans who had average or low levels of centrality. In both studies, the relationship between the meaning of being black (as measured by private regard) and psychological functioning was only predictive when race was a central identity for the individuals.

Even though these studies did not explicitly assess race-related phenomena other than racial identity, significant relationships were found between identity and varied indicators of functioning. We suspect that racial identity may play an even larger role when mental health and functioning is investigated in the context of other race-related phenomena like the experience of racial discrimination. In this next section, we will briefly review the existing literature on racial discrimination's impact on mental health. We then address the potential role that racial identity may play in buffering or exacerbating the adverse consequences of racial discrimination on mental health, using the MMRI as a conceptual frame.

IDENTITY AND MENTAL HEALTH IN CONTEXT: RACIAL DISCRIMINATION AND MENTAL HEALTH OUTCOMES

Many African Americans are regularly and frequently treated badly because of their race. For instance, a number of researchers have reported that 65 percent or more of African American adults typically encounter racial discrimination in their lifetime (Landrine & Klonoff, 1996; Thompson, 1996; Williams, Yu, Jackson, & Anderson, 1997). This proportion would probably be higher if discriminatory incidents did not involve a certain degree of ambiguity, and if institutionalized racial discrimination could be easily observed. Such discriminatory experiences can have adverse mental health consequences because they are subjectively experienced as stressful (Broman, 1997; Burke, 1984; Carter, 1993; Fernando, 1984; Landrine & Klonoff, 1996; Williams et. al., 1997; Thompson, 1996; Outlaw, 1993; Peters, 1978; Pierce, 1975). Unlike many typical stressful events, racial discrimination can be especially detrimental to psychological health because it is often inherently demeaning, degrading, and highly personal (Delgado, 1982; Landrine & Klonoff, 1996).

There is a growing body of empirical evidence linking racial discrimination to adverse mental health among African Americans. For example, using data from the 1979–1980 National Survey of Black Americans (NSBA), Williams and Chung (in press) found that respondents who experienced bad treatment because of their race were likely to report lower levels of life satisfaction and happiness. Landrine and Klonoff (1996) recently developed a racial discrimination inventory that asked respondents about eighteen lifetime and past year events. They found that the lifetime prevalence and prevalence of discriminatory events within the past year were both related to greater psychiatric symptoms (i.e., anxiety, depression, obsessive-compulsive, interpersonal sensitivity, somatization). Landrine and Klonoff also found that the individuals' appraisals of the level of stress experienced as a result of the event were also associated with greater psychiatric symptoms, independent of the total number of events that the individuals experienced.

In another study, Jackson, Brown, Williams, Torres, Sellers, and Brown (1996) found that African American respondents in the NSBA panel sample who experienced unfair treatment because of race were likely to have low subjective well-being. They also found that multiple experiences of racial discrimination over time had a cumulative, adverse impact on subjective well-being. Using the same panel data, Brown, Williams, Jackson, Sellers, Brown, Torres, and Neighbors (in press) found the experience of racial discrimination to be associated with high psychological distress, and a greater likelihood of clinical depression. In a small study of married African American police officers, Johnson (1989) found a significant relationship between experiences of racial discrimination and low marital well-being and quality. Two measures of discrimination at work were included in this study. One measure was a report of individual experiences; the other measure was a perception of institutional racial discrimination. Both measures were found to be directly associated with lower marital well-being and lower marital quality.

In a sample of 200 African Americans from the St. Louis metropolitan area, Thompson (1996) examined the relationship between racial discrimination and the psychiatric symptoms of intrusion and avoidance. She found that experiencing discrimination during the past year or the past six months were associated with high psychiatric symptoms. She further categorized the experiences of discrimination into three categories (minor, moderate, and major) based on their level of stressfulness. She found that the more stressful experiences of racial discrimination were associated with the reporting of more intrusion symptoms. In another study conducted on African Americans in an urban area, Brown (1998) distinguished between major discriminatory life events and daily discriminatory events in his investigation of the link between discrimination and mental health. Using data from the 1995 Detroit Area Study (DAS), he found that both types of discriminatory incidents, major and daily, were associated with increased psychological distress and depressive symptomatology among African Americans.

Given the evidence suggesting an adverse relationship between racial discrimination and mental health, many researchers are beginning to consider factors that may moderate this relationship. Because it represents the significance and meaning that African Americans attach to race and because race is the basis of the unfair treatment in racial discrimination experiences, racial identity may be one of these important moderating factors. Unfortunately few studies have examined this issue. Those few studies that have, however, suggest some evidence that racial identity might influence the relationship between racial discrimination and mental health. For instance, Williams, Brown, Sellers, and Forman (1999) investigated how psychological resources, social support, and racial identity moderated the relationship between racial discrimination and mental health in the NSBA. In reference to racial identity, they found that, in addition to having beneficial main effects on psychological distress and subjective well-being, closeness to blacks moderated the association between discrimination and mental health. African Americans who experienced racial discrimination and felt close to most blacks reported lower distress and higher well-being than those that experienced discrimination but did not feel close to most blacks. While the results from the Williams et al. (1999) study is suggestive, more studies that characterize how racial identity might buffer the damaging impact of racial discrimination on mental health status are needed. In addition, studies are needed that delineate the *process* by which racial identity may influence both the experience of racial discrimination as well as potentially buffer or exacerbate the impact of racial discrimination.

THE STRESS AND COPING PARADIGM: RACIAL IDENTITY, RACISM, AND WELL-BEING

Racial discrimination is so pervasive in our society that it is almost impossible to adequately model its effects using the tools available to psychologists. It has proven to be particularly difficult to adequately operationalize the concept of racism in all of its many forms. While there is a long tradition of research on prejudice in the psychological literature, this literature has focused mainly on those who hold prejudice attitudes to the exclusion of those who are targets of this prejudice. Recently, a number of researchers have begun to conceptualize racist events within a stress and coping paradigm (Harrell, Merchant, & Young, 1997; Landrine & Klonoff, 1996; Thompson, 1996). The conceptualization of racism as a stress stimuli (or stressor) has a number of advantages. It links it to well-established research literature, describes mechanisms through which racial discrimination can be linked to mental and physical health outcomes, and provides a basis by which racial identity may be linked to mental and physical health outcomes. Psychological stress resulting from racial discrimination and mechanisms for coping with racism are considered as predictors of psychological well-being. Psychological stress has been defined as "a particular relationship between the person and the environment that is appraised by the person as taxing or exceeding his or her resources and endangering his or her well-being" (Lazarus & Folkman, 1984, p. 19). Three distinct approaches to stress are prevalent in psychological research: (1) the life events approach, (2) the daily hassles approach, and (3) the transactional approach to stress and coping. Each of these perspectives is amenable to an investigation of the relationships among racial identity, racial discrimination, stress, and coping. As few of these relationships have been empirically tested, our primary goal in the following section is to initiate a discussion of the myriad ways that racial identity potentially influences the impact of racial discrimination on mental health for African Americans. We intend to elucidate the process by which racial identity might affect stress and coping for each of the three approaches.

Major Life Events

Physicians made the first attempts to describe stress from a life events approach (Smith, 1993). They noticed that illnesses clustered around times when major life events occurred in patients' lives, and deduced from this correlation that major changes in people's lives were sources of stress that decreased physical health. Drawing upon this work, Holmes and Rahe (1967) identified nine categories of life events that represented major changes and required adaptive or coping behavior. As a result, major life events became defined as those events that require significant change in an individual's life. An implicit assumption of this approach is that the number of events experienced and the amount of change associated with the events are indicative of the amount of stress that an individual is currently experiencing. Early on, researchers consistently reported modest associations between major life events and experiences of physical and psychological health (Holmes & Rahe, 1967; Rahe, Mahan, & Arthur, 1970). More recently, efforts have begun to explore potential buffers of major life event stress (see Figure 2.3A). Person factors such as hardiness and personal control have been found to play an important role in buffering the deleterious consequences of major life events (for examples, see Kobasa, 1979; and Pearlin, Menaghan, Lieberman, & Mullan, 1981).

Some discriminatory experiences result in major changes in the lives of African Americans. For example, being denied admittance to a private school due to racial discrimination can require significant restructuring of an African American child's life. There is evidence that suggests experiencing major racist events can significantly impact African Americans' psychological well-being (Landrine & Klonoff, 1996). Yet not all African Americans are equally impacted by racist events. Just as a number of researchers have found that person factors such as personal control, hardiness, and social support may moderate

Figure 2.3
(A) Pictorial Representation of a Major Life Events Approach to Studying Stress and Mental Health; (B) Pictorial Representation of a Major Life Events Approach to Studying Racist Events, Racial Identity, and Mental Health

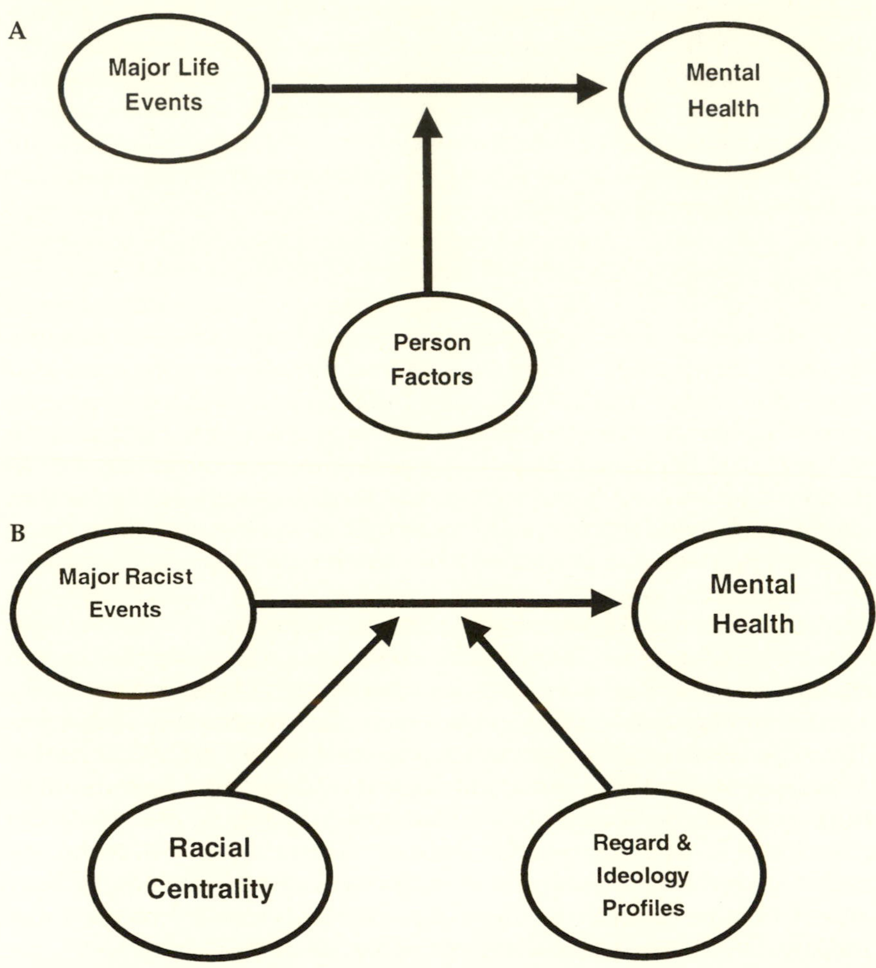

the relationship between major life events and mental health, racial identity can be similarly considered an attribute of individuals that may moderate the impact of major racist events on mental health (see Figure 2.3B).

The nature of this impact is also likely to vary according to the dimension of racial identity and the context of the life event. As such, one could argue that racial identity operates in two different ways. It could either exacerbate or buffer the deleterious impact of experiencing racist events on their psychological functioning. Certain racial identity attitudes may make one especially vulnerable to the impact of racist events. For example, one might speculate that experiencing more racist events could be particularly damaging for African Americans whose racial identity is central to their self-concept. Individuals for whom race is a central identity may be more likely to internalize an experience of racial discrimination as a personal threat to who they are. At the same time, low race-central African Americans may be able to distance themselves psychologically from the discrimination. Because they tend not to see themselves in the context of race, they may not view racial discrimination as being personally relevant. An alternative argument can be made, however, suggesting that higher levels of racial centrality may be protective and buffer against the impact of racial discrimination. One might argue that because African Americans who are highly race central are more likely to interpret race ambiguous situations as being racially relevant, they may be inoculated in some ways to the adverse impact of the racist event in comparison to low race-central African Americans. As a consequence of the sheer practice of interpreting more negative events as being the result of racial discrimination, high-central individuals may have developed a greater number of strategies in which to deal successfully with racist events. Meanwhile, low race-central individuals' deemphasis of race in defining themselves may leave them with fewer coping resources and strategies for dealing with racial discrimination.

A different logic might follow for how an individual's beliefs about the meaning of being black (ideology and regard) may moderate the relationship between experiences of major racist events and well-being. The extent to which the experience of a major racist event is consistent or inconsistent with the racial ideological worldview of an individual is likely to have consequences for how the major racist event impacts the individual's psychological well-being. For instance, African Americans with a strong nationalist or oppressed minority ideology may expect to experience racist life events and as a result may be more prepared to deal with them. The concept of racial discrimination is not foreign to the way in which they engage the world. On the other hand, African Americans with a strong humanist ideology are less likely to view themselves and others on the basis of race. The experience of a major racist event is likely to be inconsistent with their previous experience and their current worldview. As a result, these individuals have to engage in the psychologically taxing task of reconciling the inconsistency between their worldview and their experience. Such a task may be very stressful. The influence of a strong assimilationist ideology would likely depend on whether the worldview of the African

American who experienced racism was challenged by the event(s). Regard might operate in a similar fashion for African Americans. People who believe that other groups have relatively negative opinions of African Americans (low public regard) may be less affected by racism because it is consistent with their worldview. Private regard may buffer the consequences of racism. African Americans who feel positively about their racial group membership may be psychologically prepared to shield themselves from messages of social devaluation that are often communicated in racist experiences.

Daily Hassles

While major life events may show a consistent relationship with mental and physical health outcomes, some stress researchers have presented evidence that suggests that the experience of minor events or "daily hassles" may be more predictive of health (Kanner, Coyne, Schaeffer, & Lazarus, 1981). Hassles are defined as "the irritating, frustrating, distressing demands that to some degree characterize everyday transactions with the environment" (Smith, 1993, p. 18). Examples of daily hassles include being stuck in a traffic jam, misplacing or losing things, waiting in line, and having difficulty making small decisions. Daily hassles may be more predictive of mental health outcomes because the cumulative impact of a number of these hassles may serve to wear an individual down (Taylor, 1999). For most individuals, daily hassles are much more prevalent than major life events. Daily hassles also seem to have a synergistic effect. The combination of two or more hassles seems to increase the level of stress that an individual experiences exponentially. The experience of one daily hassle often increases the likelihood that another event is experienced as a hassle. For instance, a person is more likely to experience waiting in line for concert tickets as a hassle if the person has just spent an hour in a traffic jam than if he or she just walked up to the line. Because hassles are minor events, they are much more dependent on the person's interpretation of the event as stressful than major life events. While variation in the circumstances surrounding the death of a loved one may result in the event being appraised somewhat differently, it is highly unlikely that an individual would not experience such an event as being at least somewhat stressful. On the other hand, whether a person experiences waiting in line as stressful is much more dependent on who the person is and what other circumstances surround the event (see Figure 2.4A).

While a major life events approach to studying racial discrimination would focus on those racist events that lead to significant changes in an individual's life, a daily hassles approach would focus on more

Figure 2.4
(A) Pictorial Representation of a Daily Hassles Approach to Studying Stress and Mental Health; (B) Pictorial Representation of a Daily Hassles Approach to Studying Racist Events, Racial Identity, and Mental Health

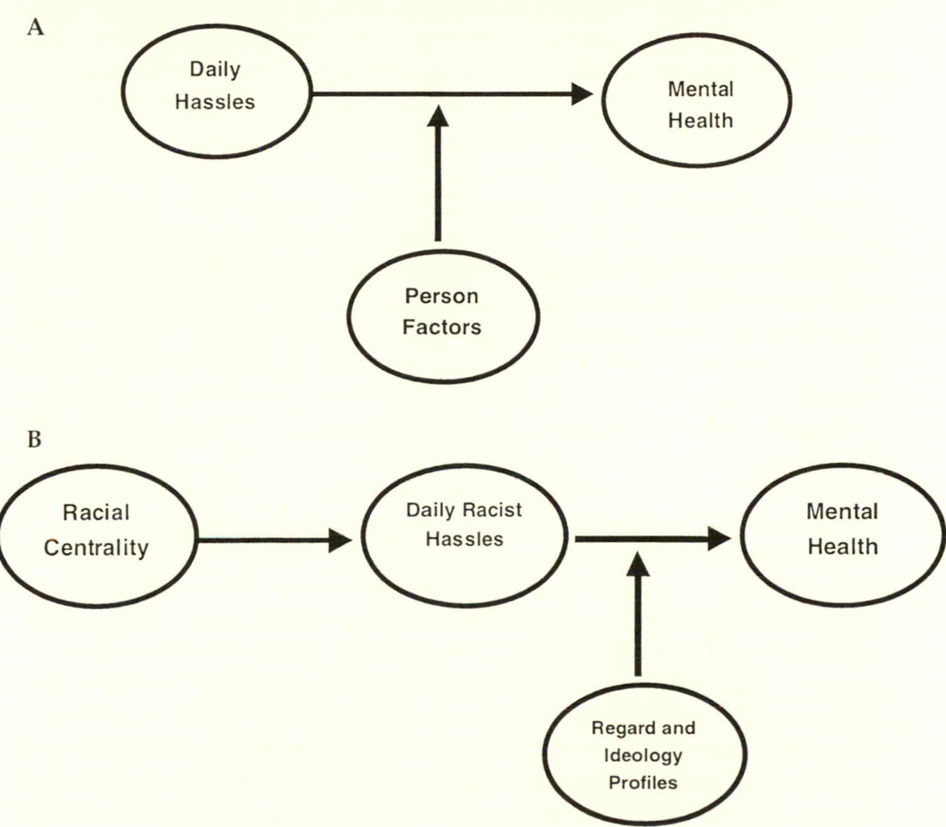

subtle experiences of racism that are likely to occur much more frequently. Not being called on by the teacher in class when he or she knows the answer is an example of daily racist experience that an African American child may face. While major racist events are generally blatant, minor events and daily hassles are more ambiguous and must first be construed as racist in order to be considered a racist daily hassle. Racial centrality and ideology may play an important role in this attribution process (see Figure 2.4B). A previous study by Shelton and Sellers (2000) demonstrated that African Americans who are highly race central were significantly more likely to attribute ambiguous discriminatory events to race than African Americans who were less race central. Fifty-five African American college students were given a scenario in which an African American student was told by a professor that "people like you usually don't do well at this school." When the professor was white, high race-central and low race-central participants were equally likely to attribute the comments to race. In the racially ambiguous situation where the professor was African American, however, race attributions were more likely for the high race-central group. The same relationship may hold for daily hassles: African Americans who are high race central will likely construe ambiguous events as racist and thus report experiencing a greater number of daily racist hassles than those who score lower on racial centrality. Once experienced as a racist hassle, the moderating impact of regard and ideology should operate in the same manner as described with major racist events and mental health. Some identity profiles may exacerbate the impact of racist hassles, while other profiles may exhibit a buffering effect.

The Transactional Model

The major life events and daily hassles approaches provide a mechanism for determining the moderating role of identity in the long-term health consequences of experiencing racist events. Many questions are left unanswered, however, by these outcome-oriented approaches. The previously proposed models of racist events, racial identity, and well-being do not provide a framework for an event-level examination. These models do not describe a process by which a specific racist event affects a person's immediate mental health status. The transactional model of stress as developed by Lazarus and Folkman (1984) provides such a framework. The transactional model of stress and coping describes the processes by which person and situation characteristics interact to determine (1) whether a specific event is experienced as stressful, (2) what coping strategies are employed, and (3) what are the psychological consequences of the event and the person's attempts to cope (see Figure 2.5A). Whereas the relationships we proposed based on the major life events and daily hassles approaches *implicitly* assume that one's appraisal of and ability to deal with racist event is the driving force behind the relationship between racial discrimination and subjective well-being, the relationships we propose within the transactional framework *explicitly* define the role of appraisal and coping. As a result, it is possible to empirically assess when and for whom a particular racist event is likely to be appraised as stressful, what coping strategies are likely to be employed, and what are the possible consequences of these appraisals and coping responses.

Figure 2.5
(A) Pictorial Representation of a Transactional Approach to Studying Stress and Mental Health; (B) Pictorial Representation of a Transactional Approach to Studying Racist Events, Racial Identity, and Mental Health

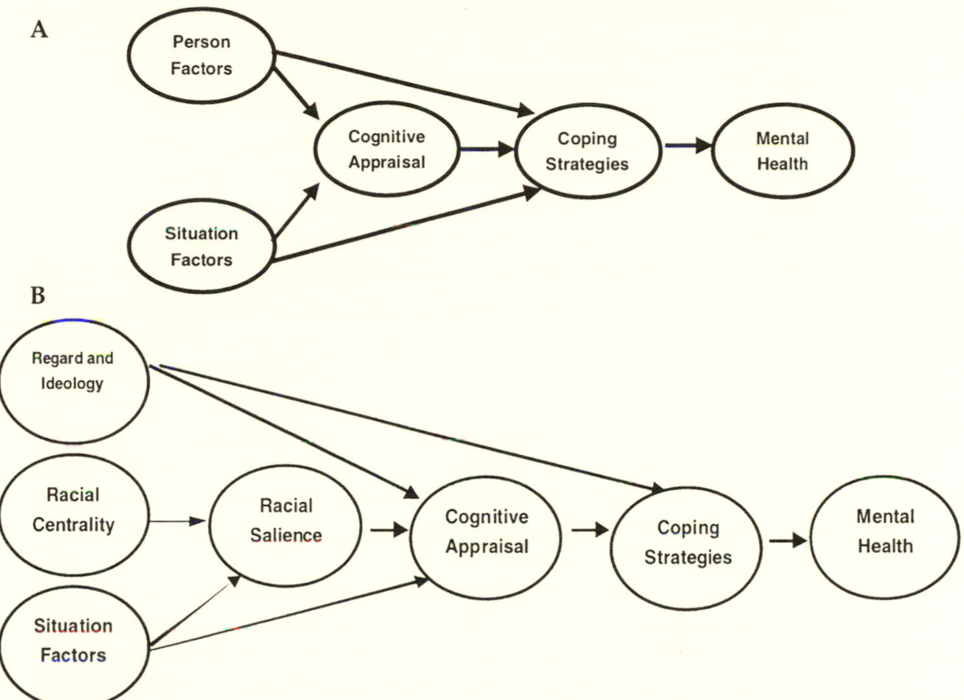

According to Lazarus and Folkman (1984), we are under stress when something we need or want is threatened and we do not think we can do much about the situation. As such, it is centered on a transaction concerning needs and wants. The two important processes in this model are cognitive appraisal and coping. Cognitive appraisal is defined as the continuous "categorizing of an encounter, and its various facets, with respect to its significance for well-being" (Lazarus & Folkman, 1984, p. 31). There are two types of cognitive appraisals: primary appraisal and secondary appraisal. Primary appraisal concerns the stakes of a stressful encounter (whether one thinks that damage has or will come from the situation), while secondary appraisal refers to coping prospects (one's perceived ability to deal with the situation effectively). Lazarus and his colleagues define coping as "the person's cognitive and behavioral efforts to manage [reduce, minimize, master, or tolerate] the internal and external demands of the person–environment transaction that is appraised as taxing or exceeding the person's resources" (Folkman, Lazarus, Gruen, & Delongis, 1986, p. 572). Both person factors (e.g., hardiness, control) and situation factors (e.g., context) are proposed to affect cognitive appraisal and coping strategies. As such, racial identity should indirectly influence the impact of a given racist interaction on mental health through its direct influence on appraisal and coping.

The first step in the transactional model for racist events, racial identity, and mental health is the attribution of the event as one that is or is not racist. Both racial centrality and the situational context play an important role in the attribution process. As noted previously, Shelton and Sellers (in press) found that both an individual's level of centrality and situational cues were predictive in determining when a person perceived a situation as being race relevant. An implicit assumption in the Shelton and Sellers' study was that the racial centrality and situational cues interacted to result in race becoming a salient construct for the individual which, in turn, leads the individual to interpret the professor's actions as either being the result of race or of some other reason (see Figure 2.5B). Clearly, further research is needed to explicitly test this assumption. Nonetheless, this assumption provides a hypothesized process for explaining the mechanism by which racial centrality, racial salience, and situational cues may influence how an individual interprets a situation.

While determining whether race is relevant to the particular event, African Americans must also determine whether the experience is stressful. Primary appraisal refers to whether something that is important to the individual is at stake. Racial centrality, ideology, and regard may all affect an individual's appraisal of what is at stake. Individuals who are high race central may be more likely to appraise a race-relevant event as being one for which there is a great deal at stake than an individual for whom race was less central. Those who strongly endorse humanist and assimilationist ideologies might also see such events as having a great deal at stake because the events may pose a threat to these individuals' goals of integrating into mainstream society or deemphasizing the importance of race in the way in which people treat each other. On the other hand, African Americans who strongly endorse the nationalist and oppressed minority ideologies have alternate goals—to build coalitions within the race or with others who are similarly oppressed. Therefore, a racist experience might be less threatening because it often does not challenge these goals. Individuals' levels of private regard may also influence whether they view a particular event as one in which there is a lot at stake. Situations that have deleterious consequences for blacks are more likely to be appraised as being threatening for individuals who feel more positively about African Americans.

Secondary appraisal refers to whether the individual thinks she or he has adequate resources to deal with a racist experience. Again, the various dimensions of the MMRI are likely to influence secondary appraisal differently. African Americans who generally think of themselves in terms of their racial group membership and feel positively about their racial group may be more prepared to deal with racism. Centrality, nationalism, and oppressed minority ideologies should be positively related to perceived resources, as racism should be consistent with the worldview of African Americans who strongly endorse these dimensions. Because they are more likely to experience situations with ambiguous race cues as being racial, over the years they have had greater practice dealing with race and may have developed a stronger arsenal for dealing with racist events. Similarly, high private regard may buffer the impact of negative information about African Americans. On the other hand, African Americans who believe that other groups have positive attitudes toward African Americans (i.e., high public regard) and strongly endorse humanism may be more surprised by racist experiences and thus less prepared to deal with them. They may appraise the situation as one for which they are less confident in their ability to cope.

Clearly, additional factors beyond racial identity determine the amount of resources African Americans have to deal with racial discrimination. For example, finances, social class, and social and institutional support remain important determinants of perceptions of available resources to deal with racist experiences. In addition, other personality characteristics play into secondary appraisal of racism. Feelings of personal control can dictate assessments of whether a racist event is stressful. While an African American who scores high on racial centrality may feel threatened by a racist experience, she may also think that she has adequate resources on hand to deal with the situation. The level of stress that she experiences in this event may ultimately depend largely on the amount of control she has in the situation. If she has enough control in the situation to utilize her resources, she will be in a better position to deal with the racist experience. However, if her control is limited, she may be more psychologically vulnerable.

Once the racist event is appraised as stressful, African Americans employ a variety of coping strategies to deal with the stress of racism. Racial identity should be related to the frequency and the qualitative nature of coping strategies that African Americans use to deal with racism. A variety of strategies fall under the umbrella of coping with stress: Problem-focused strategies involve active attempts to reduce stress by changing the situation at hand, while emotion-focused strategies describe attempts to change one's internal response to the situation. Avoidance-coping strategies are attempts to reduce stress by ignoring the situation. Because of their greater experience with racist events, high race-central African Americans and those who endorse nationalism or the oppressed minority ideologies may be more likely to employ problem-focused strategies to change the situation in which racism occurred. Private regard might serve as a cognitive buffer and therefore might be positively related to the use of emotion-focused strategies, while the humanist ideology might be positively correlated with avoidance strategies, due to the desire not to deal with race.

Although both regard and ideology attitudes may help us predict whether individuals are likely to choose more problem-focused or emotion-focused strategies in a particular racist event, their ability to predict more specific coping behavior may be an even greater contribution. Private regard and ideology attitudes may allow us to make more fine-grain behavioral predictions with respect to the individuals coping behavior beyond the intent of their coping efforts (problem-focused versus emotion-focused). For example, an African American who strongly endorses an assimilationist ideology might choose a problem-focused coping strategy of fighting racism in the workplace by using the Equal Employment Opportunities Commission to promote integration. On the other hand, an African American who strongly endorses nationalism might choose a problem focused strategy that is consistent with his/her political ideology and initiate an entrepreneurial venture with other African Americans. In both instances, problem-focused coping strategies are employed; the actual behavioral responses, however, are very different.

The benefit of using a stress and coping framework to understand how racial identity may moderate the association between racial discrimination and mental health is the flexibility it affords in examining each of the potential pathways by which racial identity may influence appraisal and coping. As we have mentioned, many other factors beyond identity, racism, stress and coping are important in determining the mental health of African Americans (e.g., age, gender, marital status, socioeconomic status, and personality traits). As such, it is not likely that any one path described in the previous models will independently explain a large proportion of the statistical variance in mental health. However, the goal of this particular line of research is to delineate the mechanisms by which racial identity influences the link between experiencing racist events and the psychological well-being in African Americans. We also recognize the complexity of the relationships that we have proposed. The importance of parsimony in science notwithstanding, we feel it is very important that we as researchers incorporate the natural complexity inherent in the role that race plays in the lives of African Americans.

SPECIAL CONSIDERATIONS FOR UNDERSTANDING AFRICAN AMERICAN CHILDREN

A major hurdle in our understanding the links between racial identity, racial discrimination, and mental health in African American children is the dearth of strong empirical research supporting our conceptual understanding of how children experience these constructs. Nowhere is this need more critical than in the racial identity development literature. Despite the popularity of developmental models, there is an alarming dearth of empirical studies of racial identity using longitudinal designs (Deaux, 1993). This lack of research impedes our understanding of how racial identity develops and changes. The MMRI provides a strong basis for propositions regarding the development and change of racial identity dimensions over the lifespan. As conceptualized by the MMRI, it is quite likely that different dimensions of racial identity develop at different ages due to African American children's cognitive resources. The ability to use racial categories in a consistent and meaningful way is a necessary cognitive prerequisite for the formation of a racial identity. There is no consensus regarding the age at which the ability to use racial categories first develops, but recent research suggests that children as young as three years old are able to use racial categories (Katz & Kofkin, 1997). Once children are able to use racial categories, it is likely that children will develop stable attitudes regarding the significance that race plays in their own conceptualization of self (defined as racial centrality by the MMRI) before they develop stable attitudes about what being black actually means.

The formation of attitudes regarding the meaning of being black often must take place within the context of exposure to other racial groups. This is often necessary so that the contrast between the racial groups can stimulate the child to develop meaning for the racial groups, in order that he or she can discriminate between the racial categories. The meanings that the child attributes to being black are likely to be initially shaped by individuals within his/her immediate social context. For instance, research by Clark and Clark (1947) suggests that African American children develop racial group preferences, a proxy for private regard, as early as age nine. Knowledge of others' opinions of African Americans, synonymous with the MMRI dimension of public regard, however, might be constructed only after African American children have engaged in sophisticated interactions with members of other racial groups. These types of interactions may become a part of African American children's social life only after they have reached school age. Racial ideology is likely the last dimension of racial identity to develop among African American children. These types of attitudes are dependent on both the development of a cognitive capacity to integrate complex and sometimes conflicting ideas into coherent ideologies, as well as exposure to enough social experiences in which the child must consider the impact of race in his or her assessment of the situation.

Currently, these suggestions regarding racial identity development are speculative. In order to determine the ages at which these dimensions of racial identity develop, qualitative research (e.g., focus groups, interviews) is needed with children of various age groups. Such research should assess the relevance of each dimension to African American children's racial self-schemas. Further, longitudinal designs should be employed to assess how the MMRI's dimensions of racial identity develop and change over time in children, given their life experiences.

Along with longitudinal designs, another imperative for research examining racial identity in African American children is the use of measures that are both age appropriate and derived from a theoretical model of racial identity that considers identity across the life span. As noted earlier, experience and cognitive ability make many existing paper-and-pencil measures of racial identity inappropriate for younger children. Not only may the underlying construct be inaccessible to younger children, the mode of instrumentation may not be suited for children. Research must understand the phenomenological experiences of the individuals they are assessing when developing instruments of racial identity for children. Thus, it is preferable to develop measures specifically for children rather than attempting to simply adapt items and change vocabulary from existing measures. In developing these new instruments, it is also imperative that these instruments are grounded in conceptual models of racial identity that are not age limited by design. Otherwise, it becomes difficult to integrate the findings generated from these new instruments into an overall framework for understanding racial identity across the life span.

An example of the issues associated with development of a racial identity instrument for children can be found in our efforts to develop a version of the Multidimensional Inventory of Black Identity for African American adolescents (ages 12 to 15). We have started with focus groups in which we ask African American adolescents what they think it means to be black. We use this question to elicit self-generated responses from the adolescents. We provide to the group definitions of the various dimensions and subdimensions of the MMRI. We ask the group whether they understand the definition. We ask the adolescents to redefine the concept of the dimension in their own words to make sure that they really do understand the concept. Next, we ask them to give us an example from their experience that is related to the dimension or subdimension of the MMRI. Finally, we ask them to help us generate items that they think capture the underlying construct. We believe that such an approach to developing a new instrument insures that the instrument is valid and that the constructs we are tapping are actually relevant to the population that we are trying to assess.

In this chapter, we have argued that racial identity's relationship with mental health outcomes is moderated by contextual factors. We propose that the relationships between particular racial identity attitudes and indicators of psychological well-being are likely to differ in different situations (e.g., experiences of racial discrimination). In order to learn more about African American children's racial identity development and mental health, it is especially important to empirically examine the impact of racist events on stress, coping, and mental health. It is important that such research consider age-appropriate racist life events and hassles. The role of racial socialization messages should also be explored as they potentially influence African American children's expectations of racial discrimination, appraisals of racist events, and racial coping strategies. Further, long-term longitudinal designs must be employed in order to gain better insight as to the causal directions of the relationships among racial identity, experiences of discrimination, and mental health. It is very likely that the relationships among these variables are bidirectional. For instance, over time, racist events may affect a child's attitudes about his or her racial group or racial identity. The subsequent change in racial identity may in turn influence how the child appraises and copes with subsequent racist events. The consequences of a subsequent racist event may then influence the significance and meaning of race in a child's self-definition. This reciprocal process of racial identification and racial coping is likely to impact the child's short-term and long-term mental well-being.

CONCLUSION

In conclusion, this chapter has attempted to explicate ways in which racial identity may be related to the psychological well-being of African Americans. While many of the relationships that we proposed are currently untested, each of the relationships proposed in this chapter is testable using current theories of racial identity. The primary goal of this chapter was to provide a blueprint for future research. In laying out this blueprint, we have tried to make three points about the nature of African American racial identity. First, African Americans are not monolithic in the way that they view themselves in the context of race. Second, African American racial identity has implications for our understanding of both behaviors and functioning, particularly in the context of racism and mental health. Finally, African American racial identity is a complex phenomenon, and its complexity should be taken into account as researchers continue to explore its development and its associations with experiences of racial discrimination and mental health.

NOTE

All correspondence should be directed to the first author at the Department of Psychology, University of Michigan, Ann Arbor, MI 48109 or via e-mail at rsellers@umich.edu.

REFERENCES

Akbar, N. (1989). Nigrescence and identity: Some limitations. *Counseling Psychologist, 17* (2), 258–263.

Anderson, L. P. (1991). Acculturative stress: A theory of relevance to black Americans. *Clinical Psychology Review, 11*, 685–702.

Austin, N. L., Carter, R. T., & Vaux, A. (1990). The role of racial identity in black students' attitudes toward counseling and counseling centers. *Journal of College Student Development, 31* (3), 237–244.

Baldwin, J. A. (1984). African self-consciousness and the mental health of African Americans. *Journal of Black Studies, 15* (2), 177–194.

Baldwin, J. A., & Bell, Y. (1985). The African self-consciousness scale: An Africentric personality questionnaire. *The Western Journal of Black Studies, 9* (2), 61–68.

Banaji, M. R., & Prentice, D. A. (1994). The self in social contexts. *Annual Review of Psychology, 45*, 297–332.

Banks, W. C. (1976). White preference in blacks: A paradigm in search of a phenomenon. *Psychological Bulletin, 83* (6), 1179–1186.

Bargh, J. A., Bond, R. N., Lombardi, W. J., & Tota, M. E. (1986). The additive nature of chronic and temporary sources of construct accessibility. *Journal of Personality and Social Psychology, 50*, 869–878.

Billingsley, A. (1992). *Climbing Jacob's ladder: The enduring legacy of African American families*. New York: Simon & Schuster.

Broman, C. L. (1997). Race-related factors and life satisfaction among African Americans. *Journal of Black Psychology, 23* (1), 36–49.

Brown, T. N., Williams, D., Jackson, J. S., Sellers, S., Brown, K., Torres, M., & Neighbors, H. (in press). *"Being black and feeling blue": The mental health consequences of racial discrimination*. Race and Society.

Brown, T. N. (1998). *Racial stratification and the mental health status of African Americans and white Americans in Detroit, Michigan*. Ph.D. diss., University of Michigan, Ann Arbor.

Burke, A. W. (1984). Racism and psychological disturbance among West Indians in Britain. *International Journal of Social Psychiatry, 30* (3–2), 50–68.

Burlew, A. K., & Smith, L. R. (1991). Measures of racial identity: An overview and proposed framework. *Journal of Black Psychology, 17*, 53–71.

Carter, J. H. (1993). Racism's impact on mental health. *Journal of the National Medical Association, 86* (7), 543–547.

Carter, R. T. (1991). Racial identity attitudes and psychological functioning. *Journal of Multicultural Counseling and Development, 19* (3), 105–114.

Carter, R. T., & Helms, J. E. (1988). The relationship between racial identity attitudes and social class. *Journal of Negro Education, 57* (1), 22–30.

Clark, K. B., & Clark, M. P. (1939). The development of consciousness of self and the emergence of racial identification in Negro pre-school children. *Journal of Social Psychology, 10,* 591–599.

Clark, K. B., & Clark, M. P. (1947). Racial identification and preference in Negro children. In T. M. Newcomb & E. L. Hartley (Eds.), *Readings in social psychology* (pp. 169–178). New York: Holt.

Crocker, J., & Luhtanen, R. (1990). Collective self-esteem and in-group bias. *Journal of Personality and Social Psychology, 58,* 60–67.

Crocker, J., Luhtanen, R., Blaine, B., & Broadnax, S. (1994). Collective self-esteem and psychological well-being among white, black and Asian college students. *Personality and Social Psychology Bulletin, 20,* 503–513.

Cross, W. E. (1971). Negro-to-black conversion experience. *Black World, 20,* 13–27.

Cross, W. E. (1991). *Shades of black: Diversity in African-American identity.* Philadelphia: Temple University Press.

Cross, W. E., Parham, T. A., & Helms, J. E. (1998). Nigrescence revisited: Theory and research. In R. L. Jones (Ed.), *African American identity development: Theory, research, and intervention.* Hampton, VA: Cobb & Henry.

Deaux, K. (1993). Reconstructing the social identity. *Personality and Social Psychology Bulletin, 19,* 4–12.

Delgado, A. K. (1982). On being black. In F. X. Acosta, J. Yamamoto, & L. A. Evans (Eds.), *Effective psychotherapy for low-income and minority patients* (pp. 109–116). New York: Plenum Press.

Demo, D. H., & Hughes, M. (1990). Socialization and racial identity among black Americans. *Social Psychology Quarterly, 53,* 364–374.

Fernando, S. (1984). Racism as a cause of depression. *International Journal of Social Psychiatry, 30* (1–2), 41–49.

Foard, F. (1991). A year of progress. *Minority News, 2* (3), 1–10.

Folkman, S., Lazarus, R. S., Gruen, R., & DeLongis, A. (1986). Appraisal, coping, health status, and psychological symptoms. *Journal of Personality and Social Psychology, 50,* 571–579.

Franklin, A. J. (1998). Treating anger in African American men. In *New psychotherapy for men* (pp. 239–258). New York: John Wiley & Sons.

Hacker, A. (1995). Two nations: *Black and white, separate, hostile, unequal.* New York: Ballantine Books.

Harrell, S. P., Merchant, M. A., & Young, S. A. (1997). *Psychometric properties of the racism and life experiences scales (RaLES).* Paper presented at the meeting of the American Psychological Association, Chicago, IL.

Helms, J. E. (1984). Toward a theoretical explanation of the effects of race on counseling: A black and white model. *Counseling Psychologist, 12* (3–4), 153–165.

Higgins, E. T. (1990). Personality, social psychology, and person–situation relations: Standards and knowledge activation as a common language. In L. A. Pervin (Ed.), *Handbook of personality: Theory and research* (pp. 301–338). New York: Guilford Press.

Holmes, T. H., & Rahe, R. H. (1967). The social readjustment rating scale. *Journal of Psychosomatic Research, 11*, 213–218.

Horowitz, R. (1939). Racial aspects of self-identification in nursery school children. *Journal of Psychology, 7*, 91–99.

Horowitz, R., & Murphy, L. B. (1938). Projective methods in the psychological study of children. *Journal of Experimental Education, 7*, 133–140.

Hughes, M., & Demo, D. H. (1989). Self-perception of black Americans: Self-esteem and personal efficacy. *American Journal of Sociology, 95*, 132–159.

Jackson, J. S., Brown, T. N., Williams, D. R., Torres, M., Sellers, R., & Brown, K. (1996). Racism and the physical and mental health status of African Americans: A thirteen year national panel study. *Ethnicity and Disease, 6* (1, 2), 132–147.

Johnson, L. B. (1989). The employed black: The dynamics of work–family tension. *The Review of Black Political Economy, 17*, 69–85.

Kanner, A. D., Coyne, J. C., Schaeffer, C., & Lazarus, R. S. (1981). Comparison of two modes of stress measurement: Daily hassles and uplifts versus major life events. *Journal of Behavioral Medicine, 4*, 1–39.

Kardiner, A., & Ovesey, L. (1951). *The mark of oppression*. New York: Norton.

Katz, P. A., & Kofkin, J. A. (1997). Race, gender, and young children. In S. S. Luthar, J. A. Burack, D. Cicchetti, & J. R. Weisz (Eds.), *Developmental psychopathology: Perspectives on adjustment, risk, and disorder* (pp. 51–74). New York: Cambridge University Press.

Kobasa, S. C. (1979). Stressful life events, personality, and health: An inquiry into hardiness. *Journal of Personality and Social Psychology, 37*, 1–11.

Landrine, H., & Klonoff, E. A. (1996). The schedule of racist events: A measure of racial discrimination and a study of its negative physical and mental health consequences. *Journal of Black Psychology, 22* (2), 144–168.

Lazarus, R. S., & Folkman, S. (1984). *Stress appraisal and coping*. New York: Springer.

Locke, D. (1992). *Increasing multicultural understanding: A comprehensive model*. Newbury Park, CA: Sage.

Luhtanen, R., & Crocker, J. (1992). A collective self-esteem scale: Self-evaluation of one's social identity. *Personality and Social Psychology Bulletin, 18*, 302–318.

Marks, B., Settles, I. H., Cooke, D. Y., Morgan, L., & Sellers, R. M. (in press). African American racial identity: A review of contemporary models and measures. In R. L. Jones (Ed.), *Black psychology* (4th ed.). Hampton, VA: Cobb & Henry.

Markus, H., & Nurius, P. (1986). Possible selves. *American Psychologist, 41*, 954–969.

Marriette, G. C. (1990). *Racial identity attitudes as predictors of ego functions/defense mechanisms in African American adult school students*. Unpublished Ph.D. diss., California Graduate Institute, Los Angeles.

Milliones, J. (1980). Construction of a black consciousness measure: Psychotherapeutic implications. *Psychotherapy: Theory, Research, and Practice, 17* (2), 175–182.

Munford, M. B. (1994). Relationship of gender, self-esteem, social class, and racial identity to depression in blacks. *Journal of Black Psychology, 20* (2), 157–174.

Neal, A. M., & Brown, B.J.W. (1994). Fears and anxiety disorders in African Americans. In S. Friedman (Ed.), *Anxiety disorders in African Americans*. New York: Springer.

Outlaw, F. H. (1993). Stress and coping: The influence of racism on the cognitive appraisal processing of African Americans. *Issues in Mental Health Nursing, 14*, 399–409.

Parham, T. A., & Helms, J. E. (1981). The influences of a black student's racial identity attitudes on preferences for counselor's race. *Journal of Counseling Psychology, 28* (3), 250–256.

Parham. T. A., & Helms, J. E. (1985). Relation of racial identity attitudes to self-actualization and affective states of black students. *Journal of Counseling Psychology, 32* (3), 431–440.

Parham, T. A., & Williams, P. T. (1993). The relationship of demographic and background factors to racial identity attitudes. *Journal of Black Psychology, 19* (1), 3–16.

Pearlin, L. I., Menaghan, E. G., Lieberman, M. A., & Mullan, J. T. (1981). The stress process. *Journal of Health and Social Behavior, 22* (4), 337–356.

Penn, M. L., Gaines, S. O., & Phillips, L. (1993). On the desirability of own-group preference. *Journal of Black Psychology, 19*, 303–321.

Peters, M. (1978). Psychosocial determinants of depression among blacks. *Transnational Mental Health Research Newsletter, 20* (1), 5–9.

Phinney, J. S. (1992). The multigroup ethnic identity measure. *Journal of Adolescent Research, 7* (2), 156–176.

Pierce, C. M. (1975). The mundane extreme environment and its effect on learning. In S. G. Brainard (Ed.), *Learning disabilities: Issues and recommendations for research* (pp. 1–28). Washington, DC: National Institute of Education.

Ponterotto, J. G., & Wise, S. C. (1987). A construct validity study of the Racial Identity Attitude Scale. *Journal of Counseling Psychology, 34*, 218–223.

Pyant, C. T., & Yanico, B. J. (1991). Relationship of racial identity and gender-role attitudes to black women's psychological well-being. *Journal of Counseling Psychology, 38*, 315–322.

Rahe, R. H., Mahan, J. L., & Arthur, R. J. (1970). Prediction of near future health change from subjects' preceding life changes. *Journal of Psychosomatic Research, 14* (4), 401–406.

Rosenberg, M., & Simmons, R. G. (1971). *Black and white self-esteem: The urban school child*. Arnold and Caroline Rose Monograph Series. Washington, DC: American Sociological Association.

Rowley, S.A.J., & Sellers, R. M. (1998). Nigrescence theory: Critical issues and recommendations for future revisions. In R. L. Jones (Ed.), *African American identity development: Theory, research, and intervention* (pp.141–150). Hampton, VA: Cobb & Henry.

Rowley, S.A.J., Sellers, R. M., Chavous, T. M., & Smith, M. (1998). The relationship between racial identity and self-esteem in African American college students. *Journal of Personality and Social Psychology, 74* (3), 715–724.

Sellers, R. M. (1993). A call to arms for researchers studying racial identity. *Journal of Black Psychology, 19* (2), 327–332.

Sellers, R. M., Caldwell, C., Zimmerman, M., & Hilkene, D. (1999, June). *Racial identity and substance abuse in a sample of academically at-risk African American high school students*. Presented at the biennial meeting of the Society for Community Research and Action, New Haven, CT.

Sellers, R. M., Rowley, S.A.J., Chavous, T. M., Shelton, J. N., & Smith, M. (1997). Multidimensional inventory of black identity: Preliminary investigation of reliability and construct validity. *Journal of Personality and Social Psychology, 73*, 805–815.

Sellers, R. M., Shelton, J. N., Cooke, D., Chavous, T., Rowley, S.A.J., & Smith, M. (1998). A multidimensional model of racial identity: Assumptions, findings and future directions. In R. L. Jones (Ed.), *African American identity development: Theory, research, and intervention*. Hampton, VA: Cobb & Henry.

Sellers, R. M., Smith, M., Shelton, J. N., Rowley, S.A.J., & Chavous, T. M. (1998). Multidimensional model of racial identity: A reconceptualization of African American racial identity. *Personality and Social Psychology Review, 2* (1), 18–39.

Shelton, J. N., & Sellers, R. M. (2000). Situational stability and variability in African American racial identity. *Journal of Black Psychology, 26* (1), 27–50.

Smith, E. (1989). Black racial identity development: Issues and concerns. *The Counseling Psychologist, 17*, 277–288.

Smith, J. C. (1993). *Understanding stress and coping*. New York: Macmillan.

Stokes, J. E., Murray, C. B., Chavez, D., & Peacock, J. M. (1998). Cross' stage model revisited: An analysis of theoretical formulations and empirical evidence. In R. L. Jones (Ed.), *African American identity development: Theory, research, and intervention* (pp. 121–140). Hampton, VA: Cobb & Henry.

Taylor, S. E. (1999). *Health psychology* (4th ed.). Boston: McGraw-Hill.

Terrell, F., & Taylor, J. (1980). Self-concept of juveniles who commit black-on-black crimes. *Journal of Corrective and Social Psychiatry, 26*, 107–109.

Terrell, F., & Terrell, S. L. (1981). An inventory to measure cultural mistrust among blacks. *Western Journal of Black Studies, 5* (3), 180–184.

Thompson, V. S. (1996). Perceived experiences of racism as stressful life events. *Community Mental Health Journal, 32* (3), 223–233.

Utsey, S. O. (1998). Assessing the stressful effects of racism: A review of instrumentation. *Journal of Black Psychology, 24* (3), 269–288.

Watts, R. J. (1992). Racial identity and preferences for social change strategies among African Americans. *Journal of Black Psychology, 18* (2), 1–18.

Weiner, B. (Ed.). (1974). *Cognitive views of human emotion*. New York: Academic Press.

Williams, D. R., Brown, T. N., Sellers, S., & Forman, T. (1999). *Racism and mental health: Risk factors and resources*. Unpublished manuscript.

Williams, D. R., & Chung, A-M. (in press). Racism and health. In R. Gibson and J. S. Jackson (Eds.), *Health in black America*. Thousand Oaks, CA: Sage.

Williams, D. R., Yu, Y., Jackson, D. S., & Anderson, N. B. (1997). *Racial differences in physical and mental health: Socioeconomic status, stress, and discrimination*. Unpublished manuscript.

Wyer, R. S., & Srull, T. K. (1981). Category accessibility: Some theoretical and empirical issues concerning the processing of social stimulus information. In E. T. Higgins, C. P. Herman, & M. P. Zanna (Eds.), *Social cognition: The Ontario symposium* (Vol. 1, pp. 1–43). Hillsdale, NJ: Erlbaum.

3

Parental Characteristics, Racial Stress, and Racial Socialization Processes as Predictors of Racial Coping in Middle Childhood

Deborah J. Johnson

Ecological models of human development over traditional developmental models consider contexts but fall short on the serious consideration of culture in family processes associated with socialization. Parental characteristics, perceptions, and practices in child rearing are the primary and critically influential factors in the development of competent children (Bugental & Goodenow, 1998). Key components of emerging developmental models inclusive of ethnic minority children centralize the contexts and experiences associated with economic and racial discrimination as contributing determinants of parental socialization processes and child outcomes (Garcia-Coll et al., 1996). In these contemporary models, competent children, particularly children of color, must necessarily develop race-related strategies to cope with the experiences and consequences of societal prejudice and discrimination. Few studies have addressed these parental racial socialization processes and child outcomes simultaneously. Among those who have investigated these relations, the principal outcome of interest is most often children's personal and racial identity development (Marshall, 1995; Spencer, 1983; Stevenson, 1995). The relation between parental socialization processes and children's coping in relation to race is only beginning to be addressed empirically.

Among the studies of racial socialization that do exist, many have pursued the investigation of adolescent experiences. Stevenson and his colleagues (e.g., Stevenson, 1995) are notable in this regard, focusing especially on adolescent outcomes and parental socialization issues, with some emphasis on what happens in the development of African American males. In particular Stevenson has found that parental socialization messages impact the development of identity among black youth. Importantly, he has also found that parental messages are predictive of adolescent recall about those messages and their own experiences. Still, the relation between adolescents and their parents, cognitive development, and the lived experiences of urban adolescents may make poor comparisons to the less developed experiences and cognitive prowess among those in middle childhood and in early adolescence. These developmental periods are difficult to compare at best. In this regard it is important to assess and further explore the relations between younger children and their parents.

Like studies of adolescence, childhood studies of racial socialization have often emphasized child racial identity (Spencer, 1983) or academic achievement (Bowman & Howard, 1985; Marshall, 1995) as the outcome of importance. Here too parental practices and intentional messages around race and prejudice have been critical (e.g., Spencer, 1983). One recent study of parental socialization among children and adolescents 5 to 14 years old becomes particularly important. Hughes and Chen (1997) investigated timing and emphasis of parents' socialization focus depending upon the child's age (Hughes & Chen, 1997). Still, how parental racial socialization processes influence the ability to cope with racial situations among children in middle childhood has not been studied. The foregoing studies do, however, indicate with a great deal of consistency the important role of parents in shaping children's more global coping with respect to race. Parenting style and child rearing is mediated by parental context and self-esteem (MacPhee, Fritz, & Miller-Heyl, 1996). Parental practices sifted through these characteristics and contexts subsequently affect child development. In the present study, the relation between maternal personal characteristics (self-esteem and personal stress), racial stress, and racial socialization practices–attitudes and how children cope with racial situations in middle childhood was investigated.

With the conceptual link of parent practices associated with race and children's competencies associated with race firmly rooted in previous studies, it makes sense, in the present study, to focus upon the relation of these racial socialization messages to children's coping outcomes. Moreover, the literature indicates that parenting influences on these particular outcomes are likely to be multifaceted and multidimensional; thus it is important to make sense of these factors in the conceptualization. Parental characteristics and parental perceptions of context are likely to have important associations with child adjustment and coping. Parental self-esteem, a personal characteristic of parents to be distinguished from parenting self-esteem (efficacy about the parenting role), has been associated with child adjustment, especially, behavioral problems in children (Finken & Amato, 1993; Klebanow, 1976). Mothers with low self-esteem (Crnic & Greenberg, 1990) have children who experience more behavioral problems or perhaps poorer coping–social skills.

Maternal stress is also linked to behavioral adjustment and psychological well-being among children. Maternal depression is also linked; however, some researchers find that it is difficult to disentangle the stressful environment in which depressed mothers are located from their depressive symptoms (Saarni, Mumme, & Campos, 1998). Stress levels of adults are profoundly affected by the racial stresses they experience daily (Utsey & Ponterotto, 1996). This is important because both children and parents are affected by these circumstances. The effects of parental stress on children, however, may offset personal characteristics and parenting skills. The work of McLoyd and her colleagues (McLoyd, Jayaratne, Ceballo, & Borquez, 1994; McLoyd & Wilson, 1990) underscores this relation among maternal stressors, maternal context, and child adjustment among working class and poor African American families. Maternal stress related to joblessness, parenting stress, and maternal psychological health were directly and indirectly associated with children's adjustment and coping.

Distal factors associated with prejudice affect children's competencies through the circuitous routes that Garcia-Coll and colleagues (1996) outlined in their model (via adaptive culture and family socialization processes). Racism–prejudice and social location indicators such as race–ethnicity or poverty represent distal factors in the model. These experiences and social status contexts are funneled through social historical factors peculiar to African Americans (e.g., slavery, the Jim Crow era) but also through cultural mechanisms which make use of these experiences and factors, but within the parameters of cultural systems of meaning and cultural ways of being. Using that lens, individual families working at their best develop child-rearing practices and provide messages infused with contemporary and historical experiences related to race or other social location indicators (e.g., poverty, minority status), but mediated through cultural approaches. Racial socialization as a family function is a response to both ecological contexts and minority status, but the mechanisms or processes through which children's racial coping competencies are socialized are culturally defined.

An older study (Peters, 1981) demonstrated the interrelations among distal and proximal factors influencing child outcomes when parents experienced particular hardships associated with race. In this study very young children were affected by context and the lived experiences of their African American parents with discrimination (e.g., poverty, job loss). Moreover, many parents responded to the particular stressor (and the ecology of racial stress ensuing) with depression and disrupted parenting practices, which strained interactions with their children. Subsequent changes in parents' behaviors had an impact on the adaptive and maladaptive competencies developed and displayed by their young children (e.g., more clingy, easily crying, withdrawn, more independent). Extrapolation from this and other work suggests that parent self-esteem and general stressful life events will be predictive of children's strategies that have a critical and problematic behavioral component (Crnic & Greenberg, 1990).

While somewhat understated, the work underscores the relation between the parent's ecology of racial stress or assessment of the racial climate based upon lived experiences and anticipated prejudices and the child's coping outcomes. Several researchers have promoted the notion that African Americans experience the following types of race-related stressors:

Chronic Overt–tangible events; lived experiences with racial discrimination
Mundane Anticipated prejudices; perceived heightened racial climate (Peters & Massey, 1983; Pierce, 1975).

These factors, when combined, comprise their racial ecology (Johnson, 1994; Peters & Massey, 1983; Pierce, 1975). Utsey & Ponterotto (1996) empirically noted that the relation between lived experience with prejudice heightened perceptions of racial stress among adults. This ecology of racial stress exists over and above other major stressful life events to which all American children and families are vulnerable. In this regard, parents' assessments of racial stressors may influence the socialization messages given to children. Peters's (1981) observational work underscored how this lived experience of racial stress among parents becomes another kind of racial ecology with its own consequences for children. Do these parental perceptions of racial stress represent a more formidable force in the development of children's racial coping than parental socialization messages? If racial stress has more power, then the strength of the messages would be diminished, weakened, or eliminated in their predictive value once racial stress is accounted for in a model.

METHODS

Participants

The larger study included 97 African American children in grades 3 through 6 and 37 parents. Only children of the participating parents (n = 37) were included in the analyses presented. Nearly one-third of the families represented were of middle income or better; other families were working class or lower SES families. The data were collected in two sessions of face-to-face interviews with children and one interview with their parent(s), typically a mother (see Table 3.1).

Parental Constructs and Measures

Four variables were used as independent measures or predictors of children's racial coping domains. These were parental self-esteem (see the Culture Free Self-Esteem Inventory, Battle, 1981), general life events stress of parents (see Coddington, 1972), racial stress as assessed by perceived prejudice (see the Prejudice Subscale of Generations Interview Schedule, Johnson & Chung, 1995), and parental racial socialization strategies (see the Parental Experiences and Racial Socialization Scale, Stevenson, 1994). Table 3.1 contains key constructs as well as the means and distributions for the measures.

Table 3.1
Distribution and Means: Mother and Child Constraints

Constructs	Parents (n = 37)	Children (n = 37)
Child characteristics		
Child gender (%)		
Male		57.1
Female		42.9
Maternal characteristics		
Family income (%)		
Less than $9,000	30.6	
$10,000-$19,900	38.9	
$20,000 or more	29.6	
Mother's marital status (%)		
Never married	50.0	
Married	23.7	
Separated	7.9	
Divorced	15.8	
Widowed	2.6	
General stress (maternal)		
Life-Event Readjustment Scale	64.14(4-183)	
Self esteem (mean)		
Culture free SEI total	25.06(9-30)	
Racial stress (mean)		
Perceived prejudice	28.24(0-32)	
Racial socialization messages		
*PERS pride	20.65(12-24)	
PERS racial struggles	23.59(15-32)	
PERS spiritual coping	17.05(9-21)	
PERS cultural survival	27.03(16-39)	

*Parent Experiences of Racial Socialization Scale.

Parental self-esteem was derived from the total score of the 40-item Culture Free Self-Esteem Inventory, which has four dimensions: attitudes toward school, global self-esteem, satisfaction with parenting role, and social competence. The Life Events Readjustment Scale measured personal stressors of parents and their judgment or appraisal of adjustment to a stressor. The version of the scale used here has 30 items. With each item the participant was to consider the last 12 months in their life and how much readjustment the stressor may have caused them on a 10-point scale (e.g., moving, loss of job, separation from significant relationship, serious illness).

Racial stressors were approximated using the two questions from the Prejudice Subscale of the Generations Interview Schedule. Parents were asked two questions with several response categories. The first question, "Have you ever lived in a neighborhood where neighbors or their children made life difficult for your family or children?" represented lived experience with prejudice. The second question, "Do you anticipate future problems in your child's life for any of the following reasons?" represented mundane or anticipated prejudice. Response categories for both questions included race, ethnicity, and physical characteristics. The combined scores from these questions provided the base for the effect of mundane and chronic stressors associated with race.

All four subscales (40 items) of the Parental Experiences Racial Socialization Scale (Stevenson, 1994) were used. The subscales included Racial Struggles, Cultural Survival, Spiritual Coping, and Pride Development; each contained 8 to 13 items. Definitions of the subscale domains and examples of items within each domain are as follows:

Domains	**Definition**	**Examples**
Racism struggles	Racial barriers and overcoming those barriers	1. Blacks don't always have the same opportunities as whites 2. Blacks have to work twice as hard as whites to get ahead in this world
Cultural survival	Maintenance of cultural heritage and family bonds; importance of struggling with racial hostilities	1. Need to learn how to live in black and white world 2. Relatives can help black parents raise their families
Pride development	Teaching pride and knowledge of African American heritage	1. You should be proud to be black 2. Never be ashamed of your color

Spiritual coping	Role of religious involvement in racial struggles	1. A belief in God can help a person deal with tough life struggles 2. Black children should be taught early that God can protect them from racial hatred

Child Outcome Measures

Outcomes or child racial coping domains were measured by the Racial Stories Task (Johnson, 1994, 1996). In this version of the measure, children were administered six closed-ended vignettes, each depicting an overt racial conflict involving both adults and children. The stories are of two types. The first type was characterized by between-group conflict vignettes with themes of interracial exclusion, racially laden verbal assaults (confrontation), and overt discrimination. These between-group conflicts characterized four of the six stories given to the children. The remaining two stories were characterized by within-group conflict, where the themes challenged group identification–affiliation and cultural authenticity. Each story required the child to make choices about what the child in the story should do. The child had to complete the vignette by choosing a "coping strategy" from among those provided. Across the stories, ten racial coping domains were represented (e.g., conflict avoidance, confrontational, moral reasoning, support seeking), although only six were presented within any one-story item. These domains were derived from previous work, validating the open-ended version of the RST (see the appendix to this chapter for definitions of the racial coping domains). In the analyses, eight domains were used.

Example of Between-Group Conflict: Jacob (Janice) (confrontation; prejudice by exclusion)

Jacob (Janice) is a black boy (girl) about your age. He (she) is very smart and his (her) classmates really like him (her). Jacob (Janice) is the only black person in his (her) classroom, all the other children and the teacher are white. Sometimes Jacob (Janice) raises his (her) hand to answer the questions the teacher asks. Almost all the time the teacher chooses someone else to answer the question. Jacob (Janice) feels this is unfair because he (she) almost always knows the answer. What should Jacob (Janice) do about this problem?

Example of Within-Group Conflict: Aisha (Terrell) (group affiliation, cultural authenticity)

Aisha (Terrell) is a black girl (boy) about your age. All the students in Aisha's (Terrell's) school are black. Her (His) classmates tease her (him) because they say she (he) "talks proper" and "tries to act like a white girl (boy)." What should Aisha (Terrell) do about this problem?

FINDINGS

Intercorrelation of Parent Variables

Although sparse in terms of significance, intercorrelations among parent variables showed several important relationships (Table 3.2). Mother's self-esteem was inversely associated with general life stress and was correlated with grade level. Mothers with lower self-esteem had a greater number of stressful events for which psychological adjustment had been difficult. Mothers of older children had higher self-esteem. Self-esteem and general life stress did vary by income and by grade level of child. Gender of child appeared to have a relation to maternal self-esteem and general life stress. The associations found in the correlation table were subjected to further means tests. The results of t-tests indicated that mothers of girls (M = 27.36) had significantly higher self-esteem than did mothers of boys (M = 23.05; t = –2.69, p = 0.01). Consistent with this finding was that the mean score for stressful life events among mothers of boys (M = 85.79) was more than twice that of stressors among mothers of girls (M = 39.47; t = 3.47, p = 002).

Intercorrelation of Parent Variables with Child Racial Coping Domains

Again the intercorrelations showed sparse associations of parent constructs with children's racial coping domains (Table 3.3). Family income, child gender, and grade level were not associated with any of the domains. Maternal self-esteem was inversely correlated with the child's *confrontational* domain. Perceived prejudice or racial stress (lived and anticipated) was inversely related to the child's *support-seeking* domain. The four components of parental racial socialization provided no significant relations to children's racial coping domains. Although constraints related to sample size prevented inclusion of all four components in the regressions conducted in the next step, the magnitude of the relation of children's coping domains and parental racial socialization were used to provide guidance as to which components to include in the regressions.

Table 3.2
Intercorrelations of Parent Characteristics, Stress, and Racial Socialization Domains

	1	2	3	4	5	6	7	8	9	10
1 Family Income	--	-.20	.19	.07	-.23	.03	.20	.30	.07	.02
2 Child Gender		--	-.05	.44*	-.52**	-.18	-.06	-.12	-.20	.05
3 Grade Level (3-4 & 5-6)			--	.35*	.21	.17	.29	.27	.23	.22
4 Self-Esteem				--	.55**	-.18	-.30	-.02	-.22	-.17
5 General Stress					--	.09	-.03	-.02	.08	.04
6 Racial Stress						--	.29	-.04	.14	.22
7 PERS Pride							--	.76**	.74**	.82**
8 PERS Spritual								--	.68**	.74**
9 PERS Race Struggles									--	.81**
10 PERS Cultural Survival										--

*$p < 0.05$; **$p < 0.01$

Hierarchical Regressions

That parental self-esteem and general stress factors of mothers should have a direct impact on children's adjustment or coping can be anticipated from the literature reviewed. The central investigation in this study was, however, to understand the impact of racial stress on child outcomes and, beyond that, to understand the power of racial socialization messages over and above parental stress related to race. Thus, based on the literature, we anticipated that maternal self-esteem and maternal stressors might behave as controls in most instances where they are entered. Hierarchical regression allows for the exploration of two questions. First, how powerful are parental perceptions of racial stressors in relation to socialization messages in influencing children's racial coping (after removing the powerful effect of self-esteem and general stress)? And, is this effect more powerful than these intentional socialization messages of parents in determining the racial coping domains of children? These questions encapsule the crux of the analysis conducted here.

A series of hierarchical regressions was conducted, such that parental predictors were regressed on eight children's racial coping domains

Table 3.3
Intercorrelations of Parent Variables with Children's Racial Coping Domains

	Racial Coping Domains							
Parental Characteristics (Stress, Racial Socialization Domains)	Authority	Avoidance	Confront	Forbearance	Moral	Proactive	Strategic	Support Seeking
Family income	.09	-.02	-.12	.09	.04	-.14	-.06	.04
Child gender	.02	-.03	-.05	-.17	.00	.11	.02	.01
Grade level (3-4 and 5-6)	-.01	-.06	-.02	.02	-.09	.16	.12	.12
Self esteem	-.04	-.11	-.34*	-.10	.20	.08	.03	.07
General stress	-.04	.08	-.08	.27	-.26	-.03	-.05	.01
Racial stress	.29	.18	.02	-.13	.06	-.10	.18	-.43*
PERS pride	.25	.07	.17	.06	-.26	-.06	-.01	-.12
PERS spiritual	.21	.03	-.06	.07	-.22	-.04	-.16	.10
PERS race struggles	.09	-.02	.15	.16	-.20	-.12	.11	-.04
PERS cultural survival	.18	-.04	.01	.21	-.10	-.16	.06	-.23

*$p < 0.05$

(i.e., conflict avoidance, conflict confronting, moral, support seeking, adult authority, proactive competence, strategic planning, and forbearance). In each regression analysis, the predictors (parental self-esteem and personal stressors) were entered as controls in block 1; racial stress was entered in block 2; and the domain(s) of parental racial socialization attitudes–practices were entered in block 3.

Generally, significant R2 changes in any block of the complete model indicated that four of eight children's racial coping domains were predicted by the model, although parental racial socialization messages–practices only predicted two of the models. Table 3.4 presents findings from the significant regression analyses only. The conflict-confronting domain was primarily predicted by the control variables (Table 3.4). The variance accounted for particularly by maternal self-esteem and, to a lesser degree, by stressful life events was consistent with the finding in previous studies, where maternal self-esteem predicted behavior problems of children. In the confrontational domain, physical and verbal aggressions are selected as the most appropriate coping mechanism in response to the story situations presented ($F[2,29] = 3.6$, $p < 0.05$; change in $R^2 = .20$).

The regression models revealed specified racial stressors, that is, lived and anticipated stressors, and once again predicted children's use of the support-seeking domain in an inverse relation—so much so that no variance was left in the model (see Table 3.4). These findings were difficult to interpret, but they were robust. The support-seeking domain typically indicates children's interest and willingness to seek support through increased contact with African Americans ("make more black friends") or insulation within an African American context ("change to a black school" or "join a black club") ($F[2,28] = 8.9$, $p < 0.01$; change in $R^2 = .23$). Few reports of adult lived experiences with prejudice coupled with nonanticipation of racial stressors for their children predicted an increase in the use of the support-seeking domain by children. Essentially, children whose parents reported fewer racial stressors were more likely to engage in support-seeking behavior. This was not expected since the coping domain indicates an attempt on the part of children to achieve buffering–protection from overtly discriminatory experiences within the insular African American context (e.g., black friends, schools, and clubs). Numerous experiences with prejudice and highly anticipated future experiences with racial stressors and other stressors associated with prejudice interfered with the use of this strategy by children. Perhaps this strategy on the part of children represents an immature and inexperienced coping approach to an overt situation in a context where parents are relatively free of racial stressors or where racial stressors are not discussed. Is it naive to think that "changing schools" or "increasing friendships

Table 3.4
Betas from Hierarchical Regressions Predicting Children's Racial Coping Strategies

	Confrontational			Support Seeking			Moral Reasoning			Strategic Planning		
Predictors	Model 1	Model 2	Model 3	Model 1	Model 2	Model 3	Model 1	Model 2	Model 3	Model 1	Model 2	Model 3
	ß	ß	ß	ß	ß	ß	ß	ß	ß	ß	ß	ß
Parent self-esteem	-.53**	-.53*	-.55*	.21	.15	.11	.14	.16	-.01	.10	.12	.24
Stressful live events	$-.35^+$	$-.35^+$	$-.41^+$	.21	.24	.23	-.12	-.13	-.22	.08	.06	.05
Racial stress		-.04	-.04		-.49**	-.46**		.11	.18		.17	.02
PERS pride development			-.19			.03			-.41*			
PERS spiratual coping												-.71**
PERS racial struggles			-.20									-.68**
PERS cultural survival						-.17						
R^2	.20*			.04			.05			.01		
Change in R^2		.00	.03		.23	.03		.01	.14*		.03	.24*

$^+p < .10$; $^*p < 0.05$; $^{**}p \leq 0.01$

with African Americans" will truly insulate one from discriminatory experiences?

Parental racial socialization messages–practices alone were the significant predictors of two racial coping domains; *moral reasoning* ($F[2,29] = 4.9$, $p < 0.05$; change in $R^2 = .14$) and *strategic planning* ($F[2,29] = 4.3$, $p < 0.05$; change in $R^2 = .24$) (see Table 3.4). The lack of parental messages associated with racial pride development increased the use of the reasoning domain, where fairness is promoted and unfairness of prejudice is underscored by children. Perhaps messages from parents that underscore race in an explicit manner are antithetical to children's usage of moral reasoning.

The strategic-planning domain appeared to increase when messages from home emphasized spiritual coping less and coping around racial struggles more (see Table 3.4). In this coping model children are focused on the hierarchy of power and how to employ it toward the resolution of a problem. Parental messages around racial struggles perhaps increase the child's rudimentary understanding and awareness of power in a variety of ecological systems. Many of the messages describe truncated opportunities in the workplace and in school. These messages are explicit, and they emphasize the pervasive macrolevel influence of prejudice and racial discrimination. Alternatively, parents with low perceived racial stress may have those perceptions because they have been afforded opportunity and means to preempt these race-laden situations through just these types of support-seeking measures, and thus children are reflecting the strategies modeled by their parents. These measures by parents may effectively and dramatically reduce family experiences with discrimination and expectations of future experiences.

DISCUSSION

The findings indicate a not too simple story about the relation between parental components and child outcomes. In the simple relations of the correlations, few significant associations were found, and thus little was revealed in these analyses. Out of the more complex view of these relations between parent and child constructs, represented by the hierarchical regressions, emerged additional information. In the more complex analysis, the interconnections between who parents are, how they see the world, their child-rearing approaches, and children's racial coping are revealed. These data support some of the alternate routes described in the Garcia-Coll and colleagues (1996) model. More important, the findings demonstrated that not all distal factors related to race are funneled through adaptive culture relative to children's developing competencies. Some distal factors like racial climate are experienced through the inhibiting environment of the parent (e.g., neighborhood, workplace, community experience) which excludes interpretation through a cultural lens; rather, it has a direct link to family socialization processes like parenting practices or fluctuations in the parent–child interaction. When racial stress experienced by the parent has a direct effect on children's coping and is not necessarily mediated through family racial socialization processes, it is evidence that these other influential pathways to the child's development do exist, while the parent still remains the vehicle. This occurs through the interaction of the parent's ecology with the child's ecology. In each instance the practice or how the child is influenced by the parent is still racialized because the context was racialized. The parental constructs used in these models were helpful in predicting children's racial coping, but were not perfect in their ability to do so. Only about half of the racial coping domains included were predicted by the parental constructs selected. Because the story is complex, it is of the utmost importance that we continually go back and rethink the model used to predict children's coping in order to capture more information about parental socialization influences on these developmental processes in children. One issue of the model is that the age of child could not be disentangled. Because of the overall size of the sample used, these groups were collapsed. Hughes and Chen's (1997) study tells us that parents' racial socialization practices are adjusted to developmental changes in children. In the regressions provided, the last entry might be affected if different models of children of various ages could be run.

The relation between parental self-esteem–stress and child adjustment–behavioral problems appeared to be supported in the relation between maternal self-esteem and children's physically confrontational coping approaches (Crnic & Acevedo, 1995; Crnic & Greenberg, 1990; Finken & Amato, 1993; Saarni et al., 1998) and is consistent with the developmental literature. Confrontational coping (e.g., hitting, fighting) is not necessarily linked to race but likely gets generalized by the child and applied to any number of situations, including those emerging as a consequence of racial discrimination or prejudice. Although the emphasis of African American parents on independence of children at early ages (Martin & Martin, 1978; McAdoo, 1998) would support a cultural style of "self-assertion," and this would be considered competence, demonstrations of this competence would rarely include violence. The confrontational coping in this study, however, goes beyond expressions of competence, is more problematic, and is more likely to indicate low impulse control than confidence and independence.

The finding that a parental ecology of low racial stress predicts children's attempts to racially buffer themselves is quite intriguing and not easily explained. Further study is required in order to better understand this finding and replicate it. In addition, it is noted that racial stress did not consistently predict children's racial coping. Indeed, if children's competencies developed entirely in relation to parental experiences and sensitivities or even reactivity to prejudice, rather than through more thoughtful integration of the realities of discrimination, knowledge of child development, cultural prescriptions, and good child-rearing practice, there would be cause for concern. If only parental racial stress predicted child coping, then by what mechanisms shall we intervene in children's development around racial issues? Thoughtful child-rearing practice should be at the forefront of parental socialization processes, given the innumerable and uncontrollable forces also influencing children's coping.

Finally, we need to better understand this tangential finding regarding parental self-esteem, stress, and children's gender. The idea that mothers of boys at this age have lower self-esteem and higher appraisals of their stressors needs to be replicated and explored more fully in larger samples. While mothers of African American boys can successfully raise them, perhaps they do so under enormous duress and with some cost to themselves. Another view would incorporate the consequences of rearing the "endangered black male" (Gibbs, 1988; Kunjufu, 1985). In this scenario single mothers are taxed at higher rates for rearing black boys; that is, they have more anxiety about intervening in their child's interface with social institutions, including the school and the legal system. And indeed, there may be more events like these in the lives of mothers of boys. Inevitably, the institutions win sometimes. Heightened negative interactions (greater number or greater intensity) with social institutions would then undermine the mothers' sense of efficacy around parenting and lower their personal self-esteem.

In this study unique aspects of maternal contributions to children's individual coping strategies were assessed. The findings imply that some coping on the part of children is more likely linked to parent characteristics, while other coping is more likely influenced through cultural means like racial socialization messages. What we know is that children are multiply influenced from multiple sources. While children might have orientations to coping which emphasize certain racial coping domains and not others, in each instance they are likely to be using several domains. Thus, parental influence from all sectors, albeit at variable levels of influence, would play some role in the development of all children's competencies in coping with race. Across children, there are both overlapping and unique contributions from their parents in this regard.

The research on racial socialization clearly needs to look at additional outcomes for children that go beyond global coping issues of ethnic identity development and to do so with more attention towards development in middle childhood.

APPENDIX: RACIAL COPING DOMAINS—DEFINITIONS

Adult authority. This dimension is defined by the child's reliance on adult authority for problem solving. The child has in mind that the problem will be resolved or abated by adults working with children or with other adults. The complete confidence of the child in adult authority or power is typified by the child's unspecified conclusion to the event.

Proactive competence. Positive, self-promoting, and self-reflective actions and attitudes are included in this dimension. Central to its theme are the child's ability to think of himself or herself as a competent individual in relation to adults and/or children and to provide coping behaviors and attitudes consistent with a self-assured perception of self.

Moral. Humanism, altruism, fairness, righteousness, and social convention are themes of this dimension. The moralistic considerations of children extend to racial and nonracial content or issues of prejudice and discrimination. These behaviors and attitudes also extend to religious doctrine, as well as to their understanding of the social rules and the law.

Conflict avoidance. To escape a difficult, stressful, painful, or otherwise challenging situation, children employ avoiding or evasive behaviors designed to separate a perhaps fearful child from confronting others. The child exhibits no particular control over the situation, the child is more determined to "get away" from the problem.

Forbearance. The child's ability to "pick the fight" by ignoring or walking away from a situation suggests that the child may be exhibiting some competence in this more passive coping dimension. The control–restraint element in this coping dimension is critical in distinguishing it from conflict avoidance.

Support seeking. The strategies which make up this coping dimension reflect efforts to acquire support or to optimize support from specific individuals, especially peers (e.g., develop support systems), or from implied groups of people (e.g., changing schools, changing neighborhoods, changing clubs). In particular children want to extend or increase their contact with other African Americans.

Conflict confronting. The suggestion of verbally or physically assaultive behaviors as a way of concluding the offensive behaviors of others is an indicator of this coping dimension. Verbal assaults typically take the form of quips or return name-calling. The child exhibits competence, but it is a reactive type of competence. Suggestions of physical assaults range from punching, hitting, and slapping, to shooting, stabbing, and gang beatings.

Strategic planning. Thoughtful and complex plans are often described in this coping dimension. Children often demonstrate their understanding of adult chains of command to be used to resolve their problem. Others may describe complex plans that are more subversive in nature to accomplish the desired end.

REFERENCES

Battle, J. (1981). *The Culture Free Self-Esteem Inventory*. Seattle: Special Child Publications.

Bowman, P. J., & Howard, C. (1985). Race-related socialization, motivation, and academic achievement: A study of black youths in three generation families. *Journal of the American Academy of Child Psychiatry, 24*, 131–141.

Bugental, D., & Goodenow, J. (1998). Socialization processes. In W. Damon (Series Ed.) & N. Eisenberg (Vol. Ed.), *Handbook of child psychology*: Vol. 3. *Social emotional and personality development* (5th ed., pp. 389–462). New York: Wiley.

Coddington, R. D. (1972). The significance of life events as etiologic factors in the diseases of children, II: A study of normal population. *Journal of Psychosomatic Research, 16*, 205–213.

Crnic, K., & Acevedo, M. (1995). Everyday stresses and parenting. In M. H. Bornstein (Ed.), *Handbook of parenting*: Vol. 4. *Applied and practical parenting* (pp. 277–297). Mahwah, NJ: Erlbaum.

Crnic, K., & Greenberg, M. (1990). Minor parenting stresses with young children. *Child Development, 61*, 1628–1637.

Finken, L., & Amato, P. (1993). Parental self-esteem and behavioral problems in children: Similarities between mothers and fathers. *Sex Roles, 28*, 569–582.

Garcia-Coll, C. G., Crnic, K., Lamberty, G., Wasik, B. H., Jenkins, R., Garcia, H. V., & McAdoo, H. P. (1996). An integrative model for the study of developmental competencies in minority children. *Child Development, 67*, 1891–1914.

Gibbs, J. T. (Ed.). (1988). *Young, black and male in America: An endangered species.* Dover, MA: Auburn House.

Hughes, D., & Chen, L. (1997). When and what parents tell children about race: An examination of race related socialization among African American families. *Applied Developmental Science, 1*, 200–214.

Johnson, D. J. (1994). Parental racial socialization and racial coping among middle class black children. In J. McAdoo (Ed.), *XIII Empirical Conference in Black Psychology* (pp. 17–38). Madison: University of Wisconsin.

Johnson, D. J. (1996, August). *The racial stories task: Situational racial coping of black children*. Paper presented at the meeting of the International Society for the Study of Behavioral Development, Quebec City, Quebec, Canada.

Johnson, D., & Chung, J. K. (1995). *Generations: American Family Heritage, Family Socialization and Cultural Adaptation (Measure)*. Unpublished survey, NICHD Study of Early Child Care, Site Specific, University of Wisconsin, Madison.

Klebanow, S. (1976). Parenting in the single parent family. *Journal of the American Academy of Psychoanalysis, 4,* 37–48.

Kunjufu, J. (1985). *Countering the conspiracy to destroy black boys.* Chicago: Afro-American Publishing.

MacPhee, D., Fritz, J., & Miller-Heyl, J. (1996). Ethnic variations in social networks and parenting. *Child Development, 67,* 3278–3295.

Marshall, S. (1995). Ethnic socialization of African American children: Implications for parenting, identity development, and academic achievement. *Journal of Youth and Adolescence, 24,* 377–396.

Martin, E., & Martin, J. M. (1978). *The African American extended family.* Chicago: University of Chicago Press.

McAdoo, H. P. (1998). African American families. In C. Mindel, R. Haberstein, & R. Wright (Eds.), *Ethnic families in America: Patterns and variations* (4th ed., pp. 361–381). Upper Saddle River, NJ: Prentice Hall.

McLoyd, V. C., Jayaratne, T., Ceballo, R., & Borquez, J. (1994). Unemployment and work interruption among African American single mothers: Effects on parenting and adolescent socioemotional functioning. *Child Development, 65,* 562–589.

McLoyd, V. C., & Wilson, L. (1990). Maternal behavior, social support, and economic conditions as predictors of distress in children. *New Directions for Child Development, 46,* 49–69.

Peters, M. F. (1981). Parenting in black families with young children: A historical perspective. In H. P. McAdoo (Ed.), *Black families* (pp. 211–224). Beverly Hills, CA: Sage.

Peters, M. F., & Massey, G. C. (1983). Mundane extreme environmental stress in stress family theory: The case of the black family in white America. In H. I. McCubbin & C. Figley (Eds.), *Stress and the family: Advances and developments in family stress theory and research* (pp. 1921–1218). New York: Haworth.

Pierce, C. M. (1975). The mundane extreme environment and its effect on learning. In S. G. Brainard (Ed.), *Learning disabilities: Issues and recommendations for research* (pp. 1–28). Washington, DC: National Institute of Education.

Saarni, C., Mumme, D., & Campos, J. (1998). Emotional development: Action, communication and understanding. In W. Damon (Series Ed.) & N. Eisenberg (Vol. Ed.), *Handbook of child psychology*: Vol. 3. *Social emotional and personality development* (5th ed., pp. 237–310). New York: Wiley.

Spencer, M. B. (1983). Children's cultural values and parental child rearing strategies. *Developmental Review, 3,* 351–370.

Stevenson, H. C. (1994). Validation of the scale of racial socialization for African American adolescents: Steps towards multidimensionality. *Journal of Black Psychology, 20,* 445–468.

Stevenson, H. C. (1995). Relationship of adolescent perceptions of racial socialization to racial identity. *Journal of Black Psychology, 21,* 49–70.

Utsey, S., & Ponterotto, J. (1996). Development and validation of Index of Race-Related Stress (IRRS). *Journal of Counseling Psychology, 43,* 490–501.

4

Being Black: New Thoughts on the Old Phenomenon of Acting White

Angela M. Neal-Barnett

Acting white is one of the most negative charges that can be hurled against an African American (AA) adolescent. Being accused of this behavior can result in an AA teen hiding his or her intelligence, allowing his or her grades to drop, withdrawing from his or her white friends, or withdrawing from black adolescent society (Fordham & Ogbu, 1986; Graham, 1995; Kunjufu, 1988). The acting white literature has focused primarily on adolescents in predominantly black schools. Little attention has been paid to blacks in predominantly white or integrated schools or those in predominantly white suburban and small town schools. As data emerge that indicate middle-class black adolescents are performing poorly in the classroom and on standardized tests (Weissert, 1999) however, scholars and researchers are recognizing that the acting white phenomenon crosses all social classes. Fitting in is a salient issue for most adolescents. Its importance may be heightened for African American adolescents because of the fictive kin network and extended sense of kinship common to many African Americans. This sense of kinship gives African Americans a feeling of connection to one another. When an African American adolescent is accused of acting white, they are essentially being told they do not belong in the black race. The emotions and cognitions generated by the acting white accusation have psychological as well as educational ramifications for African American adolescents.

In this chapter, the author closely examines the acting white phenomenon. Drawing from the racial identity literature and qualitative data collected from eight adolescent focus groups and one adult focus group, a new conceptualization of the phenomenon is proposed. Implications for future research are discussed.

CURRENT CONCEPTUALIZATION OF ACTING WHITE

The current understanding of acting white is derived from the cultural anthropological work of Signithia Fordham and John Ogbu (1986). Based on previous research from the cross-cultural–ethnic identity literature, Fordham and Ogbu hypothesize that African Americans, who historically and currently have been in a subordinate position in American society, develop as part of their social identity a sense of collective identity that is in opposition to the social identity of whites. This sense of collectiveness is manifested in the form of the fictive kin network, an extended sense of kinship manifested in many African American households. The development of this oppositional social identity also involves the development of an oppositional cultural frame of reference that allows African Americans to protect their identity and set and maintain boundaries between themselves and white Americans. Within the oppositional cultural frame of reference, certain behaviors, events, symbols, and activities are perceived as being white and therefore not appropriate, whereas others are perceived as being black and appropriate. African Americans whose cognitions, behaviors, or speech fall outside the oppositional cultural frame of reference are seen as acting white and, in many cases, are negatively sanctioned by other African Americans.

ACTING WHITE OR BEING BLACK

Fordham and Ogbu's conceptualization of "acting white" is predicated on a deficit model of racial identity. Inherent in this model is the belief that living in a racist environment *must* have a negative impact on the African American psyche. The negative effect results in African Americans either devaluing parts of themselves or devaluing the broader society. It is the act of devaluing the broader society that leads to the formation of an oppositional identity and the oppositional cultural frame of reference. The self-esteem literature indicates, however, that a number of African Americans do not engage in the devaluing process (Gibbs, 1985; Richman, Clark, & Brown, 1985; Ward, 1990). Failure to engage in the devaluing process results in the failure to develop an oppositional identity. Yet, the absence of an oppositional identity does not necessarily result in an individual being seen as acting white. An additional drawback to the oppositional identity model is that it is difficult to test, and limited empirical evidence exists that supports its existence.

Given the drawbacks to the oppositional identity conceptualization of acting white, this author began to systematically gather data on the acting white phenomenon. As part of data collection, six focus groups with black adolescents and one focus group with black parents were run. Transcripts of interviews with anxious black women who had been accused of acting white since junior high school were also studied. The information gathered from these sources suggested a conceptualization of acting white that differed from the one offered by Fordham and Ogbu.

In this new conceptualization, the focus is on what it means to be black. It would appear that in this country there exists a continuum of the significance and meaning of being black. On either end lie the extremes. One end is represented by what African Americans term "hardcore Black". This consist of stereotypical generalizations of the significance and meaning of being black. The other end is represented by the philosophy that being black is no different than being white, brown, or purple. Different groups of African Americans assign different significance and meaning to being black. These differences stem from experience, socialization, and opportunity. The accusation of acting white appears to occur when individuals at divergently different points on the continuum interact. Stated another way, the accusation of acting white occurs when one individual's definition of being black (racial identity) clashes with another individual's definition (racial identity). Such a conceptualizations does not have its roots in a deficit model, but emphasizes strengths and heterogeneity within the race.

In this volume and elsewhere, Sellers and colleagues (Sellers, Smith, Shelton, Rowley, & Chavous, 1998; Sellers, Chavous, & Cook, 1998) have delineated the Multidimensional Model of Racial Identity. Unlike many models of racial identity, Sellers and colleagues believe that racial identity is comprised of more than one dimension. Within the MMRI model, four dimensions exist: salience, centrality, regard, and ideology.

Salience refers to the extent to which one's race is a relevant part of one's self-concept at a particular moment or in a particular situation. *Centrality* refers to the extent to which a person normatively defines himself or herself with regard to race. Unlike salience, centrality remains stable across situations. *Regard* is made up of two components: public and private regard. *Public regard* is the extent to which an individual believes that others view African Americans positively or negatively. *Private regard* is defined as the extent to which an individual feels positively or negatively toward African Americans as well as how positive or negative they feel about being African American. *Ideology*, the fourth dimension, is composed of the individual's beliefs, opinions, and attitudes with respect to the way he or she feels that members of the race should act, interact, and live with society (Sellers, Smith, Shelton, Rowley, & Chavous, 1998; Rowley, Sellers, Chavous, & Smith, 1997; Sellers, Chavous, & Cook, 1998). At present, Sellers and colleagues identify four ideological philosophies: (1) the nationalist philosophy which emphasizes the uniqueness of being of African descent, (2) the oppressed minority philosophy which emphasizes the similarities between African Americans and other oppressed groups in the United States, (3) the assimilationist philosophy which emphasizes similarities between African Americans and general American society, and (4) the humanist philosophy which emphasizes the commonalties between all human beings (Sellers, Smith, Shelton, Rowley, & Chavous, 1998; Rowley, Sellers, Chavous, & Smith, 1997; Sellers, Chavous, & Cook, 1998). Sellers suggests that many African Americans can be categorized as having a predominant ideology, but can hold a variety of ideologies that vary across areas of functioning (Sellers, Morgan, & Brown, this volume).

Seller's model provides a testable theoretical framework for the continuum conceptualization of the acting white phenomenon. Using the MMRI dimensions of centrality and ideology, one can operationally define various points on the significance and meaning of being black continuum. From a continuum conceptualization, the level of centrality and the ideology preference typically embraced directly impacts who is perceived as acting white, by whom, how the accusation of acting white is processed by the accused, and the resulting behavior. For example, two adolescents may have relatively equal levels of centrality; in other words, both teens may find being black to be a very relevant (significance) part of their racial identity. However, their ideological preferences (meaning) are different. Adolescent X sees performing well in school as an important part of what it means to be black. Adolescent Y sees that high academic performance has nothing to do with being black. In this case, it would be the ideological difference that led Adolescent Y to perceive Adolescent X as acting white.

PSYCHOLOGICAL IMPLICATIONS

To attach a high level of importance to being black (centrality) and yet be perceived by same race peers as acting white appears to create psychological distress. Adolescents who fall into this category on most occasions embrace either a humanist or assimilation ideology, whereas their high race-central counterparts are typically embracing a nationalist or oppressed minority ideology. It is their ideological preference that results in the accusation. Focus group discussions with adolescents who appear to be high race-central seem to support this hypothesis. A clear example of the distress is illustrated in the following exchange with Wynter, a 17-year-old honor student at a predominantly white high school.

FACILITATOR: What type of feelings do you experience when you're accused of "acting white?"

WYNTER: Angry and I'm envious. (The other two group members nod their heads in agreement.)

FACILITATOR: Envious?

WYNTER: Yes. Envious of black kids who get to be themselves and don't get accused of acting white and envious of white kids who never get accused of acting white.

FACILITATOR: What about anxious?

WYNTER: They are judging the whole person, so its harsher than just experiencing anxiety, it's something beyond anxiety. When someone accuses you of acting white it's a judgment against the core of which you are.

The attack on her sense of racial identity and the resulting psychological distress led Wynter to engage in the following behavior.

At first I was defensive, I became the militant Black, I didn't care about school, I dressed Black, but it was displaced. . . . I realized that I did belong, I became more involved and interested in school. . . . I wore what I wanted to wear.

Wynter's initial response illustrates the "acting white trap" that ensnares many black adolescents. The desire to have their identity confirmed and to be accepted leads to the development of a different persona. For Wynter, this appeared to have involved a change in ideology. To alleviate the psychological distress, Wynter adopted a nationalist ideology. Wynter's experiences are similar to those of other adolescents in the focus groups who appear to be high race central and adopt an assimilationist or humanist ideology. Many describe going through a brief "ghetto" (*sic*) phase. Based on the focus groups and interviews, it would appear that spending some period of time in the acting white trap is an important part of successfully negotiating the trap. For high-centrality adolescents with an assimilationist or humanist ideology, time spent in the trap gives them the opportunity to come to terms with their racial identity.

The psychological distress experienced by high race-central adolescents with humanist or assimilation ideologies appears different from that experienced by low race-central adolescents who embrace a strong humanist or assimilation ideology. These adolescents appear to see themselves as people rather than as members of a specific race. Fordham in her seminal research on acting white has described these students as raceless and suggests that in coping with the accusation of acting white they adopt a strategy of racelessness. She defines racelessness as the desired and eventual outcome of developing a raceless persona and is either a conscious or unconscious effort on the part of such students to disaffiliate themselves from the fictive kinship (1988, p. 58).

Fordham's (1988) interviews with Rita, a 16-year-old junior at predominantly black Capital High School, appears to illustrate the feelings and cognitions of the low race central humanist ideology adolescent.

> They [my family] go to all the shows go out to the Capital Center and all that crap, and listen to all that trash—as far as I am concerned. But I don't really like going out [there], you know, but if I ask them to go see the Washington Philharmonics with me, they won't go. "Is that opera [they want to know]. . . . And they don't go to museums with me either, 'cause they don't think, they'd go crazy, they'd rather go to the movies to see Eddie Murphy in *48 Hours* than to go see "To Fly" at the Air and Space Museum. (p. 68)

Later in the interview Rita reveals:

> I identify with Blacks and whites alike—I don't—see, that's one thing I don't go for: I don't like when people ask me do I identify with Black people or do I identify with white people? I identify with *people.* People are people. Black or white. Spanish, red, white, or blue, we're all the same. (p. 68)

Rita's distress appears to differ in quality and quantity from the distress experienced by Wynter. Indeed, based on the focus groups and interviews conducted by the author and Fordham's work, it appears that adolescents with low levels of centrality may experience the least amount of psychological distress from the acting white accusation. Indeed, they appear less likely to become caught in the acting white trap. This is *not* because this group sees themselves as white, but because they do not see being black as central to their social identity. If being black is less relevant to one's social identity then the accusation of acting white has little meaning and thus limited psychological impact. Indeed, the distress experienced is related to exasperation and frustration that others appear to want them to choose a racial identity.

A third group of adolescents exists who are midrange race central and have not adopted a dominant ideological preference. These adolescents' racial identity seems less stable than the previous two groups. For this reason, adolescents in the midrange of centrality and without a dominant ideological stance may be most affected psychologically by the acting white accusation. Being black has some level of importance for them; the assigned importance, however, is tenuous. The tenuous nature of this particular group's centrality and the lack of an ideological stance may give more power to the accusation of acting white. As a result, adolescents in this group may exhibit more distress than those in the other two groups and may be more likely to remain mired in the acting white trap. Joyce, a 19-year-old college sophomore who attended an integrated high school, exemplifies the midlevel group.

> In high school a lot of Black kids acted in a certain way that I couldn't understand. There was bitch [*sic*] and nigga [*sic*] kind of culture. They were nothing like me. . . . I always see these Black guys wearing such baggy clothes and girls with outfits so tight they look like they are painted on. They always seem so loud in the cafeteria. Sometimes, I'll admit that they even scare me.
>
> We all have to do twice as well just to be half as good. I have to be more conscious of what I do and how I act. I feel bad sometimes because I am not "black enough" for them. (Jenkins, 1999, p. 10)

Adolescents without a dominant ideology and midrange race centrality appear less skilled in coping with the acting white accusation. Ineffective coping appears to heighten the adolescent's psychological distress. Some adolescents in this category appear to go on to develop clinically significant anxiety and depression directly related to the attacks on their racial identity.

A classic example is Lela, a 16-year-old honor student at a predominantly white high school. In response to the frequent accusations of acting white, Lela became anxious every time she approached another black student in the hallway. To alleviate this anxiety she began to carry around a sipper bottle that contained coke and vodka. When a fellow black student approached she took a sip (Neal-Barnett, 1997).

Thus far, the author has presented a new psychological conceptualization of acting white. The new conceptualization suggests that acting white has little to do with being white and everything to do with what it means to be black. In this next section, the author examines the laypersons' definition of acting white. Specifically, what do adolescents mean when they accuse other adolescents of acting white? Does the adolescent's version of acting white support the continuum conceptualization of acting white?

Being Black: The Adolescent Perspective

Whereas psychologists define acting white from a racial identity perspective, it is also important to understand how those who live with the accusation and those who make the accusation define the term. Psychological and anthropological definitions aside, how do adolescents conceptualize "acting white?" To answer this question, this author conducted six focus groups with 35 African American adolescents. Teenagers in the focus groups defined acting white in terms of attitudes and behaviors. When asked to define what acting white meant, black teenagers gave answers that related to speech, dress, academic performance, and home training. Speaking Standard English, dressing in clothes from the Gap or Abercrombie and Fitch rather than Tommy Hilfiger and FUBU, wearing shorts in the winter, and being in honors or advance placement classes are all common examples of the adolescents' definition of acting white. Kunjufu (1988) in his book *To Be Popular or Smart* also finds that the adolescent definition of acting white focuses on speaking proper English and attending educational activities. Adolescents differentiated between acting white and "bougie." Being bougie was seen as thinking you were better than everyone else and appeared to stem from a materialistic–economic base. Adolescents agreed that one can be seen as bougie, but not necessarily be labeled as acting white.

On the surface, the adolescent definition of acting white would appear to support the existence of an oppositional culture framework (e.g., wearing Tommy is black and wearing Abercrombie & Fitch is white; speaking Standard English is white and speaking slang is black). When one goes beyond the definition and investigates the feelings and cognitions experienced by adolescents accused of acting white, however, one begins to see that the phenomenon is far more complicated than what one wears, how one talks, and enrollment in honors–advanced placement courses. The emotions and cognitions expressed support the continuum conceptualization.

> I felt disowned because they said I was acting white and I came from the hood.
>
> Ron, 18-year-old male

> They told me I thought I was too good. It made me mad and upset.
>
> Shenese, 17-year-old female

> It makes me mad because someone black is always telling someone else black they act white. If the teacher asks a question and I know the answer, I am acting white. If you speak with intelligence, you are trying to be white. That implies you can't be black and intelligent.
>
> Jamal, 18-year-old male

> Mixed feeling, angry and upset. I wish I could tell all black people you don't have to talk ghetto slang to be black. I'm not acting like this, it's me.
>
> Niecy, 16-year-old female

> I was so hurt. My mom and grandma had to talk to me. They said you are being you. You are sociable and all you can do is be yourself.
>
> Kamela, 15-year-old female

Many of the adolescents saw the accusation as unfair, because their identity is that of a black adolescent and questioned why one group of black students "got to determine what is black." The perceived unfairness produced feelings of envy. The same type of envy articulated by Wynter in an earlier section of this chapter. The in-depth information generated regarding thoughts and feelings supports the idea that what students are dealing with is not the "notion of acting white" but the act of defining for themselves what it means to be black. It also suggests that most of the focus groups' participants were high to mid-level race central.

Perhaps the most intriguing information to emerge from the focus groups was black students' insistence that the author speak with white students. To quote the adolescents: "Who would know best what acting white is; someone who is white." Fifteen white females and two white males participated in two focus groups. White adolescents fell into two categories: those who were familiar with the term and those who were unfamiliar with the term. White adolescents familiar with the term gave the same definition of acting white as black adolescents and pointed out that the term related to when a black adolescent engaged in the behavior. White adolescents who were unfamiliar with the term attended school with a small number of blacks. When both groups of white students were asked how a white adolescent acts white, the response was blank stares. Students could describe, however, how a white student could act black. This involved the wearing of clothing associated with blacks and listening to black music. This individual would be labeled a "wigger."

It would appear that white students familiar with the term "acting white" have adopted the black definition of the term. The question arises whether they are simply repeating what they have heard or if they have in part internalized a negative impression of being black. It also underscores the fact that racial identity is more salient for black adolescents than it is for white adolescents and in many cases may not be salient at all for white adolescents. In their insistence that the author talk to white students, the black adolescents were engaging in misattribution. Simply stated, black adolescents believed that because racial identity was a salient issue for their social identity, it would be a salient issue for white adolescents. In reality, white focus group participants appeared never to have given much though to the significance and meaning of being white.

Peers, Parents, and Nonparental Adults

The accusation of acting white can arise as early as elementary school. It appears most significant, however, and to have the most deleterious effects during high school. Developmentally, it is not until adolescence that an individual develops the cognitive ability to conceptualize and internalize the personal meaning of racial identity. Adolescence is also the development period when peer perceptions take on an added importance. Developmentally, the first two years of high school appear to be the critical period. During this time, the perceptions of peers, parents, and nonparental adults influences the choices made by an adolescent accused of acting white.

To be perceived as acting white can result in sanctions from one's black peers. These can range from comments about one's blackness to ostracism both within the school and other traditional social outlets for African American adolescents. Depending on the school's racial make-up, adolescents labeled as acting white have several options in terms of peer relations. In integrated or predominantly white schools, they can achieve a delicate balance between the black and white worlds, develop peer relations primarily with whites, or give up the behaviors that led to the accusation and become a member of the black peer group. All three choices have costs and benefits. Black students who choose the balancing option have a foot in both worlds. They must negotiate the questions and comments of both blacks and whites. At times, this can require the skills of a diplomat. Choosing this option does not bring an end to the acting white accusation. Rather, the adolescent develops the strategies and skills to adeptly cope with the accusation and gain respect (in some cases grudging respect) from their black peers. Adolescents who balance learn how to depersonalize the accusation. These are students who can say with confidence and conviction "I'm not acting white, I'm being myself." These adolescents appear to be high race central. In order to reach this point, however, these adolescents have undergone some period of questioning their racial identity and have spent some time in the acting white trap.

To function primarily within a white peer group leads to ostracism from most black peers in the school. The accusations cease because the other black students see the adolescent as a lost cause or not worth bothering. An individual who associates with white peers in school may or may not socialize with black peers outside the school setting. These students talk about having a double life; one that neither group of their peers is aware exists. Those who do not socialize with black peers outside of the school setting report that despite their efforts to do so, they do not fit in. Rather than continue trying, they simply socialize with whites outside the school setting as well.

The third option has been the subject of much discussion in the literature on acting white and academic performance, as it has been identified as the major cause of African American academic underachievement (Fordham & Ogbu, 1985; Kunjufu, 1988; Weissert, 1999). By giving up behaviors and activities perceived to be white, the accusations cease. It appears that in the mind of their black peers, the adolescents' racial identity is no longer in question. The adolescent's classroom and academic performance also appears to decline. What have not been discussed are the psychological costs and benefits of this choice. Qualitative data (Fordham & Ogbu, 1985; Kunjufu, 1990, Neal-Barnett, 1997) indicates that whereas students may change their behavior, they do not subscribe to the ideology espoused by others in the peer group. As a result, these students fear being exposed as imposters, and some go to great lengths to conceal their true self (ideology).

Some black adolescents are enrolled in high schools where assimilationist–humanist ideology and midlevels of centrality are the norm. Within the school setting these students are protected from the acting white accusation. When they leave that school setting, however, either for a black social setting or for another school, the acting white accusation is raised. These students are then faced with a dilemma of how to respond to the accusation.

The options are more limited for adolescents in predominantly black or all black high schools. In this arena, a white peer group does not exist. Many of these adolescents end up either isolated and alone or hiding their true ideology.

Interestingly, the qualitative data appears to indicate that African American students who are viewed as acting white do not form within their school a separate peer group. The variation in dimensions of racial identity among this group may account for this behavior. A low race-central student with a humanist ideology may be reluctant to seek friendship with a high race-central adolescent with an assimilationist ideology. Also, it should be noted that some African American adolescents are not in schools with large enough black populations to form a second black peer group.

White Peers

According to African American students in the focus groups, white peers do not accuse their black peers of acting white. Instead they make statements such as, "Gee, you don't act black or you're different than the other black kids in school." These statements are viewed as insulting by black adolescents, although most recognized their white peers believed they were paying them a compliment. High to midlevel race-central adolescents view the statements as insulting because being black is important to them. Low race-central adolescents see it as insulting because they see themselves as simply a person and race should not matter.

Perhaps the peer relationship issue is best summed up by Jamal, a participant in one of the black adolescent focus groups.

> Everyone black tries to make you fit their definition of black. Everybody white tries to make you fit their definition of black. Both try to make you an ignorant, weak-minded person.
>
> Jamal, 18-year-old black male

Parents and the Community

The accusation of acting white is predominantly put forth by an adolescent's black peers. Rarely does one find incidents of parents accusing their adolescents of acting white. However, particularly among midlevel race-central adolescents, one may find parents expressing concern over the children's behavior and fearful that their child may "want to be white." Parents of adolescents who live in predominantly white neighborhoods and attend predominantly white schools often voice this concern. This parental concern is reflected in an interview with actor Samuel L. Jackson and his wife actress LaTanya Richardson (Weathers, 1999). Ms. Richardson begins to describe the Onyx Village, a group she and her husband cofounded to bring together African Americans in the entertainment industry around activities that will help their children learn more about their heritage.

LATANYA RICHARDSON: We want them to learn the tradition of being colored. We're very proud of that tradition. We want them to know about the Civil Rights Movement and the ancient kingdoms of Africa. . . .

SAMUEL L. JACKSON: (interrupting) We want them to know who Jackie Wilson is. These kids go to school with mostly white kids. We decided to make them all be black together (p. 198).

Whereas parents do not accuse their children of acting white, unwittingly in conversations they and other adults may confirm adolescents' perceptions that certain behaviors, activities are "white." A parent in a focus group described how he had inadvertently done so.

> I'm in the store and I said that person is acting white. The moment I said it, I realized I had given my child a definition. Now, I've given my child a definition.
>
> 43-year old African American father

Nonparental adults have been documented to affirm adolescents' perceptions of a peer as acting white (Weissert, 1999; Kunjufu, 1988).

Many adolescents who speak Standard English relate stories of how the bus driver or an acquaintance's mother or father have commented that they "sound like a white person." Frequently in conversations, adults may perpetuate the idea that certain behaviors and goals are white. Adolescents' responses to adults' views would appear to be directly related to levels of centrality.

SUMMARY AND CONCLUSIONS

In this chapter, the author has presented a new conceptualization to the old accusation of acting white. This new conceptualization provides more information into the psychological implications of being the recipient of the accusation. It also provides new insight into the relationship between acting white and racial identity.

Clearly, this chapter is only the beginning. More qualitative and quantitative research is needed to fully understand the acting white phenomenon and to develop interventions that prevent adolescents from becoming permanently ensnared in its trap. Providing adolescents with a safe forum to discuss the issue and their experiences appears to be a start. Whereas the focus groups served as a place to collect information, adolescents also received support and reinforcement from peers and realized they were not alone.

The literature has virtually ignored the adolescents who make the accusations. The psychological implications for these adolescents also should be explored.

Acting white *is* the most negative accusation that can be hurled at black adolescents. It is incumbent that African American adolescents, parents, teachers, researchers, and other adults realize and vocalize that room exists in the fictive kin network for more than one definition of being black.

NOTE

The author would like to thank Fannie Brown, Robert Sellers, Michelle Mitchell, and Maurice Evans for their assistance and feedback. Special thanks also to all the adolescents and parents who participated in the focus groups. Please address all correspondence to Angela Neal-Barnett, Department of Psychology, Kent State University, Kent, Ohio 44242–0001, or aneal@kent.edu.

REFERENCES

Fordham, S. (1988). Racelessness as a factor in black students' school success: Pragmatic strategy or Pyrrhic victory? *Harvard Educational Review 58* (1), 54–84.

Fordham, S., & Ogbu, J. (1986). Black students' success: Coping with the burden of acting white. *The Urban Review, 18*, 176–206.

Gibbs, J. T. (1985). Psychosocial adjustment of urban black females. *SAGE, 2,* 28–36.

Graham, L. G. (1995). *Member of the club: Reflections of life in a racially polarized field.* New York: HarperCollins.

Jenkins, M. (1999, April 13). Racism a reality in one student's life. *Daily Kent Stater,* 10.

Kunjufu, J. (1988). *To be popular or smart.* Chicago: African American Images.

Neal-Barnett, A. M. (1997). To be young, anxious, and black. In F. Serifica (Chair), *Ethnic minority children and psychopathology: A developmental–cultural approach.* Presented at 105th annual convention of the American Psychological Association, Chicago, IL.

Richman, C. L., Clark, M. L., & Brown, K. P. (1985). General and specific self-esteem in late adolescent students: Race, gender, SES effects. *Adolescence, 20,* 555–566.

Rowley, S.A.J., Sellers, R. M., Chavous, T. M., & Smith, M. (1998). The relationship between racial identity and self-esteem in African American college students. *Journal of Personality and Social Psychology, 74* (3), 715–724.

Sellers, R. M., Chavous, T. M., & Cooke, D. Y. (1998). Racial identity and racial centrality as predictors of African Americans college students academic performance. *Journal of Black Psychology, 74* (3), 715–724.

Sellers, R. M., Smith, M. A., Shelton, J. N., Rowley, S.A.J., & Chavous, T. M. (1998). Multidimensional model of racial identity: A reconceptualization of African American racial identity. *Personality and Social Psychology Review, 2* (1), 18–39.

Ward, J. V. (1990). Racial identity formation and transformation. In C. Gilligan, N. P. Lyons, & T. J. Hamner (Eds.), *Making connections: The relational worlds of adolescent girls at Emma Willard School* (pp. 215–231). Cambridge: Harvard University Press.

Weathers, D. (1999, December). Survival of a Hollywood marriage. *Essence 30,* (8), 132–134, 194, 198.

Weissert, W. (1999, October 18). Report suggests a strategy to confront minority students' academic problems. Available <http://chronicle.com/daily/99/10/99101804n.htm>.

5

Psychological Adjustment of Urban, Inner-City, African American Adolescents

Ronald D. Taylor

Urban ethnic minority parents and children often face conditions and circumstances including economically distressed communities, crime, unemployment, and poor quality schools, that may be detrimental to their psychological and physical well-being. These families also are more likely to experience problems with food or housing shortages and have less access to health care. The impact of the problems of cities and urban families extend well beyond cities' boundaries and are problems that the nation must address. It is estimated that by 2020 as much as 30 percent of the children in the United States will be ethnic minorities (America's Children, Key National Indicators of Well-Being, 1998). The failure to educate and socialize healthy youngsters to become healthy and productive adults will have ramifications for the nation's competitiveness in global markets and the quality of life in the United States. Thus, an important starting point for the discussion of the psychological and physical well-being of urban inner-city youngsters is the access of urban, ethnic minority families to sufficient social and financial resources.

The work of this chapter is organized by the conceptual model shown in Figure 5.1. The hypothetical model suggests that families' economic resources have an effect on adolescents' well-being through their influence on parents' psychological functioning and parenting. Thus, economic disadvantage is predicted to have a negative association with

Figure 5.1
Conceptual Model of the Relationships between Families' Economic Resources, Parenting, and Adolescent Well-Being

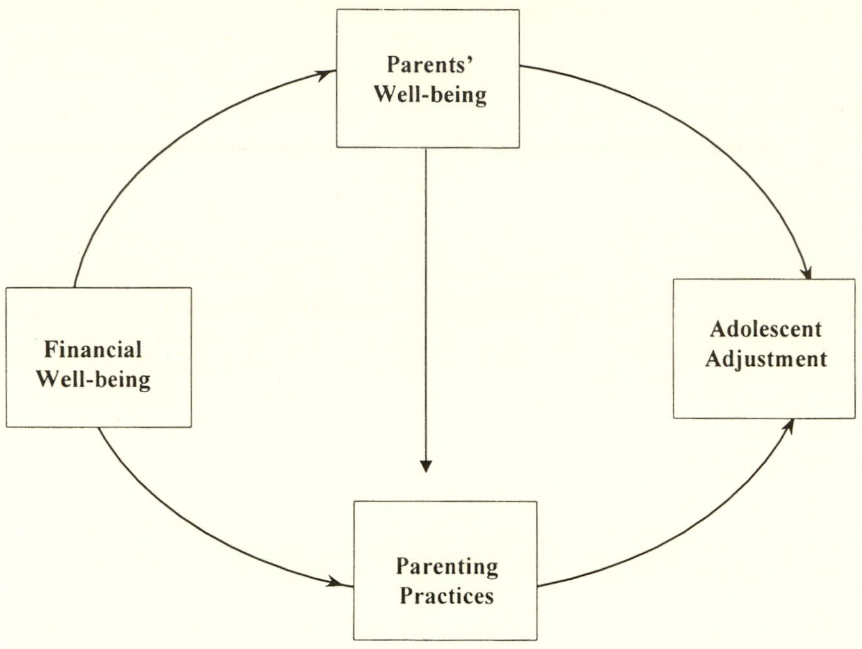

parents' psychological and emotional adjustment. Parents living in economic hardship are also expected to display less adequate parenting practices. Adolescents whose parents are psychologically distressed, and who experience less adequate parenting are expected to function less well. Adolescents' personal attributes and especially social support are expected to moderate the effects of economic resources and parents' well-being and parenting practices.

FAMILIES' SOCIAL AND ECONOMIC RESOURCES

Research has shown that economic hardship during adolescence is linked to less adequate functioning in the areas of problem behavior, depression, self-image, and positive relations (McLoyd, 1997). In inner-city neighborhoods, the effects of industrial downsizing, economic restructuring, and racism have been evident for decades. In 1996, 40 percent of African American and 40 percent of Latino families were poor. For female-headed, African American families, the poverty rate was 58 percent; for Latino female-headed homes, 67 percent (America's Children, Key National Indicators of Well-Being, 1998). Also, as is often the case, the poverty experienced by inner-city, ethnic minority families is of a long duration. For example, approximately 25 percent of African American children who are poor early in life remain poor for as much as 10 to 14 years (Duncan, 1988).

African American and Hispanic children are also less likely than white children to have a parent working full time, all year. In 1996, 56 percent of African American and 64 percent of Hispanic families had a full-time, full-year, working parent, compared to 79 percent of white children (America's Children, Key National Indicators of Well-Being, 1998). African American and Hispanic children also are more likely to experience shortages of food. In 1996, 15 percent of poor children reported that they sometimes did not have enough to eat. In 1995, 15.6 percent of poor children experienced food insecurity and were moderately to severely hungry. In terms of access to health care, Hispanic children are less likely to have health insurance than either African American or white children. In 1996, 71 percent of Hispanic children were covered by health insurance, compared to 86 percent of whites and 81 percent of African American children.

ECONOMIC AND SOCIAL RESOURCES AND ADOLESCENT ADJUSTMENT

Research assessing the link between families' socioeconomic status and adolescents' functioning has generally shown a positive association between socioeconomic disadvantage and socioemotional problems (McLoyd, Ceballo, & Mangelsdorf, in press). In the model underlying this work, it is expected that the effects of resources on adolescent adjustment are mediated by parents' adjustment and parenting. Numerous investigations have shown that poverty is associated with problems in peer relations, depression, somatic symptoms, and conduct disorders, as well as social maladaptation and psychological disorder (for a review, see Taylor, 1997). Elder and associates (Elder, 1974; Elder, Van Nguyen, & Caspi, 1985) in research on families facing the Great Depression found that mothers in families experiencing economic hardship were likely to report that their adolescents had emotional problems. Conger and colleagues (1992) have shown that family income is associated with adolescent school performance and self-confidence. In other research with preadolescent children, McLeod and Shanahan (1993) found that the length of time children had spent in poverty is positively related to internalizing symptoms (e.g., anxiety, sadness, depression, dependency). For children currently being in poverty in comparison to long-term poverty is linked to externalizing problems (e.g., disobedience, difficulty getting along with others).

An increasing amount of research has examined the role of social resources such as neighborhood or community characteristics or factors in the adjustment and social and psychological well-being of African American adolescents (Brewster, 1994; Brooks-Gunn, Duncan, & Aber, 1997; Crane, 1991; Hogan & Kitagawa, 1985; Jarrett, 1995). Neighborhoods contain resources that may either enhance or be a detriment to the functioning of adolescents and their families. Sampson (Sampson & Laub, 1994; Sampson & Morenoff, 1997) suggests that structural features of a community, for example, poverty–resource deprivation, and/or inadequate health care resources are linked to youngsters' behavior through their parents. In disadvantaged and socially disorganized communities, parental problems are more likely to arise because of the stressful experiences to which families are exposed (e.g., violence, criminal activities). Parents, because of the stressors they experience, are expected to display less adequate parenting practices, and poorer parenting is expected to be linked to negative outcomes for children.

Research has shown that for white male adolescents, poverty is associated with less effective parental monitoring and erratic, harsh discipline, which in turn are positively linked to delinquency (Sampson & Laub, 1994). Research has also shown that stressors to which African American mothers are exposed may be detrimental to their parenting and their psychological well-being (Taylor, Roberts, & Jacobson, 1997), which would be expected to be negatively associated with adolescents' behavior and adjustment. Taylor and colleagues (1997) found that for poor African American mothers, stressors (family disruption, health, and work problems) are linked to mothers' well-being and parenting.

Other research has shown that the teenage pregnancy and drop-out rates increased among African American youngsters as the proportion of high status workers (e.g., those holding professional of managerial positions) in neighborhoods declined (Crane, 1991). Also, neighborhood variables including median family income and the female employment rate are significant predictors of nonmarital sexual intercourse during the adolescent years (Brewster, 1994). Findings have also revealed that having concerned neighbors (neighbors who look out for them and are interested in their lives) is associated with lower depression among inner-city, African American adolescents (Stevenson, 1998). Other research findings have shown that the more that mothers reported that crime and physical deterioration were problems in their neighborhood, the lower were adolescents' self-esteem and self-reliance (Taylor, 1998). Also, the more that mothers reported that resources were inaccessible in their neighborhood the lower adolescents' self-esteem and self-reliance and the higher their problem behavior and psychological distress (Taylor, 1998).

Community impoverishment (e.g., poverty, abandoned housing, population loss) is also positively associated with delinquency (Coulton, Korbin, Su, & Chow, 1995). Exposure to violence in the community is positively associated with increased violence in African American adolescents. Results have shown that adolescents who have been exposed to violent incidents including beatings, shootings, and stabbings in the community are more likely to engage in violence themselves (Farrell & Bruce, 1997).

Research has also shown links between neighborhood conditions and educational outcomes. For African American males, school performance is negatively associated with the concentration of jobless males in the neighborhood (Halpern-Felsher et al., 1997). In other research, results have shown that neighborhood risk (e.g., vandalism, gang activity, crime) is negatively associated with adolescents' school achievement (Gonzales, Cauce, Friedman, & Mason, 1996). Also, other indicators of neighborhood risk (e.g., percentage of low SES neighbors, percentage of jobless) are significantly related to school departure of African American males (Connell & Halpern-Felsher, 1997). Related research has shown that for African American females living in a neighborhood with a higher percentage of affluent neighbors is positively linked to school completion (Duncan, 1994). For African American males living in a community that is integrated is positively associated with completing schooling.

ECONOMIC AND SOCIAL RESOURCES, PARENTS' WELL-BEING, AND PARENTING PRACTICES

Economic Resources and Parents' Well-Being

The effects of economic and social resources on adolescents are expected to be mediated by their impact on parents' psychological well-being and parenting. Research has generally shown that economic hardship is positively associated with parents' psychological distress (Conger, Ge, Elder, Lorenz, & Simons, 1994; McLoyd, 1990, 1997). McLoyd (1990) has suggested that among the factors explaining the elevated mental health problems of the poor are the large number of frustrating and stressful events and conditions that are beyond individuals' power to control. McLoyd has argued that the poor are subjected to an "unremitting succession of negative life events" (e.g., criminal assault, illness) while living in the context of chronically stressful living circumstances (e.g., unsafe neighborhoods, poor housing). A number of researchers have indeed found a positive link between economic hardship and depression (Brody, Stoneman, Flor, McCarary, Hastings, & Conyers 1994; Conger et al., 1994; Dressler, 1985; McLoyd, Jayaratne, Ceballo, & Borquez, 1994).

Other research has revealed a positive association of families' economic pressures and parents' emotional distress (Elder, Eccles, Ardelt, & Lord, 1995). This literature also importantly revealed that for single-parent households, social support did not buffer parents from emotional distress associated with economic hardship. In other work, Brody and colleagues (1994) found that families' financial resources are positively associated with parents' optimism and negatively linked to depression. Brody and colleagues obtained their findings with rural African American families. There is reason to believe that even stronger links between hardship and depression exist for urban African American families because they may lack some of the resources available to rural, African American families (e.g., greater proportion of two-parent families, stronger kinship networks). Indeed, McLoyd and colleagues (1994) found that among urban, single African American mothers, unemployment was associated with depressive symptomatology, and others have shown that job loss is associated with sadness and depression among African American men and women (Brown & Gary, 1988; Thomas & Ensminger, 1989).

As McLoyd (1990) notes, it is not simply poverty that increases parents' distress but also other stressors that may accompany economic distress, such as dangerous neighborhoods and stressful events. In a recent study of African American mothers, Taylor, Roberts, and Jacobson (1997) found that health-related stressors (e.g., personal illness or injury to a family member) were positively associated with mothers' depression. Also, stressors in the areas of family disruption or work were negatively linked to mothers' self-esteem. Roberts and Taylor (1994) found that the more that mothers perceived their neighborhood as deteriorated and unsafe, the more depressed they were.

Economic Resources and Parenting

In addition to the links with parents adjustment, families' economic resources are associated with the quality of parenting that parents exhibit. Research has shown that poverty is associated with mothers' lower emotional responsiveness to children' needs and more frequent use of physical punishment among African American, Hispanic, and non-Hispanic whites (McLeod & Shanahan, 1993). Mothers may be less responsive because of the stressors they face, and their emotional distress may dim their views of parenting and parental responsibilities. Research has in fact shown that financial strain is related to mothers' negative perceptions of the maternal role (McLoyd et al., 1994).

McLoyd (1997) has noted that investigations of poor and low-income African American families reveal that parents are more likely to use harsher, power-assertive discipline techniques and are less supportive of their children. In addition, poverty has been associated with the use of less reasoning in disciplining and controlling children and more use of physical punishment. Poverty has also been linked to diminished expressions of affection (for a review, see McLoyd, 1990).

Research (Taylor et al., 1997) again suggests that it is stressors accompanying economic distress that may compromise parents' parenting behavior. Findings have revealed that, among urban, low-income, African American families, the more that families experienced family disruption and work problems, the less emotional support they report for their youngsters (Taylor et al., 1997). Other work has shown that the more mothers reported that their neighborhood was socially isolated, the less supportive they were of their children (Taylor, 1998).

Finally, research has clearly shown that there is a positive relation of poverty with abusive parenting. Although a relatively small number of poor and nonpoor parents abuse their children, child abuse is higher among the poor than the more affluent (Pelton, 1989). Even the degree of poverty has an effect on abuse, as the poorest of poor families tend to engage in more severe forms of abuse than those who are less poor.

Parental Well-Being and Parenting Practices

It is important to note that parents' well-being and parenting practices are linked in that, for example, mothers' depression has been linked to harsher discipline and lower emotional support of their children (McLoyd, 1990). McLoyd and colleagues (1994) found that mothers' depression is associated with harsh parenting and negative perceptions of the maternal role among single, African American mothers. Also, Taylor and colleagues (1997) found that mothers' self-esteem is positively related to their acceptance and control and supervision of their adolescent. In related work with rural African American families, Brody and colleagues (1994) revealed that parents' optimism and low depression are associated with greater mutual support among parents and low conflict concerning child care. Finally, Ge, Conger, Lorenz, and Simon (1994) found that parents' depressed mood was positively related to harsh and inconsistent parenting. In all of the work reviewed, the common feature is that parents' financial resources are linked to parents' mental health, and parents' mental health is linked to parents' parenting practices.

MODERATORS OF THE EFFECTS OF ECONOMIC RESOURCES

It is important to note that some of the potential effects of economic hardship may be offset by resources (personal and social) available to adolescents and their families. Work in the area of resilience has shown that personal qualities like good intellectual skills, self-worth, hopefulness, and/or religious faith are features that distinguish youngsters who are well adjusted in spite of being economically disadvantaged and living in high risk neighborhoods (Masten, 1994).

A growing body of research has suggested that social support may also moderate the effects of economic hardship and may lessen parents' distress and punitive parenting behavior. Research with African American families has indeed shown that in times of financial need, individuals typically receive help from extended relatives (Dressler, 1985). Poor parents receiving emotional support are less likely to display poor quality parenting behavior (e.g., nagging, scolding, threatening) and report being more satisfied with themselves as parents (Crnic & Greenberg, 1987; Zur-Szpiro & Longfellow, 1982). A number of investigations have shown that child-care support to at-risk mothers and their children is associated with better parenting and lower risk of negative outcomes for children (Crockenberg, 1987).

PARENTAL ADJUSTMENT, PARENTING, AND ADOLESCENT ADJUSTMENT

In the conceptual model on which this chapter is based, parenting practices and parents' psychological well-being are factors that mediate the association of families' economic resources and their correlates and adolescent functioning. Research linking parents' psychological well-being with adolescents' functioning has shown that mothers' self-esteem and self-acceptance are positively linked to adolescent self-reliance and independence and negatively associated with problem behavior. There is also a trend for adolescent's psychological distress to increase as mothers' distress increases (Taylor & Roberts, 1995).

A growing body of research has revealed that African American youngsters benefit from being raised in homes that are structured and organized. Structured and organized homes are those in which both parents and children experience regular routines (e.g., bedtimes, dinnertime, time period for homework) and a home life that is stable and predictable. Clark (1983) in an ethnographic study of the factors that distinguish high- from low-achieving, low-income, African American adolescents found that high-achieving adolescents had parents who worked to structure and manage the adolescents' time and activities by establishing daily and weekly routines and schedules. These adolescents had regular sets of chores and regular times for doing homework. They also were expected to be home at specific time and knew that their parents would be home at designated times as well. Other research has shown that a structured and organized family environment (e.g., curfews, clear family schedules) is positively associated with adolescents' self-reliance and grades and negatively associated with problem behavior and psychological distress (Taylor, 1996; Ensminger, 1990).

Research has also examined the role of parents' parenting style and the association with adolescent adjustment. Findings have revealed that poor parenting (defined as neglectful, rejecting, cold, and aggressive) is positively associated with hard drug use among urban, African American adolescents (Myers, Newcomb, Richardson, & Alvy, 1997). Restrictive parenting has also been linked to problem behavior (Mason, Cauce, Gonzales, Hiraga, & Grove, 1994).

In the burgeoning literature on the effects of authoritative parenting (i.e., parenting that combines warmth, control, and democracy), findings have shown that African American adolescents in authoritative working-class and middle-class homes are more likely to report feelings of self-reliance and independence and less likely to engage in problem behavior (Steinberg, Mounts, Lamborn, & Dornbusch, 1991). Research has also revealed that among poor inner-city African American families, parental acceptance and firm behavioral control (two components of authoritative parenting) are positively related to adolescent adjustment (Taylor & Roberts, 1995). Findings have also shown that strong parent–child attachment is negatively related to delinquent behavior. Also, positive relations with parents are positively associated with self-esteem (Luster & McAdoo, 1995).

KINSHIP SUPPORT AND ADOLESCENT ADJUSTMENT

An important feature of family life for many urban, African American families is their relations with extended kin. Research work (e.g., Aschennbrener, 1973; Billingsley, 1968; Hill, 1978; McAdoo, 1982) has long noted the importance of kin support and involvement as a key feature of family life and a factor in families' adaptation, extending as far back in history as the period of slavery. Research has shown that support from adult relatives is positively associated with adolescents' autonomy and self-reliance and grades and negatively associated with anxiety and problem behavior (Taylor, Casten, & Flickinger, 1993; Taylor & Roberts, 1995; Taylor, 1996). McLoyd and colleagues (1994) found that the availability of instrumental support to single, African American mothers is negatively associated with adolescents' depression and cognitive distress.

The impact of kin support on adolescent functioning is at least partially explained by the positive association of kin social support with the quality of parenting adolescents experience when kin are involved with the family. Low-income parents are less likely to display punitive parenting when they perceive that they have social support (Hashima & Amato, 1994). Also, African American mothers with support are less likely to use punitive forms of discipline, and adolescents in turn, are less likely to be psychologically distressed and to report negative relations with their mother (McLoyd et al., 1994). Similarly, mothers report higher self-esteem and are more accepting and firm in controlling adolescents' behavior when they have the support of kin, and adolescents in turn, report lower levels of problem behavior (Taylor & Roberts, 1995). Also, families who have the support of kin are more structured and organized. Parents are more involved in adolescents' schooling, and adolescents in turn, report better grades, higher autonomy and self-reliance, lower psychological distress, and fewer problem behaviors (Taylor, 1996).

IMPLICATION FOR PREVENTION AND INTERVENTION

A clear mandate for the prevention of some of the problems of poor adolescents and their families is the investment of social and financial capital in disadvantaged communities. Wilson (1987, 1996) has argued that many of the problems of poor, inner-city families are rooted in the absence of jobs and people working for pay at regular hours. It is argued that the lack of employment means that individuals do not have regular, legitimate forms of income or models of persons using their skills to lawfully maintain a living, nor activities that structure the time and flow of events in the community.

The investment of capital may also include the introduction of resources to communities (e.g., markets, stores, banks, schools) to enhance the quality of life of its residents. The presence of greater capital would likely lead to a reduction in the stressful conditions of inner-city communities and families (e.g., lower crime, greater availability of resources). The work reviewed here has shown that residual effects of greater resources would result in fewer adjustment problems for adolescents because their parents would be less psychologically distressed and would in turn engage in more adequate parenting.

Inner-city ethnic-minority families and their children, without the introduction of increased resources, are at increased risk for problems. Thus, it is important to assess the socioemotional functioning of poor, ethnic-minority youngsters and the circumstances that pose a threat to their well-being. McLoyd (1997) has argued that comprehensive, family-centered child development programs in urban communities could, with parent consent, regularly assess the well-being of children and adolescents. It is important that such programs be designed with an awareness of the links between neighborhood characteristics, family environment, parenting, social networks, and adolescent adjustment. For example, adolescents identified with externalizing behavioral problems may also have problems at home that are rooted in the risky circumstances and stressors of their neighborhood. Treatment of the adolescents' problem behavior would thus need to consider the possibility of initiating changes in multiple domains.

As a general issue, it is important that a more concerted effort be devoted to putting empirical research on at-risk families into practice. For example, Taylor (1998) has shown that the lack of availability of vital resources in neighborhoods is associated with less adequate functioning in families. This work indicates important targets of neighborhood revitalization in terms of community resources with implications for the functioning of families and their members. For example, research has shown that mothers' psychological distress is positively associated with the lack of availability of resources such as medical or financial services. This work suggests that the introduction of such resources to communities will mean lower levels of distress and anxiety for caregivers. Lower levels of psychological distress for caregivers is likely to result in more positive interactions with youngsters in the home.

Research has also shown that there is a positive association of social support with the functioning of adults and children (Taylor, 1997). Thus, it is possible that by creating or utilizing mechanisms in the community (e.g., schools, churches, support groups) through which families have access to social support, families may function more adequately because parents and youngsters have others they can turn to for aid. Parents and adolescents, when they are linked to such support networks, may develop relations within their communities that had not existed before. Mental health workers, teachers, administrators, and others working with families can play an important role in initiating families' contact with such networks. As McLoyd (1997) has noted, attention should be payed to devising strategies that make use of "culturally indigenous structures and patterns of relations" of ethnic minorities, like kin support or flexibility in family roles played.

Also, Taylor (1999) has shown that among at-risk families, creating an organized and structured family environment helps buffer the impact of stressors that at-risk families face. Family organization is positively associated with more adequate parenting practices and with adolescent adjustment. It is important, whether through churches, schools, social agencies or other media, that information on important family practices be conveyed to families.

Finally, Taylor, Rodriguez, Seaton, and Dominguez (1999) have shown that mothers experiencing financial problems are prone toward depression because they are not hopeful about the future. Mothers' depression in turn is associated with adolescents' depression because mothers and adolescents in such circumstance are likely to have problems communicating. This work points toward potential targets of intervention, including the improvement of the economic opportunities and resources of such families and possibly therapeutic services aimed at mothers' sense of hopelessness and parent–adolescent communication problems.

It is also important to acknowledge that there are limits to the resilience of individuals and the power of social institutions to overcome problems such as poverty or racism. As important as social support may be to families, it may not enable families to overcome some of the challenges they face. For example, individuals facing discrimination in the workplace may not be as depressed as they might be because of support they receive from kin. The fact remains, however, that such discrimination limits the individuals' capacity for job advancement and increased financial resources for the family. As Halpern (1991) notes, there has been an over reliance on services in the United States when many problems of poor families have their roots in intentional social and economic policies and practices that may require controversial political solutions.

SUMMARY AND FUTURE DIRECTIONS

Urban, inner-city, ethnic-minority adolescents and their families face a host of conditions and experiences that place their well-being at risk. Chief among the risks are those associated with economic disadvantage. Economic hardship is both directly associated with adolescents' maladjustment and affects youngsters through the negative impact on parents' well-being and parenting practices. Living in neighborhoods that lack resources and are beset with crime and social and physical deterioration is linked to poor adjustment in both parents and adolescents. Some of the effects of economic distress are offset by adolescents' personal attributes and by social support to their families from extended relatives and others.

In future research, more process-oriented work examining the links between factors placing adolescents at risk and adolescents' functioning is needed. For example, it is established that economic disadvantage is linked to mothers' depression, and mothers' depression is associated with less adequate parenting and adolescent depression. It is not known, however, what the factors are leading economically distressed individuals to become more depressed. It may be that individuals are depressed because they are hopeless, ashamed of their circumstances, and feel powerless to initiate change. Adolescents' despair may also be linked to other risky behaviors (e.g., violence, drug use, problems in school). Clearly, if economically distressed persons feel hopeless, one step in a therapeutic strategy would involve efforts to alleviate feelings of despair.

More research is also needed on the connection between health and family functioning. Racial disparities spanning from differences in infant mortality to differences in life expectancy are well known. Research has also shown that health concerns are sources of stress that have a negative impact on mothers' psychological adjustment and parenting and adolescents' psychological well-being (Taylor et al., 1997). Thus, more research is needed not simply on why there are disparities in health, but also on the implications of health-related problems for family functioning.

Finally, more research is needed on the links between culture and adolescent adjustment. There may be culturally based patterns of behavior or customs that are either sources of strength or sources of stress for ethnic-minority families (see Lambert, this volume). The importance of extended family networks for African American families has been examined here. There are many other patterns and customs or culturally based child-rearing goals (e.g., flexibility in family roles) that may be linked to the adjustment of children and adolescents but have not been explored in empirical work. Also, the meaning of behaviors (e.g., parenting behaviors) may depend upon the cultural traditions and customs of the families and adolescents. For example, the correlates of the same parenting behaviors may differ depending on the ethnic groups considered (Chao, 2000). There may also be behavioral patterns in urban, ethnic-minority families that have grown as a result of cultural practices and adaptations to disadvantaged circumstances. As the United States becomes increasingly ethnically diverse, but remains highly ethnically segregated, the importance of understanding the cultural foundations of behavior will grow in importance.

REFERENCES

America's Children, Key National Indicators of Well-Being. (1998). National Interagency Forum on Child and Family Statistics. Washington, DC: U.S. Government Printing Office.

Aschenbernner, J. (1973). Extended families among black Americans. *Journal of Comparative Family Studies, 4*, 257–268.

Billingsley, A. (1968). *Black families in white America*. Englewood Cliffs, NJ: Prentice Hall.

Brewster, K. L. (1994). Race differences in sexual activity among adolescent women: The role of neighborhood characteristics. *American Sociological Review, 59*, 408–424.

Brody, G., Stoneman, Z., Flor, D., McCrary, C., Hastings, L., & Conyers, O. (1994). Financial resources, parental psychological functioning, parent co-caregiving, and early adolescent competence in rural two-parent African-American families. *Child Development, 65*, 590–605.

Brooks-Gunn, J., Duncan, G. J., & Aber, J. L. (1997). *Neighborhood poverty*: Vol. 1. *Context and consequences for children*. New York: Russell Sage Foundation.

Brown, D. R., & Gary, L. E. (1988). Unemployment and psychological distress among black women. *Sociological Focus, 21*, 209–221.

Chao, R. K. (2000). Cultural explanations for the role of parenting in the school success of Asian-American children. In R. Taylor & M. Wung (Eds.), *Resilience across contexts: Family, work, culture, and community*. Mahwah, NJ: Erlbaum.

Clark, R. (1983). *Family life and school achievement: Why poor black children succeed or fail*. Chicago: University of Chicago Press.

Conger, R. D., Conger, K. J., Elder, G. H., Lorenz, F. O., Simons, R. L., & Whitbeck, L. B. (1992). A family process model of economic hardship and adjustment of early adolescent boys. *Child Development, 63*, 526–541.

Conger, R. D., Ge, X., Elder, G. H., Lorenz, F. O., & Simons, R. L. (1994). Economic stress, coercive family process, and developmental problems in adolescents. *Child Development, 65*, 541–561.

Connell, J. P., & Halpern-Felsher, B. L. (1997). How neighborhoods affect educational outcomes in middle childhood and adolescence: Conceptual issues and an empirical example. In J. Brooks-Gunn, G. Duncan, & J. L. Aber (Eds.), *Neighborhood poverty*: Vol. 1. *Context and consequences for children*. New York: Russell Sage Foundation.

Coulton, C. J., Korbin, J. E., Su, M., & Chow, J. (1995). Community level factors and child maltreatment rates. *Child Development, 66*, 1262–1276.

Crane, J. (1991). The epidemic theory of ghettos and neighborhood effects on dropping out and teenage childbearing. *American Journal of Sociology, 96*, 1226–1259.

Crnic, K., & Greenberg, M. (1987). Maternal stress, social support, and coping: Influences on early mother–child relationships. In C. Boukydis (Ed.), *Research on support for parents and infants in the postnatal period* (pp. 25–40). Norwood, NJ: Ablex.

Crockenberg, S. (1987). Support for adolescent mothers during the postnatal period: Theory and research. In C. Boukydis (Ed.), *Research on support for parents and infants in the postnatal period* (pp. 3–24). Norwood, NJ: Ablex.

Dressler, W. (1985). Extended family relationships, social support, and mental health in a southern black community. *Journal of Health and Social Behavior, 26*, 39–48.

Duncan, G. J. (1988, June). *The economic environment of childhood*. Paper presented at a study group meeting on poverty and children, University of Kansas, Lawrence.

Duncan, G. J. (1994). Families and neighbors as sources of disadvantage in the schooling decisions of white and black adolescents. *American Journal of Education, 103*, 20–53.

Elder, G. A., Eccles, J. E., Ardelt, M., & Lord, A. (1995). Families under economic pressure. *Journal of Family Issues, 15*, 5–37.

Elder, G. H., Jr. (1974). *Children of the Great Depression*. Chicago: University of Chicago Press.

Elder, G. H., Jr., Van Nguyen, T., & Caspi, A. (1985). Linking family hardship to children's lives. *Child Development, 56*, 361–375.

Ensminger, M. E. (1990). Sexual activity and problem behaviors among urban adolescents. *Child Development, 61*, 2032–2046.

Farrell, A. D., & Bruce, S. E. (1997). Impact of exposure to community violence on violent behavior and emotional distress among urban adolescents. *Journal of Clinical Child Psychology, 26* (1), 2–14.

Federal Interagency Forum on Child and Family Statistics. (1998). *America's children: Key national indicators of well-being*. Washington, DC: U.S. Government Printing Office.

Ge, X., Conger, R. D., Lorenz, F., & Simons, R. D. (1994). Parents' stress and adolescent depressive symptoms: Mediating process. *Journal of Health and Social Behavior, 35*, 38–44.

Gonzales, N. A., Cauce, A. M., Friedman, R. J., & Mason, C. A. (1996). Family, peer, and neighborhood influences on academic achievement among African American adolescents: One-year prospective effects. *American Journal of Community Psychology, 24* (3), 365–387.

Halpern, R. (1991). Supportive services of families in poverty: Dilemmas of reform. *Social Service Review, 65*, 343–364.

Halpern-Felsher, B. L., Connell, J. P., Spencer, M. B., Aber, J. L., Duncan, G. J., Clifford, E., Crichlow, W. E., Usinger, P. A., Cole, S. P., Allen, L., & Seidman, E. (1997). Neighborhood and family factors predicting educational risk and attainment in African American and white children. In J. Brooks-Gunn, G. J. Duncan, & J. L. Aber (Eds.), *Neighborhood Poverty*: Vol. 1. *Context and consequences for children*. New York: Russell Sage Foundation.

Hashima, P. Y., & Amato, P. R. (1994). Poverty, social support, and parental behavior. *Child Development, 65*, 394–403.

Hill, R. (1978). *The strengths of black families*. New York: Emerson-Hall.

Hogan, D. P., & Kitagawa, E. M. (1985). The impact of social status, family structure, and neighborhood on the fertility of black adolescents. *American Journal of Sociology, 90*, 825–855.

Jarrett, R. L. (1995). Growing up poor: The family experiences of socially mobile youth in low-income African American neighborhoods. *Journal of Adolescent Research, 10*, 111–135.

Luster, T., & McAdoo, M. P. (1995). Factors related to self-esteem among African American youths: A secondary analysis of the High/Scope Perry preschool data. *Journal of Research on Adolescence, 5*, 451–467.

Mason, C. A., Cause, A. M., Gonzales, N., Hiraga, Y., & Grove, K. (1994). An ecological model of externalizing behaviors in African-American adolescents: No family is an island. *Journal of Research on Adolescence, 4*, 639–655.

Masten, A. S. (1994). Resilience in individual development: Successful adaptation despite risk and adversity. In M. C. Wang & E. W. Gordon (Eds.), *Educational resilience in inner-city America: Challenges and prospects* (pp. 3–26). Hillsdale, NJ: Erlbaum.

McAdoo, H. P. (1982). Stress absorbing systems in black families. *Family Relations, 31*, 479–488.

McLeod, J., & Shanahan, M. (1993). Poverty, parenting, and children's mental health. *American Sociological Review, 58*, 351–366.

McLoyd, V. C. (1990). The impact of economic hardship on black families and children: Psychological distress, parenting, and socioemotional development. *Child Development, 61,* 311–346.

McLoyd, V. C. (1997). The impact of poverty and low socioeconomic status on the socioemotional functioning of African-American children and adolescents: Mediating effects. In R. Taylor & M. Wang (Eds.), *Social and emotional adjustment and family relations in ethnic minority families.* Hillsdale, NJ: Erlbaum.

McLoyd, V. C., Ceballo, R., & Mangelsdorf, S. (in press). The effects of poverty of children's socioemotional development. In J. Noshpitz (Ed.), *Handbook of child and adolescent psychiatry.* New York: Basic Books.

McLoyd, V. C., Jayaratne, T. E., Ceballo, R., & Borquez, J. (1994). Unemployment and work interruption among African American single mothers: Effects on parenting and adolescent socioemotional functioning. *Child Development, 65,* 562–589.

Myers, H. F., Newcomb, M. D., Richardson, M. A., & Alvy, K. T. (1997). Parental and family risk factors for substance use in inner-city African-American children and adolescents. *Journal of Psychopathology and Behavioral Assessment, 19* (2), 109–131.

Pelton, L. H. (1989). *For reason of poverty: A critical analysis of the public child welfare system in the United States.* New York: Praeger.

Roberts, D., & Taylor, R. D. (1995, March). *Neighborhood characteristics, parenting, and adolescent adjustment in African-American families.* Paper presented at the biennial conference of the Society for Research in Child Development, Indianapolis, IN.

Sampson, R. J., & Laub, J. H. (1994). Urban poverty and the family context of delinquency: A new look at structure and process in a classic study. *Child Development, 65,* 523–540.

Steinberg, L., Mounts, N. S., Lamborn, S. D., & Dornbusch, S. M. (1991). Authoritative parenting and adolescent adjustment across varied ecological niches. *Journal of Research on Adolescence, 1,* 19–36.

Stevenson, H. C. (1998). Raising safe villages: Cultural–ecological factors that influence the emotional adjustment of adolescents. *Journal of Black Psychology, 24* (1), 44–59.

Taylor, R. D. (1996). Kinship support, family management, and adolescent adjustment and competence in African-American families. *Developmental Psychology, 32,* 687–695.

Taylor, R. D. (1997). The effects of economic and social stressors on parenting and adolescent adjustment in African-American families. In R. Taylor & M. Wang (Eds.), *Social and emotional adjustment and family relations in ethnic minority families.* Hillsdale, NJ: Erlbaum.

Taylor, R. D. (1998). *Association of African-American mothers' perceptions of their neighborhood with their parenting and adolescent adjustment.* Unpublished manuscript, Temple University, Philadelphia.

Taylor, R. D. (1999). *Stressful experiences and the adjustment of African-American adolescents: Moderating effects of family organization.* Unpublished manuscript, Temple University, Philadelphia.

Taylor, R. D., Casten, R., & Flickinger, S. (1993). The influence of kinship social support on the parenting experiences and psychosocial adjustment of African-American adolescents. *Developmental Psychology, 29*, 382–388.

Taylor, R. D., & Roberts, D. (1995). Kinship support and maternal and adolescent well-being in economically disadvantaged African-American families. *Child Development, 66*, 1585–1597.

Taylor, R. D., Roberts, D., & Jacobson, L. (1997). Stressful life events, psychological well-being, and parenting in African-American families. *Journal of Family Psychology, 11*, 45–56.

Taylor, R. D., Rodriguez, A. U., Seaton, E., & Dominguez, A. (1999). *Association of financial resources with parenting and adolescent adjustment in African-American families.* Unpublished manuscript, Temple University, Philadelphia.

Thomas, M. S., & Ensminger, M. E. (1989). Psychological well-being among mothers with school age children: Evolving family structures. *Social Forces, 67*, 715–730.

Wilson, W. J. (1987). *The truly disadvantaged: The inner city, the underclass, and public policy*. Chicago: University of Chicago Press.

Wilson, W. J. (1996). *When work disappears: The world of the new urban poor*. New York: Knopf.

Zur-Szpiro, S., & Longfellow, C. (1982). Fathers' support to mothers and children. In D. Belle (Ed.), *Lives in stress: Women and depression* (pp. 145–153). Beverly Hills, CA: Sage.

6

Violence and Trauma in the Lives of African American Children

Esther J. Jenkins

Despite recent declines in the violent crime rate in this country (Federal Bureau of Investigation, 1998; Taylor, 1997; Peters, Kochanek, & Murphy, 1998), violence and the threat of violence remains a central feature in the lives of many African American children. This chapter examines black children's exposure to violence and the consequences of that exposure for their development, mental health, and general welfare.

EXPOSURE TO VIOLENCE

Data from a number of sources indicate that black children, particularly those who are poor and reside in the inner city, are exposed to considerable violence as victims, witnesses, and close others of victims. The violence occurs in their homes as well as in their communities. Exposure to violence can occur either by being the victim of a violent act or by witnessing a violent act. In this next section, both forms of exposure are examined.

Victimization

Intrafamilial

Black children are overrepresented as victims of abuse. A recent report from the National Child Abuse and Neglect data system (U.S.

Department of Health and Human Services [HHS], 1998) which compiles statistics from state departments of child welfare, indicates that in 1996, black children, who comprised approximately 15 percent of the minor children in the country, were 28 percent of the reported physical abuse victims and 19 percent of sex abuse victims. Survey data, which do not have the same problem with reporting biases as official statistics, also show that black children have relatively high abuse rates (Hampton, Gelles, & Harrop, 1989). Homicide, perpetrated almost exclusively by parents or caretakers, is the second leading cause of death for 1-to-4-year-old black children (Peters et al., 1998).

Extrafamilial

African American children are at extreme risk for victimization outside the family. Black adolescent males have the highest violent victimization rate of any group (Sickmund, Snyder, & Poe-Yamagata, 1997). Despite recent decreases in violent crime, black youth and young adults are still eight times more likely than whites to die violently, and homicide remains the leading cause of death for black males and females ages 15 to 24 (Peters et al., 1998). Surveys of African American children have also found high rates of self-reported victimization, particularly of black males being shot at (see Jenkins & Bell, 1997).

Black youth's fearfulness suggests that they are aware of the danger. In a survey of students in a high violence area (Jenkins, 1995), half did not feel safe in their neighborhood, and one in ten did not feel safe in their homes. Youth seem most fearful in and around their schools (Jenkins, 1995; Sheehan, DiCara, LeBailly, & Christoffel, 1997), although they are less likely (Kaufman et al., 1998) or no more likely (Singer, Miller, Gou, Flannery, Frierson, & Slovak, 1999) to be victimized at school. Students may not attend school because of fear for their safety (Kaufman et al., 1998) and, anecdotally, youth workers and educators frequently report that youth leave or refuse to attend a school because it is located in an unsafe area.

Witnessing

Community Violence

As shown in Table 6.1, studies of African American children consistently find high rates of witnessing of community violence. Surveys of 3000 plus inner-city schoolchildren found that exposure to severe violence (e.g., witnessing of a shooting) ranged from 26 to 70 percent. These rates of exposure are much higher than those reported in a national sample of adolescents in which 5 to 6 percent had seen someone

Table 6.1
Survey Studies of African American Children's Exposure to Chronic Community Violence

			Most severe acts witnessed		
Author (year)	N	Age	Shooting	Stabbing	Killing
Jenkins & Thompson (1986); Bell & Jenkins (1993)	536	7-15	26.3	30.0	----[a]
Shakoor & Chalmers (1991); Uehara et al. (1996); Bell & Jenkins (1993)	997	10-19	39.4	34.6	23.5
Osofsky et al. (1993)	53	9-12	26.4	18.9	5.7
Richters & Martinez (1993a)	51	6-8	47.0	31.0	----
	37	9-10	31.0	17.0	----
Fitzpatrick & Boldizar (1993)[c]	221	7-18	70.0[d]	53.0	44.0
Jenkins & Bell (1994); Jenkins (1995)	203	13-18	60.6	45.0	43.0
Singer et al. (1995)[e]	227	14-19	43.0[d]	34.3	----
	228	14-19	55.5	55.5	----
	862	14-19	30.4	30.4	----
	379	14-19	5.0	5.0	----
Schubiner et al. (1993)	246	14-23	42.0[f]	42.0[f]	22.0
Farrell & Bruce (1997)	436	10-15	34.9	21.3	----
Sheehan et al. (1997)	146	7-13	42.0	37.0	----

Source: Adapted from Jenkins & Bell, 1997.

[a]Not asked.

[b]Beatings and chasings.

[c]Approximations taken from graph; sample 35 percent African American.

[d]Shot or shot at.

[e]Within the past year.

[f]Shooting or knifing.

shot (Kilpatrick, Saunders, Resnick, & Best, 1997). Exposure levels appear to be related to gender. With the exception of sexual assault, boys report more victimization than girls (Jenkins & Bell, 1994; Shakoor & Chalmers, 1991; Fitzpatrick & Boldizar, 1993; Farrell & Bruce, 1997). The findings on witnessing show no gender differences in younger samples (Attar, Guerra, & Tolan, 1994; Uehara, Chalmers, Jenkins, & Shakoor, 1996; Farrell & Bruce, 1997), but among older youth, boys report more witnessing than girls, particularly of severe community violence against strangers (Schubiner, Scott, & Tzelepis, 1993; Singer, Anglin, Song, & Lunghofer, 1995; Jenkins & Bell, 1994).

Children know and are often close to the individuals whose victimization they witness. Uehara and colleagues (1996) reported that half of those seen shot and one in four of those seen killed was a family member, friend, classmate, or neighbor. In a similar sample drawn from a high violence community, 70 percent of those witnessing a shooting or stabbing reported that the victim was a friend or a family member; one in ten reported that they had witnessed the death or serious injury of a sibling or parent (Jenkins & Bell, 1994). Richters & Martinez (1993a) found similar results in their sample of elementary schoolchildren; in addition, most of the perpetrators in their study were also known to these youngsters, with almost half the children reporting that they were family or friends.

Domestic Violence

Although it is believed that the incidence is high, determining the exact number of children who witness domestic violence has been difficult. Surveys of community violence may ask generally about identity of victim and perpetrator, but typically do not determine if the situation is one of domestic violence (i.e., that both victim and perpetrator in the same incident are family members). Data on the occurrence of domestic violence do not provide specific information on children's witnessing of parental fights. There are strong indicators, however, that many black children are aware of and witness domestic violence. A 1985 study of domestic violence in a nationally representative sample of married or cohabiting couples (Hampton, Gelles, & Harrop, 1989) found that 247 per 1,000 black couples had experienced minor or severe marital violence (wife-to-husband and/or husband-to-wife) in the year preceding the survey. Of the couples in the sample, 75 percent had at least one minor child living at home. A more recent report on violence against women that drew from official and self-report sources (Greenfield et al., 1998) found lower rates of intimate violence (women); again, the majority of these women had minor children residing with them.

Cooccurrence of Violence

There are considerable overlap and cooccurrence in the victimization and witnessing that children experience. Children who witness domestic violence are at increased risk for physical abuse and for sexual abuse, so much so that domestic violence should be considered a marker for these crimes. It is estimated that children are abused in 45 to 70 percent of the homes in which domestic violence occurs, and that children of abused women are 7 to 14 times more likely to be sexually abused by the batterer or someone outside the home (Margolin, 1998). Significant correlations exist between children's exposure to community violence and their reports of family violence (Osofsky et al, 1993) and between witnessing community violence and experiencing physical abuse (O'Keefe, 1997).

Violence exposure occurs in a cumulative pattern from witnessing to victimization and finally to perpetration. In a large sample of middle and high school students Uehara and colleagues (1996) found that many students had only witnessed violence, but rarely had a student been victimized who had not also witnessed. Similarly, students who had perpetrated a violent act overwhelmingly had experienced victimization *and* witnessing. This cumulative pattern of exposure suggests that an effective place for identification and intervention with potential youth perpetrators is with youth who have witnessed violence, and particularly those who have been victimized.

Chronicity

For many, the defining mark of life in inner city is pervasive violence. Its frequent occurrence means that youth have the opportunity for many encounters with violence, under a variety of circumstances, and from an early age. In a small sample of ten public housing mothers, Dubrow and Garbarino (1989) found that all of their children had an encounter with violence by age five. An earlier study of children's exposure to violence (Jenkins & Thompson, 1986) involving children 7 to 15 years old did not find statistically significant differences in the incidence of witnessing by age.

All the studies reviewed in this chapter have found that, when assessed, children in these high violence communities have had multiple experiences with violence as a victim, witness, and/or close other of a victim. For example, in our high school sample (Jenkins & Bell, 1994) and Richters & Martinez's (1993a) elementary school sample, seven out of ten of the children witnessing a shooting reported that they had seen more than one. In a sample of middle school students, children averaged more than four personal victimizations, seven instances of witnessing violence, and eight instances of acquaintances being victimized (Hinton-Nelson, Roberts, & Snyder, 1996). Others have found similar results, with more frequent exposure to less severe acts (Uehara et al., 1996; Richters & Martinez, 1993a; Fitzpatrick & Boldizar, 1993).

Regardless of their direct experiences, almost all of the children in these violence exposure studies are aware of the victimization of others and of the general level of violence in their neighborhoods (Osofsky, 1995). Frequently these victims are friends and family members (Shakoor & Chalmers, 1991; Uehara et al., 1996; Jenkins & Bell, 1994). Shakoor & Chalmers (1991) refer to this awareness of the victimization of close others as "co-victimization" and, as the term suggests, it has important implications for the child.

The picture that emerges is one of large numbers of children exposed to chronic violence in their homes and communities, with some violence directed at them, but most often at friends and family members. It is frequently said that these children live in "war zones." Unlike the children in Northern Ireland, the Middle East, and Eastern Europe with whom they are compared, however, African American children do so without the benefit of a clearly identifiable enemy or a political ideology to frame and explain the violence they experience.

IMPACT OF VIOLENCE EXPOSURE

Children are affected by their experiences with violence. The impact may be as obvious as impaired mental health or as insidious as a lack of trust in others and a cynical worldview. It can manifest in academic difficulties and acting out, behaviors considered endemic among poor inner-city youth, but which may be reactions to trauma. When the violence occurs within the context of many other stressors, and in harsh circumstances that afford few personal, familial, and community resources to buffer the stress, it increases the probability that violence exposure will have deleterious effects.

Most of the work on the impact of violence on children has examined psychological distress and externalizing-type problems. The former includes anxiety and depression, and symptoms of post traumatic stress disorder (PTSD). Externalizing problems focus on aggression, conduct problems, and delinquent behaviors. Although outside the scope of this chapter, there is a growing understanding of and literature on the physiological effects of violence and trauma which underlie behavioral responses (see Perry 1994, 1997).

Psychological Distress

The most frequently discussed reaction to traumatic stress is PTSD. Growing out of work with war veterans, and first included in the DSM-III (American Psychiatric Association, 1980), PTSD occurs in response to an extreme stressor and is characterized by behaviors that fall into three categories: reexperiencing the event, avoidance of reminders and psychic numbing, and increased arousal. Children display all of the symptoms of PTSD in an age-appropriate manner (Pynoos & Eth, 1984; Pynoos & Nader, 1986, 1988). In addition, children are prone to behavioral reenactments of the event, have trauma specific fears, and may develop pessimistic attitudes about people, life, and the future which manifest as a sense of hopelessness and difficulty forming close personal relationships (Terr, 1991).

Just as with adults, traumatized children can also experience, alone or with PTSD symptoms, a number of other stress-related disorders, such as depression, conduct and impulse control disorders, panic and generalized anxiety disorder, and brief reactive psychosis (Marmar, Foy, Kagan, & Pynoos, 1993; Courtois, 1988; Herman, 1992; Bell, 1997). In a study of maltreated children referred to the court, Famularo and colleagues (Famularo, Fenton, Kinscherff, & Augusstyn, 1996) found that a PTSD diagnosis was correlated with ADHD, other anxiety disorders, brief psychotic disorder, suicidal ideation, and mood disorders. In addition, traumatized children are more prone to substance abuse, eating disorders, and academic difficulties (Dyson 1990; Bell, 1997; Deykin & Buka, 1997).

Symptoms may occur immediately after the event or they may not manifest until months or years later, resulting in adult psychiatric problems such as borderline or antisocial personalities disorders. The full impact of the event may only occur when the child matures enough to fully comprehend and understand the incident (Bell, 1997). The traumatic memories may be repressed and activated by a new trauma, hearing about a similar event, or some other reminder, or conversely, the current trauma may serve as a reminder of some previous traumatic event causing a renewal or exacerbation of symptoms (Pynoos & Nader, 1988). Furthermore, the events need not be the same but rather involve similar emotions such as loss, fear, or helplessness, particularly when these issues have not been adequately addressed. This potentially cumulative affect of trauma has particular implications for children exposed to chronic violence and adversity.

Based on her work with children who have been traumatized, Terr makes the useful distinction between traumas that result from "unanticipated single events" and those that result from long-standing or repeated exposure to an event or multiple events. Unlike the sudden trauma which may have only limited effects on the individual, Terr argues that repeated trauma may lead to anger, despair, profound psychic numbing, and dissociation resulting in major personality change (Terr, 1991).

Survey studies of African American youth have found symptoms consistent with clinical descriptions of traumatized children. Violence exposed youth are more likely to report PTSD symptomatology (Martinez

& Richters, 1993; Osofsky, Wewers, Hann, & Fick, 1993; Fitzpatrick & Boldizar, 1993; Jenkins & Bell, 1994; Singer et al., 1995), depression (Fitzpatrick, 1993; Freeman, Mokros, & Poznanski, 1993; Singer et al., 1995; Gorman-Smith & Tolan, 1998; DuRant, Getts, Cadenhead, Emans, & Woods, 1995), anxiety, dissociation, and anger (Singer et al., 1995). They are also more likely to report feelings of hopelessness, less purpose in life, and a belief that they will die violently (DuRant et al., 1995; Hinton-Nelson et al., 1996).

The violence that these children witness or know about often results in the death or injury of family or friends. Thus, in addition to dealing with trauma induced distress, they must also deal with issues of grief and loss and anxiety and worry over the safety of close others (Pynoos & Nader, 1988). Grieving may be particularly difficult when the death has been sudden or grisly, making reminiscing about the deceased, which is necessary for grief resolution, difficult and anxiety provoking (Rynearson, 1986). In addition, there may be issues of guilt over the child's actions or inactions in the face of danger (Pynoos, 1993).

At least part of the violence related distress comes from traumatic reminders and secondary stresses (Pynoos, 1993, 1996). Traumatic reminders are associated with the event and can produce renewed symptoms. Almost anything can serve as a traumatic reminder, from precipitating conditions, to characteristics of the assailant, to bodily sensations and feelings resulting from the incident. Traumatic reminders are pervasive and difficult to avoid.

Secondary stresses occur as a result of the incident, but may be quite traumatic in themselves and serve as an additional source of distress (Pynoos, 1993, 1996). As with traumatic reminders, secondary stresses are wide ranging. Secondary stressors from the injury or death of a family member might include frequent and frustrating involvement with the criminal justice system, loss of the deceased's income, impaired relationships within the family as other members struggle to deal with their grief and trauma, and changing schools or residences. They are most likely to occur and are most debilitating when systems are already weakened and made vulnerable by poverty and other stressors.

Externalizing Behaviors

Increasingly, research on the consequences of violence exposure has focused on the occurrence of aggression and other high-risk behaviors. Several theories—psychoanalytic, social learning, and information processing—point to aggressive or violent behavior as a consequence of violence exposure. Younger children may engage in reenactments of the event, whereas older youth may engage in high-risk belligerent behavior in a counterphobic attempt to deny their own vulnerability. Youth may seek revenge or retaliation; those experiencing abuse and victimization often feel intense rage (Terr, 1991) which may manifest as aggression. Children often model the violence that they see and experience (Bandura, 1973), and violence exposed youth are more inclined to view the world as a hostile place in which aggressive behavior is expected and appropriate (Dodge, Pettit, Bates, & Valente, 1995).

Research has generally shown a relationship between violence exposure and aggression. Child abuse is a well documented contributing factor to criminal and violent behavior (Widom, 1989a; Lewis, 1992; Smith & Thornberry, 1995). Witnessing domestic violence is a risk factor for male and female involvement in abusive relationships (Kalmus, 1984), and victimization and/or witnessing of community violence is positively related to fighting and weapon carrying (DuRant, Cadenhead, Pendergrast, Slavens, & Linder, 1994; Jenkins & Bell, 1994; Uehara et al., 1996).

While research often shows that violence exposed children display both psychological distress and externalizing behaviors (Osofsky et al., 1993; DuRant et al., 1994; Gorman-Smith & Tolan, 1998), increasingly, studies are finding that violence exposure is significantly related to aggression and acting out but not to anxiety and depression in these children. The findings have been consistent across studies in which externalizing has been operationalized as mother ratings of confrontational behavior (Hill & Madhere reviewed in Horn & Trickett, 1998), Child Behavior Checklist (CBCL) externalizing scores (Cooley-Quille, Turner & Beidel, 1995), child's self-reports of involvement in fights and arguments (Farrell & Bruce, 1997), and peer and teacher ratings of aggression (Attar et al., 1994). At least two studies found a negative relationship between violence exposure and internalizing responses (Fitzpatrick, 1993; Hill & Madhere reviewed in Horn & Trickett, 1998).

Several explanations have been offered for this finding. As Cooley-Quille and colleagues (1995) note, most of the studies showing the stronger relationship with externalizing behaviors have been done with children who have experienced repeated exposure to violence as opposed to a single acute incident, which suggests a desensitization to the repetitive violence. Studies reporting an inverse relationship between violence exposure and depression and anxiety (Fitzpatrick, 1993; Hill & Madhere reviewed in Horn & Trickett, 1998) suggest such a possibility. It is also suggested that violence-exposed children may experience distress but mask it in order not to appear weak and vulnerable in a hostile environment (Attar et al., 1994). If in fact this is the case, this coping with violence and loss by insulating oneself from the emotional experience of it, while adaptive in that environment, may come at a considerable cost to future social and emotional development (Fitzpatrick, 1993). It also suggests that empathy with the victim is less likely to be a deterrent to one's own aggressive behavior.

Other possible explanations include the nature of the exposure and the amount of threat to self and close others, gender, and personal or familial factors. For example, research on poor black and Latino adolescent boys found that the outcomes of violence exposure were related to family processes (Gorman-Smith & Tolan, 1998) with depression or anxiety more likely to occur when family cohesiveness was low, and, somewhat paradoxically, aggression being related to violence exposure when family structure was high.

Violence Exposure and Development

Children of *any* age may be affected by trauma and the impact of the incident and the specific symptoms reflect the age and developmental level of the child (Pynoos & Eth, 1985; Pynoos & Nader, 1986, 1988). Furthermore, the trauma experience can negatively affect the child's normal developmental process (Pynoos, 1993; Pynoos & Eth, 1985; Garbarino, 1993).

Although, most of the work in this area has focused on preschool, school-age and adolescent youth, trauma symptoms have been observed in infants and toddlers (Osofsky, 1995). These very young children show increased irritability, sleep disturbances, fears of being alone, and regression in developmental tasks such as toileting and language. Preschool children have somewhat similar reactions such as regressive symptoms of bed wetting, decreased verbalization, dependency, and separation anxiety along with other manifestations of anxiety such as nightmares and sleep disturbances (Pynoos & Eth, 1985; Pynoos & Nader, 1988; Osofsky, 1995). Preschoolers are also more likely to engage in reenactment of the traumatic incident.

In addition to sleep disturbances and nightmares, school-age children suffer from more somatic complaints (headaches and stomach aches) and cognitive distortions and deficits that manifest as learning disabilities and academic difficulties. They may be both withdrawn and aggressive and have difficulty in their social relationships because of belligerency and inconsistency (Pynoos & Nader, 1988; Pynoos, 1993).

Traumatized adolescents may engage in acting out and self-destructive behaviors such as substance abuse, promiscuity, delinquent and aggressive behavior, and life threatening reenactments (Pynoos & Eth, 1985; Eth & Pynoos, 1994). Involvement in self-destructive behaviors are seen as a defense mechanism that these youth use in order to distract them from painful memories and anxiety.

Traumatizing experiences can impact the psychosocial, moral, cognitive, and general personality development of the child. Acute or chronic trauma can literally change a child's life course. At the least, the incident(s) and subsequent attempts to deal with the trauma can be a distraction from developmental tasks. Schoolwork may suffer as traumatized children have difficulty concentrating due to increased physiological arousal, are distracted by intrusive thoughts, or suffer fatigue from sleep disturbances (Pynoos & Nader, 1988; Nader, Pynoos, Fairbanks, & Frederick, 1990) with resulting academic failure and lowered self-esteem. Trauma-induced belligerency and acting out may get the child excluded from certain social groups and pushed toward associating with more antisocial peers; adolescents may choose to associate with such groups for protection. The extreme negative emotions associated with the traumatic event can be so overwhelming that the child avoids emotions—good and bad—displaying a restricted range of affect and less differentiation of affective states (Pynoos 1993). Moral development and political ideology can be affected if perpetrators are not brought to justice or are treated lightly by the courts, sending a message about the distinction between right and "might," and the worth of certain groups in society.

For younger children, living in a violent milieu may compromise their ability to complete their major developmental tasks of establishing trust and autonomy (Wallach, 1994; Osofsky, 1995). In high-violence neighborhoods parents often keep their children indoors and away from widows for fear of random shooting. Such restrictions limit the child's opportunities for exploration and new relationships. These parents may also engage in harsher discipline to keep their children in line and may be less emotionally accessible due to the stress of functioning in a dangerous environment.

Mediators

The child's reaction to violence exposure is mediated by a number of factors associated with the incident, the child, and their environment. One such factor is proximity to the incidence which is related to severity of symptomatology. Research on this "dose effect" has found that the closer children are to the incident, the more severe their symptoms (Nader et al., 1990). Such a dose effect is confounded with, or explained by, the extent of threat to the child which also has been related to symptomatology (Pynoos, 1993). However, survey data is equivocal in its support of this premise. While some research has found, as expected, that victimization is related to greater symptomotology than witnessing (Singer et al., 1995; Fitzpatrick & Boldizar, 1993) others have not found a difference in the effect (Osofsky et al., 1993; Berman, Kurtines, Silverman, & Serafini, 1996).

Gender

Although not all research has found a relationship between gender and outcomes of violence exposure (Martinez & Richters, 1993; Attar et al., 1994; DuRant et al., 1995), a growing body of evidence suggests gender differences in degree and type of symptomatology. In studies where gender differences have been analyzed, girls reported more PTSD symptoms (Fitzpatrick & Boldizar, 1993; Jenkins & Bell, 1994), anxiety, anger, and depression (Singer et al., 1995), and emotional distress than boys (Farrell & Bruce, 1997). These findings are consistent with those from national surveys (Boney-McCoy & Finkelhor, 1995; Kilpatrick et al., 1997) and occurred even though females experienced less violence exposure. Possibly, girls feel less capable of defending and protecting themselves and thus feel more vulnerable in violent environments. Gender differences in empathy (Eisenberg & Lennon, 1983) suggest that girls will feel more distress for others who are hurt. In addition, there is evidence that girls have closer relationships with the victims of the violence. In a study of 12-to-21-year-old girls visiting an urban hospital-based medical clinic, 45 percent reported that at some point in their lives, a "boyfriend, girlfriend, lover, or spouse" had been killed (Horowitz, Weine, & Jekel, 1995). Such findings (as well as the fact that boys are much more likely to be killed) suggests that girls may be more likely to have an *intimate* other die violently.

Just as girls show more psychological distress than boys, there is the expectation that they are less likely to display externalizing behaviors than boys. This is consistent with the higher incidence of antisocial behavior among males and more histrionic personality disorders among females (American Psychiatric Association, DSM-IV, 1994). Research on the impact of domestic violence on children has generally shown greater externalizing for boys (Margolin, 1998), and our research with high school students found that boys were more likely to engage in fighting and gun carrying (Jenkins & Bell, 1994). However, not all research supports this position. In her study of the impact of abuse on violent behavior, Widom (1989b) found that as adolescents, girls were more likely to have a criminal record for violence than were boys (a finding which did not, however, hold through adulthood). Recent research on the impact of violence exposure has found a stronger relationship between violence exposure and externalizing than internalizing for girls (O'Keefe, 1997; Farrell & Bruce, 1997). The involvement of girls in aggressive and violent acts is consistent with statistics which show dramatic increases in juvenile female arrests for violent offenses (Sickmund, Snyder, & Poe-Yamagata, 1997) and with anecdotal reports from educators and therapists. Perhaps as boys' and girls' risk factors and experiences with violence become more similar, so will their responses. At the least, the current research suggests that girls may be more prone than boys to both internalizing and externalizing consequences.

Familiar Others

A robust finding in the literature on violence exposure is the effect of the involvement of known others (i.e., friends and family) as either victims or perpetrators on children's response to the violence. Research comparing the effect of community and intrafamilial violence has found that the latter is a stronger predictor of distress (O'Keefe, 1997; Osofsky et al., 1993; Barbarin, 1998; DuRant et al., 1995). In their sample of fifth and sixth graders, Martinez & Richters (1993) found a relationship between victimization and witnessing and the child's distress *only* when the incidents involved known others as perpetrators or victims. Among high school students there was a significant correlation between victimization of family members and psychological distress, whether they witnessed the victimization or not (Jenkins & Bell, 1994).

INTERVENTION AND PREVENTION

Many factors determine the impact of violence exposure on the child and promote or deter the resolution of the child's distress. Children's responses to violence exposure will vary by characteristics of the incident (the proximity of the incident and the child's relationship to the victim and perpetrator), the child's developmental level, and familial and individual risk and protective factors, including previous experiences with trauma, preexisting psychiatric problems, or developmental challenges (DSM-IV, 1994; Pynoos & Nader, 1993; Pynoos, 1993). However, most children who witness a violent incident will benefit from some form of crisis intervention, particularly as immediate intervention can prevent or attenuate the development of full-blown PTSD (Schwarz & Perry, 1994). Pynoos and Nader (1988) have developed a "psychological first aid" that outlines symptoms and provides concrete responses for each developmental level and can be used by caregivers as well as professionals and paraprofessionals. Depending on the severity of the child's reaction, longer-term treatment is indicated and may include dynamic psychotherapy, cognitive–behavioral, and psychopharmacological treatment, used independently or in combination (Marmar et al., 1993). The treatment may be individual and/or group. Pynoos and colleagues (Goenjian et al., 1997) reported successful reduction in PTSD symptoms of children who survived an earthquake using a combination of brief individual and group psychotherapy which addresses grief, traumatic reminders, and secondary stresses, as well as PTSD symptoms. A similar program was implemented with inner-city children exposed to chronic violence (Murphy, Pynoos, & James, 1997).

For children whose primary response to violence exposure is aggression and violent behavior, cognitive skills training programs, grounded in information-processing theory (Dodge & Crick, 1990), show great promise (for reviews, see Guerra, 1998; Tolan & Guerra, 1994; Sherman, Gottfredson, MacKenzie, Eck, Reuter, & Bushway, 1997). Based on the assumption that children have become primed to be aggressive by their violence experiences, these programs teach children how to interpret incidents in less threatening ways and to think through and practice alternative nonviolent solutions to conflict (Guerra & Slaby, 1990). Several cognitive-based programs have been developed with African American youth (Hammond & Yung, 1991; Hudley, 1994). It is also important to work with families in addressing children's acting out and creating family relationships and values that do not encourage aggression.

Although unpopular in some circles, traumatized children may need medication. Many traumatic stress symptoms originate from increased catecholamine activity which in turn causes alterations in sympathetic nervous system responsivity. Such symptoms (e.g., startle response, lack of sleep, mood lability) may be so debilitating that psychotherapy can not occur. Under these circumstance, medications which inhibit the catecholaminergic system are recommended (Pynoos, 1993; Bell, 1997).

Toward Resiliency

Not all children develop debilitating symptoms in response to violence. Although it is often difficult to determine how many children in the community violence studies are asymptomatic, there is some indication that many, possibly the majority, of children who are exposed to violence do not display severe disturbances. In the Osofsky et al. (1993) study of black elementary school children in New Orleans, 91 percent of the children were violence exposed, but only 45 percent fell at or within the clinical range of problem behaviors. In a subsample of black elementary school students, of the more than 90 percent of whom had witnessed violence or been victimized (Richters & Martinez, 1993a), Richters and Martinez (1993b) found that 54 percent of the children displayed adaptational success, defined as appropriate progress in academic and social–emotional domains. While abuse and neglect places children at an increased risk of delinquency and adult criminality, the majority of these children do not end up in the criminal justice system (Widom, 1989a).

It is important not to minimize the effects of violence exposure for children. Symptoms in children are often not obvious or may not manifest until years afer the incident (Pynoos, 1993). In addition, the secondary stresses that result from violence exposure and existence in a violent milieu (e.g., lowered achievement and aspirations, inappropriate conflict resolutions skills, grief and loss, alienation and anger) can be life altering even in the absence of severe pathology. Surviving does not necessarily mean thriving. However, the fact that most of these violence exposed children do not succumb to the trauma is a testament to their hardiness, suggests the operation of familial and community protective factors, and quite likely is a reflection of the wide variation in the nature and extent of their violence exposure.

A number of characteristics of the child and their environment may buffer the child from maladaptive outcomes that can occur in response to violence exposure. An important such factor is the presence of and relationship to a caregiver. Work on children under conditions of war (Freud & Burlingham, 1943; Pynoos, 1993) indicates that the child's reaction to extreme threat is very much determined by the parent's response. When the adult caregiver appears appropriately calm and effective in the face of danger, while not minimizing its seriousness, the outcome for the child is much better than if the parent is not available or is overwhelmed by the situation.

Family relationships are critical in mediating the impact of the violence exposure and helping the child cope with the experience (Wallen & Rubin, 1997). In low-income, violence-exposed children, family closeness has been associated with a decrease in aggression (Gorman-Smith & Tolan, 1998), and the presence of the mother predicted lower levels of depression (Fitzpatrick, 1993). National surveys found that better child–parent relationships were associated with fewer symptoms in victimized children (Boney-McCoy & Finkelhor, 1995), and that children's connectedness to parent–family and school protected against risk behaviors that ranged from violence perpetration to substance abuse, emotional distress, and suicidality (Resnick et al., 1997). The importance of family support is underscored by Richters and Martinez's (1993b) finding that "adaptational success" for children in violent neighborhoods was predicted by the safety and stability of the child's home rather than the child's exposure to community violence.

Though not specific to violence, a number of other factors may enhance the child's general resiliency or ability to function well in the face of various adversities, of which violence may be only one (Garmezy, 1993). Resilient children have certain characteristics. In general, they tend to be high in social and cognitive competency, autonomy, and a sense of purpose (Benard, 1992). Social competency refers to characteristics that favor good relationships with adults and peers (e.g., effective communication, empathy, and a good sense of humor). Cognitive competency includes good problem-solving skills, ability to think abstractly, and active coping; autonomy is characterized by a sense of independence, internal locus of control, high self-esteem, and self-efficacy. A sense of purpose refers to goal directedness, a positive future orientation, and a belief that things will work out.

While some characteristics of resiliency appear very early and seem innate (e.g., good temperament), others are clearly malleable and can be created. Resiliency is nurtured in the home, school, and community by caring and supportive relationships with an adult; high expectations that include encouragement, discipline, clear rules and standards; and encouragement to participate in age-appropriate and worthwhile tasks (Benard, 1992). A relationship with a caring adult in or outside of the family (e.g., teacher, coach, minister) seems essential for children to have successful outcomes despite adversity (Benard, 1992; Masten, Best & Garmezy, 1991; Masten & Coatsworth, 1998).

CONCLUSIONS AND DIRECTIONS FOR FUTURE RESEARCH

Research shows that many children are exposed to considerable violence and are affected by these experiences. However, there is still much to be learned about the impact of violence on children, the processes by which it occurs, and factors that mediate specific outcomes. Areas in need of attention are the impact of exposure to chronic violence and the apparent (but possibly decreasing) gender differences in response to violence. We need to know more about the mediators of trauma, particularly how the child's subjective experience and cognitive interpretation of the event affect outcome, and the impact of other stressors. Are general protective factors the most effective for helping children deal with violence-induced stress or are there activities and behaviors that serve specifically as buffers against the impact of violence exposure? Just as we work with children severely impaired by their experiences with violence in order to document its effects, we must look closely at children and families who survive and manage to thrive in these urban war zones in order to identify truly relevant protective factors. While most of the research in this area has addressed internalizing and externalizing behaviors, greater attention must be given to other areas of functioning that exposure to violence is theorized to impact and that need empirical investigation (e.g., academic success, intimate relationships, attitudes toward marriage and family, and, possibly, spirituality).

Violence affects children and their families in obvious and not so obvious ways. It is important that we document its occurrence and impact and move to establish well-grounded interventions to ameliorate its effects. Simultaneously, we must identify and address those broader systemic factors that create the fertile ground in which familial and community violence thrive.

NOTE

Thanks to Dr. Carl C. Bell for years of collaboration and feedback around this topic and to Dr. Lynne Mock for her careful reading of this chapter.

REFERENCES

American Psychiatric Association. (1980, 1994). *Diagnostic and statistical manual of mental disorders* (3d and 4th ed.). Washington, DC: Author.

Attar, B. K., Guerra, N. C., & Tolan, P. H. (1994). Neighborhood disadvantage, stressful life events, and adjustment in urban elementary school children. *Journal of Clinical Child Psychology, 23*, 391–400.

Bandura, A. (1973). *Aggression: A social learning analysis*. Englewood Cliffs, NJ: Prentice Hall.

Barbarin, O. (1998, August). *Violence, maternal distress and psychological health of South African children*. Poster session presented at the 106th annual convention of the American Psychological Association, San Francisco.

Bell, C. C. (1997). Stress-related disorders in African-American children. *Journal of the National Medical Association, 89*, 335–340.

Bell, C. C., & Jenkins, E. J. (1993). Community violence and children on Chicago's Southside. *Psychiatry: Interpersonal and Biological Processes, 56* (1), 46–54.

Benard, B. (1992, Summer). Fostering resiliency in kids: Protective factors in the family, school, and community. *Prevention Forum Newsletter of the Illinois Prevention Resource Center, 2*, 1–16.

Berman, S. L., Kurtines, W. M., Silverman, W. K., & Serafini, L. T. (1996). The impact of exposure to crime and violence on urban youth. *American Journal of Orthopsychiatry, 66*, 329–336.

Boney-McCoy, S. & Finkelhor, D. (1995). Psychosocial sequelae of violent victimization in a national youth sample. *Journal of Consulting and Clinical Psychology, 63*, 726–736.

Cooley-Quille, M., Turner, S., & Beidel, D. (1995). Emotional impact of children's exposure to community violence: A preliminary study. *Journal of the American Academy of Child and Adolescent Psychiatry, 34*, 1362–1368.

Courtois, C. (1988). *Healing the incest wound: Adult survivors in therapy*. New York: Norton.

Deykin, E. Y., & Buka, S. L. (1997). Prevalence and risk factors for posttraumatic stress disorders among chemically dependent adolescents. *American Journal of Psychiatry, 154*, 752–757.

Dodge, K. A., & Crick, N. R. (1990). Social information-processing of aggressive behavior in children. *Personality and Social Psychology Bulletin, 16*, 8–22.

Dodge, K. A., Pettit, G., Bates, J., & Valente, E. (1995). Social information-processing patterns partially mediate the effect of early physical abuse on later conduct problems. *Journal of Abnormal Psychology, 104*, 632–643.

Dubrow, N., & Garbarino, J. (1989). Living in a war zone: Mothers and young children in public housing development. *Journal of Child Welfare, 68,* 3–20.

DuRant, R. H., Cadenhead, C., Pendergrast, R. A., Slavens, G., & Linder, C. W. (1994). Factors associated with the use of violence among urban black adolescents. *American Journal of Public Health, 84,* 612–617.

DuRant, R. H., Getts, A., Cadenhead, C., Emans, S. J., & Woods, E. (1995). Exposure to violence and victimization and depression, hopelessness, and purpose in life among adolescents living in and around public housing. *Developmental and Behavioral Pediatrics, 16,* 233–238.

Dyson, J. (1990). The effects of family violence on children's academic performance and behavior. *Journal of National Medical Association, 82,* 17–22.

Eisenberg, N., & Lennon, R. (1983). Sex differences in empathy and related capacities. *Psychological Bulletin, 94,* 100–131.

Eth, S., & Pynoos, R. S. (1994). Children who witness the homicide of a parent. *Psychiatry, 57,* 287–306.

Famularo, R., Fenton, T., Kinscherff, R., & Augusstyn, M. (1996). Psychiatric comorbidity in childhood post traumatic stress disorder. *Child Abuse and Neglect, 20,* 953–961.

Farrell, A. D., & Bruce, S. E. (1997). Impact of exposure to community violence on violent behavior and emotional distress among urban adolescents. *Journal of Clinical Child Psychology, 26,* 2–14.

Federal Bureau of Investigation. (1998). *Uniform crime reports: Crime in the United States, 1997.* Washington, DC: Department of Justice.

Fitzpatrick, K. M. (1993). Exposure to violence and presence of depression among low-income, African American youth. *Journal of Consulting and Clinical Psychology, 61,* 528–531.

Fitzpatrick, K. M., & Boldizar, J. P. (1993). The prevalence and consequences of exposure to violence among African-American youth. *Journal of the American Academy of Child and Adolescent Psychiatry, 32,* 424–430.

Freeman, L. N. , Mokros, H., & Poznanski, E. O. (1993). Violent events reported by normal urban school-aged children: Characteristics and depression correlates. *Journal of American Academy of Child and Adolescent Psychiatry, 32,* 419–423.

Freud, A. & Burlingham, D. T. (1943). *Children and war.* London: Medical War Books.

Garbarino, J. (1993). Children's response to war: What do we know? *Infant Mental Health Journal, 14,* 103–115.

Garmezy, N. (1993). Children in poverty: Resilience despite poverty. *Psychiatry, 56,* 127–136.

Goenjian, A. K., Karayan, I., Pynoos, R. S., Minassian, B. S., Steinberg, A. M., Najarian, L., Asamow, J., & Fairbanks, L. (1997). Outcome of psychotherapy among early adolescents after trauma. *American Journal of Psychiatry, 154,* 536–542.

Gorman-Smith, D., & Tolan, P. (1998). The role of exposure to community violence and developmental problems among inner-city youth. *Development and Psychopathology, 10,* 101–116.

Greenfield, L., Rand, M., Crave, D., Klaus, P., Perkins, C., Ringel, C., Warchol, G., Maston, C., & Fox, J. A. (1998). *Violence by intimates: Analysis of data on crimes by current or former spouses, boyfriends, and girlfriends.* Washington, DC: U.S. Department of Justice, Office of Justice Programs, Bureau of Justice Statistics.

Guerra, N. G. (1998). Intervening to prevent childhood aggression in the inner city. In J. McCord (Ed.), *Violence and childhood in the inner city* (pp. 256–312). Cambridge, UK: Cambridge University Press.

Guerra, N. G., & Slaby, R. G. (1990). Cognitive mediators of aggression in adolescent offenders: 2. Intervention. *Developmental Psychology, 26* (2), 269–277.

Hammond, R., & Yung, B. (1991). *Dealing with anger.* Champaign, IL: Research Press.

Hampton, R., Gelles, R., & Harrop, J. (1989). Is violence in black families increasing? A comparison of 1975 and 1985 national survey rates. *Journal of Marriage and the Family, 51,* 969–980.

Herman, J. (1992). *Trauma and recovery.* New York: Basic Books.

Hinton-Nelson, M. A., Roberts, M. C., & Snyder, C. R. (1996). Early adolescents exposed to violence: Hope and vulnerability to victimization. *American Journal of Orthopsychiarty, 66* (3), 346–356.

Horn, J. L., & Trickett, P. K. (1998). Community violence and child development: A review of research. In P. K. Trickett & C. J. Schellenbach (Eds.), *Violence against children in the family and the community* (pp. 103–138). Washington, DC: American Psychological Association.

Horowitz, K., Weine, S., & Jekel, J. (1995). PTSD symptoms in urban adolescent girls: Compounded community trauma. *Journal of the American Academy of Child and Adolescent Psychiatry, 34,* 1353–1361.

Hudley, C. (1994). The reduction of childhood aggression using the Brain Power Program. In M. Furlong & D. Smith (Eds.), *Anger, hostility, and aggression: Assessment, prevention, and intervention strategies for youth.* Brandon, VT.: Clinical Psychology Publications.

Jenkins, E. J. (1995). Violence exposure, psychological distress, and risk behaviors in a sample of inner city youth. In R. Block & C. Block (Eds.), *Trends, risk, and intervention in lethal violence: Proceedings of the third annual spring symposium of homicide research working group* (pp. 287–298). Washington, DC: Department of Justice.

Jenkins, E. J., & Bell, C. C. (1994). Violence exposure, psychological distress, and high risk behaviors among inner-city high school students. In S. Friedman (Ed.), *Anxiety disorders in African-Americans* (pp. 76–88). New York: Springer.

Jenkins, E. J., & Bell, C. C. (1997). Exposure and response to community violence among children and adolescents. In J. Osofsky (Ed.), *Children in a violent society.* New York: Guilford.

Jenkins, E. J., & Thompson, B. (1986). *Children talk about violence: Preliminary findings from a survey of black elementary school children.* Presented at the nineteenth annual convention of the Association of Black Psychologists, Oakland, CA.

Kalmus, D. (1984). The intergenerational transmission of marital aggression. *Journal of Marriage and the Family, 46,* 11–19

Kaufman, P., Chen, X., Choy, S., Chandler, K. I., Christopher, C., Rand, M., & Ringel, C. (1998). *Indicators of School Crime and Safety, 1998.* Washington, DC: U.S. Department of Justice, Office of Justice Programs.

Kilpatrick, D. G., Saunders, B. E., Resnick, H. S., & Best, C. L. (1997, August). *Patterns of violence exposure and PTSD within a national sample of adolescents*. Presented at the 105th annual convention of the American Psychological Association, Chicago.

Lewis, D. O. (1992). From abuse to violence: Psycho-physiological consequences of maltreatment. *Journal of the American Academy of Child and Adolescent Psychiatry, 31* (3), 383–391.

Margolin, G. (1998). Effects of domestic violence on children. In P. K. Trickett & C. J. Schellenbach (Eds.), *Violence against children in the family and the community* (pp. 57–102). Washington, DC: American Psychological Association.

Marmar, C., Foy, D., Kagan, B., & Pynoos, R. (1993). An integrated approach for treating posttraumatic stress. In J. M. Oldham, M. B. Riba, & A. Tasman (Eds.), *Review of psychiatry* (12). Washington, DC: American Psychiatric Press.

Martinez, P., & Richters, J. (1993). The NIMH community violence project II: Children's distress symptoms associated with violence exposure. *Psychiatry, 56*, 23–35.

Masten, A. S., Best, K. M., & Garmezy, N. (1991). Resilience and development: Contributions from the study of children who overcome adversity. *Development and Psychopathology, 2*, 425–444.

Masten, A. S., & Coatsworth, J. D. (1998). The development of competence in favorable and unfavorable environments. *American Psychologist, 53* (2), 205–220.

Murphy, L., Pynoos, R. S., & James, B. (1997). The trauma–grief-focused group psychotherapy module of an elementary school-based violence prevention–intervention program. In J. Osofsky (Ed.), *Children in a violent society* (pp. 223–255). New York: Guilford.

Nader, K., Pynoos, R., Fairbanks, L., & Frederick, C. (1990). Childhood PTSD reactions one year after a sniper attack. *American Journal of Psychiatry, 147*, 1526–1530.

O'Keefe, M. (1997). Adolescents' exposure to community and school violence: Prevalence and behavioral correlate. *Journal of Adolescent Health, 20*, 368–376.

Osofsky, J. (1995). The effects of exposure to violence on young children. *American Psychologist, 50*, 782–788.

Osofsky, J. D., Wewers, S., Hann, D. M., & Fick, A. C. (1993). Chronic community violence: What is happening to our children? *Psychiatry, 56*, 7–21.

Perry, B. (1994). Neurobiological sequelae of childhood trauma: Post-traumatic stress disorders in children. In M. Murberg (Ed.), *Catecholamines in posttraumatic stress disorder: Emerging concepts* (pp. 253–276). Washington, DC: American Psychiatric Press.

Perry, B. (1997). Incubated in terror: Neurodevelopmental factors in the "cycle of violence." In J. Osofsky (Ed.), *Children in a violent society* (pp. 124–149). New York: Guilford.

Peters, K. D., Kochanek, K., & Murphy, S. (1998, November). *Deaths: Final data for 1996. National vital statistics reports, 47 (9)*. Hyattsville, MD: National Center for Health Statistics.

Pynoos, R. S. (1993). Traumatic stress and developmental psychopathology in children and adolescents. In J. M. Oldham, M. B. Riba, & A. Tasman (Eds.), *Review of Psychiatry* (vol. 12, pp. 205–237). Washington, DC: American Psychiatric Press.

Pynoos, R. S. (1996). Exposure to catastrophic violence and disaster in childhood. In C. R. Pfeffer (Ed.), *Severe stress and mental disturbance in children* (pp. 181–208). Washington, DC: American Psychiatric Press.

Pynoos, R. S., & Eth, S. (1984). Child as a criminal witness to homicide. *Journal of Social Issues, 40*, 87–108.

Pynoos, R. S., & Eth, S. (1985). Developmental perspective on psychic trauma in childhood. In C. R. Figley (Ed.), *Trauma and its wake* (pp. 309–330). New York: Brunner/Mazel.

Pynoos, R. S., & Nader, K. (1986). Children's exposure to violence and traumatic death. *Psychiatric Annals, 20*, 334–344.

Pynoos, R. S., & Nader, K. (1988). Psychological first aid: For children who witness community violence. *Journal of Traumatic Stress, 1*, 445–473.

Pynoos, R. S., & Nader, K. (1993). Issues in the treatment of posttraumatic stress in children and adolescents. In J. Wilson & B. Raphael (Eds.), *International handbook of traumatic stress syndromes*. New York: Plenum Press.

Resnick, M. D., Bearman, P. S., Blum, R. W., Bauman, K., Harris, K. M., Jones, J., Tabor, J., Benhring, T., Sieving, R. E., Shew, M., Ireland, M., Bearinger, L., & Udry, R. (1997). Protecting adolescents from harm: Findings from the national longitudinal study on adolescent health. *Journal of the American Medical Association, 278*, 823–832.

Richters, J. E., & Martinez, P. (1993a). The NIMH community violence project: I. Children as victims of and witnesses to violence. *Psychiatry, 56*, 7–21.

Richters, J. E., & Martinez, P. (1993b). Violent communities, family choices, and children's chances: An algorithm for improving the odds. *Development and Psychopathology, 5*, 609–627.

Rynearson, E. K. (1986). Psychological effects of unnatural dying on bereavement. *Psychiatry Annals, 62*, 272–275.

Schubiner, H., Scott, R., & Tzelepis, A. (1993). Exposure to violence among inner-city youth. *Journal of Adolescent Health, 14*, 214–219.

Schwarz, E. D., & Perry, B. D. (1994). The post-traumatic response in children and adolescents. *Psychiatric Clinics of North America, 17*, 311–326. (See also American Journal of Psychiatry, March 1999.)

Shakoor, B., & Chalmers, D. (1991). Co-victimization of African-American children who witness violence and the theoretical implications of its effects on their cognitive, emotional, and behavioral development. *Journal of the National Medical Association, 81*, 233–238.

Sheehan, K., DiCara, J. A., LeBailly, S., & Christoffel, K. K. (1997). Children's exposure to violence in an urban setting. *Archive of Pediatric and Adolescent Medicine, 151*, 502–504.

Sherman, L. W., Gottfredson, D., MacKenzie, D., Eck, H., Reuter, P., & Bushway, S. (1997). *Preventing crime: What works, what doesn't, what's promising*. Washington, DC: U.S. Department of Justice, Office of Justice Programs.

Sickmund, M., Snyder, H., & Poe-Yamagata, E. (1997). *Juvenile offenders and victims: 1997 Update on Violence, Statistics Summary*. Washington, DC:

U.S. Department of Justice, Office of Justice Program, Office of Juvenile Justice and Delinquency Prevention.

Singer, M. I., Anglin, T., Song, L., & Lunghofer, L. (1995). Adolescents' exposure to violence and associated symptoms of psychological trauma. *Journal of the American Medical Association, 273*, 477–482.

Singer, M. I., Miller, D. B., Gou, S., Flannery, D. J., Frierson, T., & Slovak, K. (1999). Contributors to violent behavior among elementary and middle school children. *Pediatrics, 104*, 878–884.

Smith, C., & Thornberry, T. P. (1995). The relationship between childhood maltreatment and adolescent involvement in delinquency. *Criminology, 33* (4), 451–477.

Taylor, B. (1997, April). *Changes in Criminal Victimization, 1994–1995: National Crime Victimization Survey*. Washington, DC: U.S. Department of Justice, Office of Justice Programs, Bureau of Justice Statistics.

Terr, L. (1991). Childhood traumas: An outline and overview. *American Journal of Psychiatry, 48*, 10–20.

Tolan, P., & Guerra, N. (1994). *What works in reducing adolescent violence: An empirical review of the field*. Boulder, CO: University of Colorado at Boulder, Center for the Study and Prevention of Violence.

Uehara, E., Chalmers, D., Jenkins, E. J., & Shakoor, B. (1996). African-American youth encounters with violence: Results from the Chicago Community Mental Health Council Violence Screening Project. *Journal of Black Studies, 26*, 768–781.

U.S. Department of Health and Human Services, Children's Bureau. (1998). *Child maltreatment 1996: Reports from the states to the national child abuse and neglect data system*. Washington, DC: U.S. Government Printing Office.

Wallach, L. B. (1994). Violence and young children's development. Urbana: University of Illinois (ERIC Clearinghouse on Elementary and Early Childhood Education EDO-PS-94-7).

Wallen, J., & Rubin, R. (1997). The role of the family in mediating the effects of community violence on children. *Aggression and Violent Behavior, 2*, 33–41.

Widom, C. S. (1989a). The cycle of violence. *Science, 244*, 160–166.

Widom, C. S. (1989b). Child abuse, neglect, and violent criminal behavior. *Criminology, 27* (2), 251–271.

7

Sports and African American Male Children: What Values and Motives Do They Have?

Robert E. Stadulis, Gary Waters, and
Angela M. Neal-Barnett

For approximately the past twenty-five years, various studies have attempted to determine the importance and the perception of sports to African Americans. The term *sports*, as used in this chapter, is defined as "institutionalized competitive activities that involve vigorous physical exertion or the use of relatively complex physical skills by individuals whose participation is motivated by a combination of personal enjoyment and external rewards" (Coakley, 1998, p. 19). Typically, the studies of sports in the lives of African Americans have focused upon adult and later adolescent, especially collegiate level, athletes. Few investigations have attempted to find out if African American children's perceptions and values of sports participation are similar to their older cohorts and to other children in general. One recent exception (Lapchick, 1996) to this paucity of such research has reported that for elementary and junior high school boys, blacks and whites are about equal in aspiring to be professional athletes. During high school, however, white males tend to develop other occupational goals whereas black males continue their focus on sports, especially basketball and football (Coakley, 1998).

Related to the discussion of the relationship between sports participation and race is the growing body of literature that deals with at-risk or underserved youth. Society is fervently seeking ways to try to combat the barriers that impede at-risk children's transition to adulthood and their effective functioning within mainstream society (Martinek & Hellison, 1998). These barriers include (1) influences of gangs and the combative values associated with these groups (Bing, 1991), (2) the resistance to the school culture (Ogbu, 1997), (3) dysfunctional home life (Wallerstein, 1983), and (4) fear of making certain choices (Steihl, 1993) that leads to feelings of helplessness (Seligman, 1990).

Sports have often been perceived as the panacea for such troubled youth. Such a perception grows out of the philosophy that sports can be a major contributor, through social learning opportunities, of society's values to children (Coakley, 1998). Sports participation "is presumed to build character, teach discipline, prepare one for life's competitions, facilitate moral development and good citizenship, and cultivate desirable personality traits" (Leonard, 1988, p. 126). For North American males in general, sportsman role models are an important contributor to adult career aspirations (Leonard, 1988). However, for African American males in particular, evidence has been strong that the black professional sportsmen in society serve as more *exclusive* role models, their white cohorts broaden their range of role models to include a variety of additional occupational options (Castine & Roberts, 1974). Guttman (1988) has assailed this exclusive modeling by black males as stemming from a "folk belief" that sport is an "accessible avenue for increasing socio-economic status." As many have noted (e.g., Edwards, 1988; Guttman, 1988), there are very few opportunities for professional sports careers for the 30 million African American males. Thus, such a belief that sports will provide *the* avenue to success may lead to a great many disappointments (and much stress). Worse, as promoted by Hoberman (1997), the persona of black masculinity, as a merger of athlete, gangster rapper, and criminal, serve to perpetuate an image that makes it difficult to motivate African American males to pursue more productive cultural and intellectual interests.

The purpose of this chapter is to focus upon the role of sport in the development of occupational goals and societal values within African American children, especially males. There will be three parts to the chapter. The first part of the chapter will provide an overview of the literature relative to this issue (see previous paragraphs for some of the key sources). Given the virtual lack of data from preadolescents, we have assessed African American children's perceptions of the role of sports in their lives. Children of ages 10 to 15 years completed questionnaires designed to assess their motives for participating in youth sports. Ewing and Seefeldt's (1989) State of Michigan Youth Sports Participation Survey was adapted to assess the reasons for participation in sports. The survey has been modified to assess values, in addition to those already contained within the survey, that represent the goals and objectives frequently identified by sports coaches as outcomes from participation in sports. This second section of the chapter will end with the presentation of the results of this study and in particular determine whether findings from studies of collegiate athletes hold true for the preadolescent African American child. The concluding part of the chapter tries to integrate the study's findings with the questions we will raise concerning the relationship between sports participation and the motives and values characteristic of the African American male.

SPORTS IN THE AFRICAN AMERICAN'S LIFE

A common assertion, so common that it may have become a stereotype, is that sports in the life of the African American, especially if male, is of greater importance than that of the white cohort. As Sage noted in his introduction to Brooks and Althouse's *Racism in College Athletics: The African-American Athlete's Experience,* "excellence in sports provides one of the few opportunities for African Americans to escape the slums and ghettos in which many of them live. Thus, hours devoted to honing sport skills, combined with the desire to escape their childhood environment, seem to cause many African-American youths to approach sport with greater motivation to excel than is found in middle-class whites" (1993, p. 10).

Such a perception of the importance of sports to African American youth would seem supported by the results of a national survey of 8,000 boys and girls (Ewing & Seefeldt, 1996). When participation in youth sports was examined in terms of racial grouping, African American youth demonstrated the highest percentage involvement in the "big three sports" (i.e., baseball, basketball, and football) than of any of the racial groups studied. One interpretation to this greater extent of involvement in sports by African Americans is that sports remains as the major means to social mobility in the minds of many African Americans.

It needs to be noted that there are alternative views to the importance of sports to African Americans, males especially. One view suggests that the prominence of sport for the African American flows from the experience of living centuries in Africa before being brought to the "New World." The importance of physical activities we now call "sports" are genetically imbued in the African American as a result of evolution.[1] Others suggest there are "race-linked" superiority factors that foster greater focus by the African American male on sports (Leonard, 1988). The perception of the African American's superiority to other races in sports should result in a greater attraction to participate in sports. Some have argued for such superiority based upon physical and physiological characteristics (Kane, 1971). Others link the perception of superiority to the unique, racially specific, historical experience of African Americans (i.e., surviving the trip from Africa and then slavery) has resulted in the survival of the most fit (Edwards, 1973). Finally, Hoberman has argued that blacks have a fixation on sports and a "clan pride" that "lives on in stereotypes about black physical superiority that have become nothing less than global racial folklore" (1997, p. 5).

A positive aspect of the African American's greater involvement in sports stems from the belief that sports, as agents of socialization, have the ability to teach participants many useful and desirable skills and attributes. Sports have been seen as promoters of learning that carry over to other aspects of a person's life (Coakley, 1996). Sports are proclaimed as able to "build character" (Griffin, 1998). Thus, the greater proportional involvement of African American youth in sport could be hypothesized to lead to adults who are "better citizens" and who possess high moral values and standards. Sports may provide an effective way to overcome barriers to effective functioning in mainstream society. Unfortunately, as Coakley (1996) has noted, the results of numerous studies of socialization through sports have not provided the strong support for the long-held beliefs of the power of the sports experience to affect the psychological state and the social behaviors of the participant athlete.

For example, Spreitzer (1992), using a longitudinal design, found no evidence of a relationship between participation in high school athletics and psychological well-being six years later. He also found that although there was a modest relationship between sports participation as a high school senior and educational attainment, varsity sports involvement was a much weaker predictor than other variables. The study also indicated that this modest relationship between sports participation and educational attainment existed for white males only.

At the collegiate level, there have been few attempts to assess the relationship between college athletic participation and athletes' lives after college. As Sellers (1993) cautioned, there is little research evidence that addresses the relationship and, from the few studies that have been conducted, there is virtually no evidence that athletes lead happy, contented lives and become successful vocationally as a direct result of their participation in sports.

However, many in the sporting world share from their experiences a positive view of sports participation that lead us to hypothesize that the few studies that have been conducted may not provide the true and the only view of the effects of sports participation. For example, at Kent State University, there are two recently documented cases that serve as examples of how involvement in sports with a positive role model can influence certain athletes to complete their education and lead them to a happier existence. These two student athletes were about to end their collegiate sports experience before the completion of their playing eligibility and without their degrees. Both student athletes came from dysfunctional homes, were classified as at risk, and were labeled as unlikely to succeed. Both were ready to leave the university but were extrinsically motivated to remain in school using sports participation as the primary incentive.

Presently, one of these student athletes has since graduated and is employed in the field of choice while also considering graduate study. The other student athlete is one semester away from graduation and has just completed the most rewarding and memorable season of his collegiate experience. It is our contention that without the opportunity provided through athletic participation and the positive effects of being a member of an athletic team, these players would not have achieved success either academically or professionally. The outcome from meeting athletic and academic challenges enables at least *some* athletes to achieve success in life. Had these players left school, their "at-risk" classification would predict a less than successful future for them. The quantitative approach taken by most studies may reflect that only *some* student athletes respond to such challenges and grow. More qualitative research methodology may reveal that a significant number of individuals are profoundly affected by their sports experience.

Such methodology may enable better measurement of the mentoring relationship coaches provide; this coach–athlete relationship may be potentially a more powerful variable affecting the sports participation–race relationship.

To this point, we have focused upon high school and collegiate sports participation. When the prehigh school sport experience is considered, what is the relationship between sports participation and a person's social, emotional, and spiritual attributes? Here we find almost no study to draw upon. However, as clearly reflected by a recent *Time* magazine cover story, "Inside the Crazy Culture of Kids Sports," contemporary American parents and their children seem to view youth competitive athletics as a positive experience worthy of great sacrifice (Ferguson, 1999). While apparently no longitudinal examinations of the relationship have been undertaken, some retrospective approaches have suggested that sports may not be quite the powerful independent variable so many in our society believed it to be. Messner (1992), for example, when studying retrospectively the perceptions of masculinity in connection with men's sports careers, found that the men in his study began their first sports experiences as youth already enculturated to an "approved masculine orientation." The experience in sports then helped these men build upon their initial perceptions and further develop and construct orientations, relationships, and experiences that were in synchrony with their starting points.

Such findings have led Coakley to conclude that an "internalized model" of socialization through sports is untenable. Beginning sports participants, even those who are very young, do not enter the sport environment with "blank slates" just waiting to be "filled in" by the sports experience. Rather, the few longitudinal investigations "suggest that participation in organized, competitive sport does not so much change people as much as it provides a context in which important social relationships might be established, nurtured and maintained" (1996, p. 361).

Once again, there is the personal, more qualitative experience that suggests this *sports as context* hypothesis is true. In the early 1960s, there was a young child, age of nine, that had no prior involvement in organized sports. He was introduced to the sport of football in a youth league organization. But due to poor academic performance, he was not allowed to participate in that sport after the first month of involvement. As a result of his need to achieve, coupled with his interest in sports, he began to place much greater importance upon his schoolwork. He diligently improved his academic standing and never experienced poor academic performance again. He is presently an NCAA Division I head coach and holds three college degrees, with honors!

This example points again to the use of sports as a powerful motivator in achieving success in other aspects of life (e.g., academics and vocations). For many, motivation for academic pursuits is not very intrinsic, and an external stimulus is needed. Sports can be the avenue that allows certain individuals to succeed when other venues fail. For the person in the example, academic success was developed through the motivation to participate in athletics. However, being involved in athletics may have been the necessary stimulus context to nurture the development of confidence, honesty, integrity, and hard work, attributes which were already preformed in this individual through prior experiences. The coupling of sports participation with these personal attributes then contributed to the youngster's ultimate success.

Rudd, Stoll, and Beller (1999) have recently proposed a model that may explain why the prior research efforts typically provide such a negative perspective to the sports-character development relationship. They have proposed that it is crucial to separate *moral character* (honesty, justice, responsibility) from *social character* (i.e., cooperation, self-sacrifice, perseverence, courage). In separating character into two distinct components, they hypothesize that whereas sports participation does not build moral character, sports does build social character. Early assessment of their hypothesis (Rudd, Stoll, & Beller, 1999) has found that social values of loyalty, team work, and self-sacrifice are acquired by athletic populations, and in particular by male team-sports participants.

Given the perspective of an interactional model of sports participation and enhancement of social, emotional, and spiritual attributes, does the early socialization of the African American child in his or her culture provide a special frame of reference that fosters an interaction with the sports context that is different from other groups? For the male in particular, does the continued societal presentation of the athlete as *the* successful African American then influence the young African American participant to perceive sports differently from his white peers? Lapchick's (1996) results suggest that if this is so, it does not emerge until high school. His observation that African Americans (males especially) continue to limit their aspirations primarily to an athletic career may also lead then to proposing that there is in an additional stress factor for the African American youngster. If sports provide one of the few open avenues to "success" in American society, then success and achievement in sports may become paramount for the African American male. If success is expected but performance is less than excellent, does the young man experience this added stress of worrying about achieving a "way out" from the current life's condition to the "better life?" There must also be concern expressed for those African American youngsters, especially males, who fall on the lower side of the talent distribution. If excellent sports performance is such an important expectation for the male, what impact does nonachievement of that status have?

The potential for added stress for the African American sports performer may compromise the potential benefits of sports participation. If success, especially defined in terms of the winning of competitions, becomes the major goal of the involvement, do values of fair play and respect for others give way to the pressure of the commitment to win? Many complain that this is a problem within sports in general. As the number of years of participation in sports increase, the importance of winning to the participant also increases, even to the point that breaking rules and cheating are accepted as appropriate means to achieving the goal (Beller & Stoll, 1995). Is this challenge to ethical values more strained in the African American youth sports participant, given the greater apparent importance of sports to these youth?

Coaches often proclaim the importance of moral and ethical values as points of pride of their programs. Is the social pressure to achieve in sports so great on the African American athlete, especially for the young male whose performance has been identified as potentially superior, that the lofty goals of the coach (and society in general) concerning sportsmanship run headlong into conflict with these achievement motives?

If the stress on the African American sport athlete is indeed greater as the foregoing suggests, what are the implications for health and well-being? Do higher levels of competitive anxiety result in the African American performer than athletes in other groups? Is continued exposure to such stress a potential factor with respect to the early incidence of hypertension in African American males than other groups in the American population (Hall, Saunders, & Shuman, 1985)?

Clearly, there are multiple qualitative "testimonies" by athletes, their families, and their coaches that would dispute the quantitative, generalized finding of the lack of support for the "sports participation leads to positive psychological and social outcomes" hypothesis. These disputants hold sports dear as a positive influence in the athlete's life. In concurring with Sellers (1993), from the limited research and data gathered, it can be said that participation in sports by itself does not lead to a happier life and a more successful career. However, there are many documented cases that indicate that if an extrinsic force is involved during the sports experience that fosters values, integrity, and confidence, a person can lead a more productive life, both socially and professionally. Furthermore, practical experiences clearly provide a pattern of success when intrinsic desires and external intervention simultaneously converge. Thus, there are potential dangers in offering generalizations in this area. While statistical support may be lacking, individual difference methodologies may find numerous instances where the prophylactic outcome of the sports experience is confirmed. Investigation earlier in a person's development may be necessary to document more carefully the relationship, especially noting the child's orientation to sports from the very beginning of the child's involvement in them. A qualitative examination of the coach–athlete interactional relationship may provide more fruitful evidence of those coach-controlled actions that serve to promote more positive outcomes from the sports experience. Discovering these positive actions and behaviors by the coach can lead to formulating specific guidelines to coaches to better foster the outcomes they desire. It may be that many African American males who are able to move from primarily sports role models and focus upon other career opportunities survive the stress to more fully benefit from the sports experience in the positive ways hypothesized.

EMPIRICAL RESEARCH

Given the questions this chapter has posed, it seems imperative that there be efforts underway to examine the perceptions and beliefs of sports participants younger than the high school and college-aged youth traditionally studied. Therefore, we have undertaken the investigation of the motives and values of preadolescent and early adolescent youth concerning their participation in sports.

Children ages 10 to 15 years were asked to complete questionnaires designed to assess their motives for participating in youth sports. Ewing and Seefeldt's (1989) State of Michigan Participation Survey was adapted to assess the reasons for participation (or nonparticipation) in sports. The adaptation to the original survey represents goals and objectives frequently identified by sports coaches as desired outcomes from participation in sport and correspond to values promoted by the Kent State University men's basketball program within its summer camps for youth. In addition, children were asked to respond verbally to (and be audiotaped) for two questions, one concerning their attitude about the importance of winning versus playing and a second concerning who their role models are. To examine factors associated with stress in youth sports participants, Martens's (1977) Sport Competition Anxiety Test (SCAT-C, a trait assessment, children's form) was administered as well.

Initially, our preliminary work targeted African American boys of middle school or early high school ages (fifth through ninth graders) involved in youth sports programs at their school or within their community. This sample is younger than those typically studied previously and focuses upon sports participation before the attention of spectators (as "crowds") and the media become especially present. As we proceed with our inquiry, we will include girls, non-African Americans and nonsports participants to the sample wherever possible.

The data reported here represent two separate assessments. The first assessment sample consisted of ninth grade boys who were members of a private high school freshman basketball team (n = 10) located within a large city (population over 500,000 people). The team was balanced racially, with four boys each being African American or European American. One youngster described himself as of "black and Indian" ethnicity; he was included with the four African Americans in a "black" group for this preliminary inspection of the responses. Similarly, a boy who described himself as "white and Hispanic" was included with the four European American boys to form a "non-black" group.

The second group of children assessed represented a group of youngsters who attended the same church in a smaller city (250,000 population). This church sample consisted of both boys (n = 9) and girls (n = 5). Ages ranged from 10 to 14 years. All children in the second sample were African American.

Procedures

After obtaining the consent of all involved (i.e., the school and church officials, the players and their parents), each youngster was assessed at their school or church. At the high school, students gathered together at their coach's home room during their lunch period. After reviewing the purpose of the study and the procedures, some boys (n = 7) began completing the written questionnaires (the Participation Survey and SCAT-C). The remaining boys left the coach's home room with an interviewer to be interviewed at a different location. When the interview (asking the student to respond to the two questions focused upon winning–losing versus playing and their role models) was completed, the interviewer escorted the youngster back to the home room. Another boy then was asked to interrupt his responding to the survey and go with the interviewer to be interviewed. A similar procedure was followed at the church. Some children were first interviewed while the rest completed their questionnaires. When one part of the assessment was completed (interview or questionnaire), the second was administered.

The order of the two question areas addressed within the interview was randomized within each sample as was the initial assignment to interviewer. To provide some extrinsic motivation for the high school boys' participation in the study, a meal of pizza and soda pop was provided.

Sport Participation Questionnaire responses were coded and separated into three separate data sets: (1) motives (items 1–28); (2) values and commitment (items 29–43); and (3) the SCAT-C. Audiotaped responses to the questions concerning winning versus playing and role models were transcribed. A second evaluator checked the transcriptions for accuracy. Responses were then coded independently by three evaluators.

FINDINGS

The data collected from these two small samples are presented, recognizing that the sample size is limited; thus, our ability to offer generalizations is restricted. Our main purpose has been to assure ourselves (and others) that the assessment procedures planned are indeed functional and especially that the survey and interview items produced little confusion and difficulty for the respondents. While specific inferential statistical tests of reliability and validity have not been provided, the descriptive findings may help point the way for some of the answers to the nature of the relationship between sports participation and the motives and values of African American youth. Given the small sample sizes in two of the groups (African American girls and non-black boys), significance difference testing was deemed inappropriate.

Participation Survey: Motives

The first section of the Sport Participation Questionnaire, adapted from Ewing and Seefeldt (1989), focuses upon the reasons for participation in sports. The items (n = 27) focus upon a range of motives for sports participation, including to get exercise, to have something to do, to be with friends, to receive more attention from parents, and to have fun. Respondents are asked to circle a number for each item: a "5" meant the item was perceived to be "very important" as a reason for sports participation, and a "1" that the reason was "not at all important." The 27th item was a fill in; respondents were asked to enter any other reason they have for playing that had not been presented in the previous 26 items. As a final item to this section, respondents were requested to indicate which of the previous 27 items they would identify as "the most important" for their participation in sports.

Our children viewed only three items to be less than "somewhat important" (i.e., a group mean response of < 2.5; (see Table 7.1). These items were: item 5—"For the travel that goes with being on a team"; item 9—"My parents or close friends want me to participate"; and item 26—"To receive more attention from parents." Given a typical limited and local schedule for middle school, a ninth grade basketball team and interchurch competition, the perception of travel as less important seems quite reasonable. Both remaining items suggest that this group may have been less motivated by extrinsic factors, especially those related to parental influence and attention. From a reliability perspective, it should be noted that these three "less important items" were the same three identified by each sample separately. No other item evidenced a mean response of below "of somewhat importance" in any sample.

Given that the remaining 24 items resulted in mean response values of > 2.5, it appears that the wide majority of reasons for participation were judged to be "important." This may mean that these subjects do not discriminate to any great extent between their reasons for participation or that they have a multiple number of important reasons for their participation in sports. There were a number of items that were consistently rated as important (≥ 4) by both samples: "To improve my skills" (item 1), "To stay in shape" (item 6), "To play as a part of a team" (item 7), "For the excitement of competition" (item 8), "To learn new skills" (item 10), "To do something I'm good at" (item 12), "To get exercise" (item 15), "To go to a higher level of competition" (item 19), "For the challenge of competition" (item 21), and "To have fun" (item 23)—this final item represented the highest mean importance (overall group M = 4.7).

Table 7.1
Mean Responses on Reasons for Sport Participation for Racial and Sex Groups (for only those items reflecting racial and/or sex group differences)

Reason	Black Males (n=14)	Non-Black Males (n=5)	Black Females (n=5)	Overall (N=24)
#4 Someone I admired played this sport	3.2	3.6	1.8	3.0
#5 For the travel that goes with being on a team	2.6	2.2	2.0	2.4
#9 My parents or close friends want me to participate	2.6	2.4	1.2	2.3
#20 To be popular by being a good athlete	2.6	4.0	2.4	2.8
#22 I like the coaches	2.9	4.0	2.4	3.0
#25 To attract boys/girls attention	2.4	3.8	3.8	2.6
#26 To receive more attention from parents	2.2	2.4	1.8	2.2

The black and non-black groups' as well as the boys' and girls' mean responses were compared. Presented in Table 7.1 are only those items that resulted in a mean difference of greater than 1.25 points on the 5-point response scale when comparing the race or sex groups. "To be popular" and "to attract boys–girls attention" was rated more important by the non-black males than either group of African American children. The non-black males also indicated that their liking of the coach was an important factor for their participation.

The mean responses of the black males compared to the black females also yielded some interesting differences in perception of importance. Using again a difference of 1.25 as the criterion, girls responded differently from the boys on motive items 4 and 9 (see Table 7.1). Boys viewed someone they admired and parents or close friends as more important reasons for sports participation than did the girls. However, neither of these motives were seen as more than "somewhat important" to the boys.

With respect to item 28 (which is the most important reason for participation), great variability of response was evidenced. Twelve different items were identified by the 24 children responding. Five (four boys and one girl) chose "To go to a higher level of competition." Five children (three girls and two boys) selected "To have fun" as their most important reason for participating in sports. Three boys perceived "To be popular by being a good athlete" as their major reason for participation. Another chose his fill-in response to item 27: "To be the best of the best!"

Participation Survey: Values

The second section of the sport participation questionnaire focuses on the values of the youngsters (labeled by Ewing and Seefeldt as "commitment" in the original instrument). This section was assessed in relation to the values stressed by the second author in his summer youth basketball camps. Additional items were added to Ewing and Seefeldt's original version, resulting in a total of 15 value assessment items. The questionnaire requires the respondent to again select from a 5-point scale, in which a 1 equaled "low commitment (completely false)" and a 5 equaled "high commitment (completely true)."

As a manipulation check, one item was worded in the reverse direction (item 14, the 42nd item on the survey: "I will do whatever it takes to win even if I have to break a rule"). Indeed, this was the only item to produce an overall mean response below 3. The black male responses (M = 1.4) versus the non-black male responses (M = 2.2) indicated that these respondents were still reading and thinking about this item almost at the very end of the sport participation questionnaire. However, the mean for the girls on this item was 3.4. It is unclear as to whether rating this item as "true" means that the girls were not reading the items carefully at this point in their responding (next to the last item on the questionnaire) or if they believe that breaking the rules is acceptable in order to be successful in competition. While not achieving the previously mentioned > 1.25 point difference criterion for discussion of racial differences, it should be noted that the black males responded the most positively to the item (here a response of 1.4 indicated that winning by breaking the rules is not of high value to them).

Overall, the children responding in this study evidenced the perception that all 15 values were of some importance to them. Seven of the items achieved a mean response of greater than 4 (important) to all three groups of children (black males, black females, and non-black males): (1) "I really want to become an outstanding athlete"; (2) "I never let up or give up"; (3) "I take personal responsibility for mistakes and work hard to correct them"; (4) "I give 100% in practice"; (5)

"I give 100% effort in games"; (6) "I feel more committed to improvement in my sport than to anything else"; and (7) "I feel more successful, or gain more recognition, in my sport than in anything else."

There was little evidence of differential responding due to race differences in the boys; all 15 item means were within 1 point of each other. With respect to sex differences, a few commitment differences between boys and girls were evidenced (M difference 1.0). The girls valued becoming "an outstanding athlete," "pushing hard even when it hurts," "improvement in my sport," and gaining more success and "recognition" *less than* the boys. The female respondents also indicated they believed "being truthful" was a more important commitment than their male counterparts.

Competitive Anxiety

The SCAT-C responses indicated that the group as a whole (M =20.7) was very typical to the norms for this age group. Also in line with norms (Martens, Vealey, & Burton, 1990), the girls evidenced substantially higher levels of competitive anxiety (M = 25.5) than the boys (M = 19.5). Interestingly, the non-black males self-reported higher levels of competitive A-trait (M = 21.8) than their black counterparts (M = 18.6). While these data appear well within the normal (± 1 standard deviation) expected range of values, and represent a small sample, it is nevertheless at least curious to see the higher competitive anxiety levels in the non-black males. Is this evidence that the proposed stress hypothesis does not begin to function until later in high school or even college? Longitudinal or at least carefully controlled cross-sectional comparison studies are needed to address this question.

Interview Responses: Win–Lose

Each child was asked to indicate which of the following they would prefer: "To be a member of a team that usually wins but I do not play very much" or "To be a member of a team that usually loses but I play a lot." The boys (n = 19) were split in their preferences: Ten indicated they preferred to play on a losing team and nine boys chose playing on a winning team. The black males were split evenly (seven for the play emphasis and seven for the win emphasis). The five females were also split evenly; two preferred the winning situation, two the losing situation, and one said she "could not choose between them." This would seem to conform to the observation in prior research that winning is far down the list of priorities for the youth sports participant. Only one child indicated on the motive section of the questionnaire that "to win" was the most important reason for sports participation.

At higher levels (e.g., college) winning appears to rise in importance for the typical athlete.

Interview Responses: Role Models

Three categories of responses emerged when the children answered the role model question. Fourteen of the 24 respondents (58%) selected family members as their response to the question, "Is there one person that you would like to be most like when you are an adult?' "Dad/ Father" was the most frequent response (n = 7) by the boys. Three selected their mothers as their role model (two of the girls and one African American boy). Another chose both parents. Others (n = 3) chose relatives: a cousin, a sister, and a grandfather. Six children indicated that rather than having an external role model, they preferred to think of themselves as "my own self" or "no one else but me." Only four of the 24 children (17%) chose individuals beyond their family. These were singer Lauren Hill and basketball players Kevin Johnson (n = 1) and Michael Jordan (n = 2). Interestingly, the two players who selected Jordan as their role model were not African American.

DISCUSSION AND CONCLUSIONS

Recognizing the need for further study, especially increasing the sample size, it is nevertheless useful to speculate from these preliminary data. In general, with all but a few items, the black males did not seem to vary greatly from their non-black cohorts. Our results support Lapchick (1996) and suggest that the racial differences reported in the literature for high school and college-aged respondents have not as yet emerged during the middle school experience of children. The nonemergence of different perceptions between blacks and non-blacks of middle school age may be interpreted as support for Messner's (1992) and Coakley's (1996) assertions that in order to instill positive values in youngsters through sport, one needs to build upon already present values. The positive values are present already in these preadolescent children. For example, the males in the present study displayed a value system that was positive such that not one value was rated as "false." One of the strongest responses given concerned winning by breaking the rules; the strongest negative response to this was by the black males. One would hope that their future coaches will reinforce this value system and facilitate the positive outcome concerning desired characteristics when these boys become young adults. Prior research suggests that these youngsters are at risk, as African American males, to succumb to much social pressure to behave and think differently. Longitudinal study is necessary to see if this indeed happens to youngsters such as these who possess such positive values.

A number of males reflected the goal to succeed at the "highest level." Sport is seen as very important to most of these youngsters even to the point that one male's goal is to be "the best of the best." Becoming an outstanding athlete is already a strong motive for this 14-year-old African American male. Such motivation may prove problematic if this is a commitment that goes unfulfilled. Alternative career paths need to be fostered, especially for those who aspire to such athletic greatness. Given that the odds of reaching such a goal are so small (Coakley, 1998), preparation for the eventual "cut" needs to be provided.

The importance of the family is evident from the role models selected. Another potential effort to promote more positive outcomes might utilize this admiration and affection the athlete has for his family, especially his mother and father. It became obvious from reviewing the transcriptions that these young people who selected their parents as role models were very proud and thankful for the paths laid out by their families. One way to combat the "clan pride" (Hoberman, 1997) that presents sports and physical proficiency as the only path for success is for significant others, especially parents, to keep sports in perspective and provide alternatives for the future. Unlike the data for older sports participants, for example, college and high school levels (Castine & Roberts, 1974), the role models for the younger age group in the present study were not exclusively sports figures. In fact, only one of the African American males selected a sportsman as the person he would most like to be as an adult.

The anxiety data suggests that these African American boys have low to moderate stress with respect to competition. Further testing is needed to see if competitive stress rises in the African American male as he competes at the high school level and beyond. There was little evidence in the present study that competition and sports are threatening to the 10- to 15-year-old African American child. Although it is a very small sample (n = 5), it is of note that the African American females self-reported higher competitive anxiety levels put them somewhat above the normal finding for girls of this age. It appears that girls, regardless of race, experience stress about competition earlier than boys.

As with Ewing and Seefeldt's (1989) seminal work, winning was not viewed as very important to these youngsters. Our experience with older African American males, especially athletes, suggests that they strongly favor winning over playing. The present group not only split on this choice but also rated "fun" as of prime importance for their participation in sports. At a later age, fun and winning seem to become linked together. One must hope that these youngsters do not lose their zest for the fun they receive when they participate in sports. As noted in some of the earlier anecdotes, the enjoyment that sports provide to these youngsters may be used as a motivational tool to promote the positive values and characteristics society seeks in all its citizens.

Our data in this preliminary study suggest that the younger African American male should not be characterized as possessing similar motives and values to his older male sport counterparts. The later childhood–early adolescent African American male evidences many of the positive characteristics we desire our sports participants to possess.

NOTES

Many persons made this study possible. Students from Kent State University and the University of Akron aided the data collection under the supervision of Mary MacCracken. The analysis of the audiotapes was aided by Kent student J. Warren and University of Leipzig (Germany) students J. Boeck and A. Oberbach.

1. This view was suggested by W. Johnson, University of Chicago, during the forum.

REFERENCES

Beller, J. M., & Stoll, S. K. (1995). Moral development of high school athletes. *Journal of Pediatric Exercise, 7*, 352–363.

Bing, L. (1991). *Do or die*. New York: HarperCollins.

Castine, S., & Roberts, G. C. (1974). Modeling in the socialization process of the black athlete. *International Review of Sport Sociology, 3–4*, 59–73.

Coakley, J. (1996). Socialization through sports. In O. Bar-Or (Ed.), *The encyclopedia of sports medicine*: Vol. 6. *The child and adolescent athlete*. Oxford, UK: Blackwell Science (Human Kinetics, Distributor).

Coakley, J. J. (1998). *Sport in society: Issues and controversies*. Boston MA: WCB/McGraw-Hill.

Edwards, H. (1973). *Sociology of sport*. Homewood, IL: Dorsey Press.

Edwards, H. (1988). *Racial stratification in sport and society: The problem and the solution*. [Cassette recording]. Washington, DC: National Colloquium.

Ewing, M. E. & Seefeldt, V. (1989). *Participation and attrition patterns in American agency-sponsored and interscholastic sports: An executive summary* (Final Report). North Palm Beach, FL: Sporting Goods Manufacturers Association.

Ewing, M. E., & Seefeldt, V. (1996). Patterns of participation and attrition in American agency-sponsored youth sports. In F. L. Smoll & R. E. Smith (Eds.), *Children and youth in sport: A biopsychosocial perspective* (pp. 31–45). Dubuque, IA: Brown & Benchmark.

Ferguson, A. (1999). Inside the crazy culture of kids' sport. *Time, 154* (2), 52–60.

Griffin, R. S. (1998). *Sports in the lives of children and adolescents: Success on the field and in life*. Westport, CT: Praeger.

Guttman, A. (1988). *A whole new ballgame: An interpretation of American sports*. Chapel Hill: University of North Carolina Press.

Hall, E., Saunders, E., & Shuman, N. (1985). *Hypertension in blacks: Epidemiology, pathophysiology and treatment*. Chicago, IL: Year Book.

Hoberman, J. (1997). *Darwin's athletes: How sport has damaged black America and preserved the myth of race*. New York: Houghton Mifflin.

Kane, M. (1971, January 18). An assessment of black is best. *Sports Illustrated, 34*, 72–83.

Lapchick, R. (1996). *Sport in society: Equal opportunity or business as usual?* Thousand Oaks, CA: Sage.

Leonard, W. M. (1988). *A sociological perspective of sport* (3d ed.). New York: Macmillan.

Martens, R. (1977). *Sports competition anxiety test*. Champaign, IL: Human Kinetics.

Martens, R., Vealey, R. S., & Burton, D. (1990). *Competitive anxiety in sport*. Champaign, IL: Human Kinetics.

Martinek, T., & Hellison, D. (1998). Values and goal-setting with underserved youth. *Journal of Physical Education, Recreation and Dance, 69* (7), 47–52.

Messner, M. A. (1992). *Power at play: Sports and the problem of masculinity*. Boston: Beacon Press.

Ogbu, J. (1997). Understanding the school performance of urban blacks: Some essential background knowledge. In H. J. Walberg, O. Reyes, & R. P. Weissberg (Eds.), *Children and youth: Interdisciplinary perspectives* (pp. 190–222). Thousand Oaks, CA: Sage.

Rudd, A., Stoll, S. K., & Beller, J. M. (1999). *Measuring moral and social character among a group of Division IA college athletes, nonathletes and ROTC military cadets*. Paper presented at the annual convention of the American Alliance for Health, Physical Education, Recreation and Dance, Boston.

Sage, G. (1993). Introduction. In D. D. Brooks & R. C. Althouse (Eds.), *Racism in college athletics: The African-American athlete's experience* (pp. 1–17). Morgantown, WV: Fitness Information Technology.

Seligman, M.P.H. (1990). *Learned optimism*. New York: Pocket Books.

Sellers, R. M. (1993). Black student-athletes: Reaping the benefits of recovering from the exploitation. In D. D. Brooks & R. C. Althouse (Eds.), *Racism in college athletics: The African-American athlete's experience* (pp. 143–176). Morgantown, WV: Fitness Information Technology.

Spreitzer, E. (1992). *Does participation in interscholastic athletics affect adult development? A longitudinal analysis of an 18–24 age cohort*. Paper presented at the American Sociological Association Conference, Pittsburgh.

Steihl, J. (1993). Becoming responsible: Theoretical and practical considerations. *Journal of Physical Education, Recreation, and Dance, 64* (5), 38–71.

Wallerstein, J. (1983). Children of divorce: The psychological tasks of the child. *The American Journal of Orthopsychiatry, 53*, 230–243.

8

Young Unwed African American Fathers: Indicators of Their Paternal Involvement

Waldo E. Johnson, Jr.

Knowledge about the influence and effects of paternal involvement on family formation and child well-being has expanded over the past decade (Lamb, 1997). Much of this literature is based on the assumption that paternal involvement, defined as the degree of fathering children receive and the extent to which it reduces child-rearing burdens on employed mothers, is positive for children and family formation (Pleck, 1997). The diversity of fathers and their paternal role statuses affect their abilities to provide and sustain such involvement (Pleck, 1997). Yet, the empirical evidence to support the presumed positive effects of paternal involvement on child well-being remains ambiguous. Much of the ambiguity lies in the differences in the effect of paternal involvement when examined among the various paternal statuses (e.g., adolescent fathers, middle-aged fathers, married fathers, divorced fathers). The variation in statuses among their children also limits these studies' ability to show the effects of paternal involvement. The chronological, social, and psychological statuses of men in their roles as fathers impact their interactions and influences upon their children. Similarly, the chronological, social, and psychological statuses of children appear to impact and influence their responses to their fathers. Although paternal role functioning among young unwed fathers remains a topic of social critique, limited systematic inquiry has been conducted.

This chapter examines the indicators of paternal involvement among young unwed African American fathers. To place these indicators of paternal involvement in the proper conceptual context, the chapter proposes a sociodevelopmental perspective of young unwed fatherhood. Following the description of the indicators of paternal involvement, the chapter concludes with the implications of the indicators for policy and clinical practice interventions with these young parents and their children.

YOUNG FATHERS: WHO ARE THEY?

Adolescent or young parenthood remains one of the enduring social dilemmas facing American society as it enters the new millennium. Increased understanding of the influences and effects of paternal involvement is especially crucial when the father is barely beyond childhood and the role expectations mandate undertaking adult responsibilities.

The term "young father" is a rather amorphous term which has significant currency for describing young men who father children out of wedlock. Contemporary references to this group of fathers generally depict them as those males who became fathers prior to completing formal and postsecondary training, making a formal commitment (e.g., marriage) to their partners, securing stable and sustaining employment, and emancipating themselves from their families (Marsiglio & Cohan, 1997). Their early transition to parenthood and incomplete education and training preparation increases the likelihood that they will be economically poor. The term "young father" represents an amalgamation of teenage or adolescent father designations as well as those fathers who have chronologically entered into early adulthood (Johnson, 1999a). Traditional perspectives on adolescence, depending on the developmental theorist, suggest that adolescence can extend up to age 24 (Lee, 1994). Emerging perspectives of the chronological scale of adolescence extend to age 30, especially when considering those individuals for whom economic assistance from their family of origin remains a primary form of financial support beyond traditional emancipatory life events (e.g., completion of postsecondary education, graduate and/or professional school, securing professional employment). In addition, this perspective on adolescence also embraces those at the other end of the spectrum: individuals who have not completed secondary education nor work preparation endeavors necessary for successfully assuming socially expected paternal roles. While variation in age among young fathers exists, the term "young father" contextualizes fatherhood in poverty and social science research along socioeconomic status. Chronologically, young fathers may range in age from the early teen years to age thirty. This description, in terms of education, work readiness, and labor force experience, also aptly reflects the portrait of teenage and adolescent mothers with whom many of these young fathers partner in their parenting relationships.

The tendency among social science researchers who study fatherhood has been to compare adolescent and young males to older adult men in their roles as fathers without acknowledging how young males' social and developmental statuses affect paternal role readiness and the ability to undertake paternal obligations. Truncated educational, vocational, and resulting psychological development experienced as a premature parent, unprepared to assume personal and societal expectations of parenthood, minimizes the importance of chronological markers in examining paternal involvement. What is needed is a conceptual framework which links the social and developmental characteristics of young fathers to individual and structural factors affecting their paternal role performance.

Young Unwed Fathers: A Review of the Research Literature

Until the late 1970s and early 1980s, social science researchers concentrated very little on teen, adolescent, or young fathers, nor were developmental and social issues pertinent to these fathers (as they similarly affect teen mothers) given much consideration (Miller, 1997). Even today, it remains unclear who is or should be included in these categories. The term "teenage father" seems to be calibrated along chronology; that is, the segment of the male population who become fathers during the teenage years, usually ages 13 to 19. Elster and Panzarine (1981) studied male white, African American, and Latino teenage partners of girls enrolled in a teen maternity project. The mean age of the sixteen unwed teenage prospective fathers was 17.4 years. This article was among the first to investigate the psychosocial needs of unwed teenage prospective fathers, and it formed the basis for a psychosocial profile of teenage fathers which suggested the presence of paternal emotional responses similar to those experienced by prospective mothers during the prenatal period.

Hendricks, Howard, and Caesar (1981) and Hendricks and Montgomery (1983) made major contributions to the early research focused on teenage fathers. They conducted one of the first multisite studies of unwed teenage African American fatherhood. Their findings provided much needed direction in understanding the problems these fathers face and their sources of social support. The findings also suggested that unwed teenage fatherhood is indeed stressful. In addition, family and friends were cited as the prime sources of social support. An equally important finding suggested that 95 percent of the teen fathers expressed a high degree of readiness to attend a teenage parenting agency if it offered services for unwed adolescent fathers. Hendricks's (1982) subsequent research focused on attitudes toward abortion, contraception, and sexuality. He reported a marked sentiment against abortion, a predisposition toward espousing honesty in their emotional feelings toward their sexual partners, sharing the fact of their sexual activity with peers, and receptivity to sex education. Subsequent studies on teenage fathers expanded the research tradition began by Hendricks in examining teen fathers' developmental needs. The subsequent studies explored for possible differences among African American married and unmarried teenage fathers and white and Canadian teen fathers (Fry & Trifiletti, 1983; Robinson, 1988). Barret and Robinson (1982) provided a historical account of teenage fatherhood for examining these young men's dispositions toward paternity. Their research findings dispelled myths about teenage fatherhood and examined its effects on children.

Montemayor (1986) offered a developmental approach for examining adolescence focused on chronology, biology, psychological maturity, legal status, and life course events. As Barret and Robinson (1982) suggested, when teenage fathers are included in traditional research, information is often inferred (Adams & Pittman, 1988; Males & Chew, 1996). The early 1980s also witnessed the beginning of young fatherhood research studies framed from the adolescent perspective and aptly dubbed as "adolescent pregnancy research." It followed an earlier, firmly established research tradition that examined pregnancy, parenthood and their effects on teenage females. In fact, much of our current knowledge (both intuitive and empirical) about young fathers is based on models originally developed to study sexually active teen females who became teenage mothers. This gendered framework for examination, intervention, and practice for model development continues to permeate current perspectives of paternal research, especially that focused on adolescent and young adult parents.

Card and Wise (1978) conducted one of the first demographic studies in which fathers and mothers were compared with their nonparenting peers in terms of educational attainment and marital status at conception. This demographic research tradition became firmly entrenched during the 1980s. Marsiglio (1987) examined African American and white adolescent fathers' initial living arrangements, marital experience, and educational outcomes using the National Longitudinal Survey of Youth (NLSY). Further study by Marsiglio focused on the adolescent fathers' commitment to social fatherhood, the decision to reside with the partner and child in the event of an unplanned nonmarital conception, pregnancy resolution preferences, and family formation intentions (Marsiglio, 1988, 1989). Lerman (1993) provided a more detailed demographic look at young unwed fathers using the National Longitudinal Survey of Labor Market Experience, Youth Cohort. Such analyses as incidence of unwed fatherhood, backgrounds, and behavior and earning patterns among these young males provided in Marsiglio's and Lerman's study were neither possible nor conceptualized as important research questions during the late 1970s and early 1980s teen parenting studies. Lerman's findings suggested that the incidence of unwed fatherhood appears unlikely to decline in the future and that safeguards against unwed fatherhood include stronger family, cultural, and peer buffers, as well as better opportunities for young men to enter rewarding careers (Lerman, 1993).

Sullivan (1985) conducted a classic ethnographic study of adolescent fatherhood among African American, white, and Latinos in three Brooklyn neighborhoods. Sullivan's depiction of these young men broadened the societal view of young unwed fatherhood. It clarified the role of family as a social support in the assumption of paternity. Based on narrative interviews with young unwed fathers, Sullivan's findings introduced the role of schooling, employment, and crime among inner-city youths as antecedents to fatherhood, thus offering a compelling synthesis of social psychological constructs and poverty analysis. McAdoo (1990) examined adolescent fatherhood among married and unmarried African American adolescent fathers from a modified social exchange perspective. He examined how racial, educational, and economic barriers impede the adolescent fathers' positive contributions to their families and communities. A breakthrough in adolescent fatherhood research was achieved by McAdoo. The theoretical framework that undergirded his study yielded a richer context for understanding adolescent fatherhood. McAdoo's inclusion of young fathers in their early to mid-twenties pushed the boundaries in terms examining differences in chronological versus various developmental indicators of readiness for fatherhood.

Social Forces and Young Unwed Fatherhood

Current research depicting young fathers as uninvolved and having pathological outcomes as parents emerge out of an evolving research tradition which earlier framed young parenthood from a combined maternal and chronological perspective. Social forces contributed to this focus on young fathers. Consistently portrayed as "hit-and-run victimizers" by social researchers, policy makers, and often their partners, family services program staff traditionally excluded young unwed fathers from its support efforts aimed at young mothers and their children. The current maternal and child care system in which support services (e.g., physical and mental health, social services) is characterized by female-headed families in which unwed, noncustodial fathers are viewed as absent even when they are present. In the current welfare reform environment in which substance-addicted and terminally ill, poor mothers increasingly are compelled to relinquish parenting rights, even the most committed of unwed, noncustodial fathers often experience intense resistance from the child welfare system in their efforts to gain custody of their biological children (Johnson, 1999b). Parenting services designated for custodial parents are often interpreted by caseworkers as "maternal" even when noncustodial fathers pose no threat to their children's welfare as custodial parents.

Such unfair program practices are similarly reflected in the social research tradition where anecdotal information about young fathers portray them as uncaring and uninvolved. Such characterizations further marginalize these fathers' presence and value (Lawson & Rhodes, 1993; Luker, 1996). The truncated educational, vocational, and psychological development that is widely found among poor young urban males is heightened in the social assessment of their performance as fathers. Yet, their poor performance as fathers is often linked to sociobiological and environmental factors which are reflected in weak commitments to educational advancement and sustaining employment, their children, and their families (Marsiglio & Day, 1997). These social structural factors combined with individual inabilities exert a devastating impact on their statuses as men, partners, and fathers. Key interventions for assisting these young unwed African American fathers in overcoming their enfeebled statuses lie in deconstructing the individual and structural barriers toward forming an integrative perspective that addresses all barriers to positive paternal role functioning. Such an integrative perspective embraces the developmental and social factors that impinge on fatherhood. As previously outlined, developmental factors like support and encouragement from the families of origin often result in young fathers' attempt to carve out areas of involvement and engagement with their children (McAdoo, 1993; Johnson, 1995). Subsequently, these fathers are better prepared to meet social challenges that enhance their human capital, resulting in improved school and vocational achievement, work opportunities, and labor force participation.

An emerging research tradition focused on the psychological well-being of teen and adolescent fathers was being forged by Elster and Lamb (1982), Hendricks (1982), and McAdoo (1990). Escalating out-of-wedlock adolescent pregnancies propelled the emerging research tradition for other reasons and resulted in less than complementary depictions of these fathers. An increasingly conservative public purportedly reflected in opinion polls and alleged state and federal legislative mandates became intolerant of inflationary costs associated with maternal and child care services for young mothers and their children. Public welfare "costs in aid" to female-headed families with dependent children are considered unacceptable unless the young mothers provide public service for their doles. Poor unwed mothers with dependent children are increasingly dubbed as the "deserving poor" because of their public dependency. Incumbent legislators and hopefuls alike, armed with statistics about the millions of dollars uncollected annually in child support payments, advocated not only for cutbacks in support to AFDC families but also measured retaliation against the "deadbeat dads" who fail to financially support their children.

The multimillion dollar ripoff in unpaid child support, unfortunately, is calculated on the collection of payments from all fathers, a sizable proportion of which include poor young males who have neither the jobs nor financial means to pay child support consistently (Sorenson & Mincy, 1994; Johnson, Levine, & Doolittle, 1999). As suggested by economists Ron Mincy and Elaine Sorenson, to collect child support from these poor young fathers would be the equivalent of "squeezing blood from turnips." Mincy and Sorenson aptly refer to these poor young fathers as "turnips" instead of "deadbeats," or those who could pay but refuse to do so (Sorenson & Mincy, 1994). In spite of this reality, these poor young fathers consistently provide the public persona of the "deadbeat dad."

Welfare reform, as we currently know it, has done little to connect poor unwed fathers with their children as it was widely touted to accomplish in 1996 when the federal legislation was enacted. In fact, provisions regarding fathers are found in only two sections of the Personal Responsibility and Work Opportunities Reconciliation Act (PRWORA): paternity establishment and child support. Federal law, enforced by states, requires that unwed mothers identify the biological fathers of their children, thus setting in motion the assignment child support orders by the family court. Typically, these provisions instead have driven a wedge between the otherwise fragile relationships among poor unwed parents. In the legal as well as social determination of paternity and order for child support, the unwed fathers are not guaranteed access to visitation with their children as provided in legal separations and divorces among married parents.

INDICATORS OF PATERNAL INVOLVEMENT AMONG YOUNG, UNWED AFRICAN AMERICAN FATHERS

It is important to better understand how paternal involvement among young unwed fathers is undertaken (Waller, 1997). Theories of human development suggest that the tasks of adulthood and specifically fatherhood are better assumed when the developmental tasks of adolescence are completed (Lee, 1994). Becoming a father prior to completing the developmental tasks of adolescence or fully undertaking the expectations of adulthood minimizes the chances that the transition will be a smooth one (Elster & Lamb, 1982). The results are disastrous not only for well-being of the young father (Lawson & Rhodes, 1993; Luker, 1996) but also for his child's well-being. Improved knowledge about the factors that support and inhibit paternal involvement among young unwed fathers will lead to better public policies and interventions designed to improve paternal and family functioning.

Concern regarding the involvement of young unwed fathers in the lives of their children continues to mount. In some cases, the relationships between young, unwed, expectant African American mothers and fathers dissolve before the pregnancies come to full term. As a result, the young unwed father may become distant and uninvolved during the pregnancy and following the birth. His child becomes at risk of growing up without the economic and social well-being that is provided by the paternal parent.

The data used to develop this chapter are drawn from several sources including previous studies and the Fragile Families and Child Well-Being Study, a nationally representative, longitudinal study of the circumstances of unmarried parenthood among residents in twenty-one U.S. cities with population over 200,000. A comparison group of married parents will also be followed. The total sample size will be 4,700 families, including 3,600 unwed couples and 1,100 married couples. Findings from the Chicago pilot study (which included a baseline survey interview and follow-up semistructured interviews over the succeeding eight months) conducted by the author in 1996 and the baseline survey interviews from the Oakland, California and Austin, Texas samples conducted by the National Opinion Research Center (NORC) in 1998 are presented here. The Fragile Families Study addresses three areas of great interest to policy makers and community leaders: nonmarital childbearing, welfare reform, and the role of fathers. It will provide important information on the implementation of welfare, child support, health care, child care, and housing policies in different cities and reveal how such policies are playing out under different labor market conditions and across various racial and ethnic groups.

The subsequent examination initiates a critical first step: identifying the indicators of paternal involvement among young unwed African American fathers. The factors that promote father involvement are (1) the sustaining of a romantic relationship between the couple during pregnancy and immediately following the birth, (2) support for his paternal involvement from his family of origin, (3) support for his paternal involvement from his partner's family of origin, (4) the father's ability to provide financial support, (5) the father's financial contributions, (6) the age of the father, (7) other demographic factors (e.g., race, ethnicity, education), (8) the effects of fatherhood programs on paternal development and family functioning, (9) the fathers' values about fatherhood, and (10) the father's spiritual concept regarding his children.

Couple Relationships

Research findings suggest that the relationship between the young unwed father and mother is a critical factor in predicting paternal involvement (Hendricks, Howard, & Caesar, 1981; Hendricks & Montgomery, 1983; Elster & Lamb, 1986; Westney, Cole, & Munford, 1986; Marsiglio, 1989; Danziger & Radin, 1990; Cochran, 1997; Florsheim, Moore, & Suth, 1997; Johnson, 1999a). Johnson found that being in a romantic, cohabiting relationship was positively correlated with paternal involvement among unwed African American couples. Unwed fathers in romantic, noncohabiting relationships were less involved, but unwed fathers who neither resided nor were romantically involved with their children's mothers were uninvolved as parents. In particular, fathers who took part in decision making (especially pregnancy resolution) were highly involved in parenting (Miller, 1994).

Father's Family of Origin Influence on Paternal Involvement

Parental identity and parenting development is primarily a compilation of experiences and observations over time. The family of origin provides the context in which many of these experiences and observations are acquired. Family traditions and values passed on by parents and other adult family figures often shape the paternal behavior and activities embraced by sons in their families of procreation. While fathers and male figures are presumed to best communicate and transmit paternal behavior, in the absence of empirical evidence, maternal communication of paternal behavior remains unclear (Christmon, 1990a; Miller, 1994). The importance of this issue is most apparent in examining the paternal socialization of young urban African American males growing up in single, female-headed households.

Empirical evidence for linking adolescent males' early forays into sexual activity and parenthood to absent fatherhood among poor, urban, young African American males remains elusive. Given the large number of urban, impoverished adolescent males who reside in single, female-headed households, there is urgency in identifying how various family structures and compositions affect the young males' subsequent sexual and parenting perceptions and behaviors. It is unknown if and how the father's family of origin acts as a barrier to paternal involvement.

Earlier studies contend that the father's family-of-origin response to the pregnancy and his paternity influenced his paternal involvement (Sullivan, 1986; Rivara, Sweeney, & Henderson, 1986, 1987; Christmon, 1990a; Miller, 1994; Johnson, 1993). In contrast, more studies questioned the impact of the father's family of origin on his paternal role development (Christmon, 1990b; Anderson, 1999). Variations in study samples, variables and factors examined, and methods possibly explain these contrasting findings, but in the absence of analyses that can be drawn across studies, these findings are unclear. For example, Miller found that mothers are particularly influential in shaping their sons' paternal behavior as unwed young fathers. This contention potentially offsets concern raised about the unfulfilled role of absent fathers in shaping their son's paternal role behavior. Damon, an eighteen-year-old father, disclosed the following story about his paternity acknowledgment:

> I was unsure about being my daughter's father. Her mother and me had sex on the day after we met. I felt if she had sex with me, she could be having sex with a lot of other guys. When she was three months pregnant, she called me saying that she was pregnant but "I was not hearing that." Her father called after the baby was born, told me that I was a father and wanted to know if I was going to take care of my responsibilities. I told my mother. She and my grandmother said that they would go with me to the hospital to see the baby. When my grandmother saw my daughter, she said, "That baby got your grandfather's chin and complexion. That's your child!" My mother said, "You are going to take care of that baby. It's your responsibility." I knew there was no way I could deny it.

Damon's family of origin was instrumental in his assuming paternity for his son. In contrast, John is a fifteen-year-old father whose family of origin, namely his mother, was not thrilled with the notion of becoming a grandparent. When John told her about his son's birth, she replied that he should not expect financial support from his family. He stated,

> My mother said that she was not interested in seeing my son. I don't think she really meant it. She was angry about my having a child I could not afford to support. She said that our [household] income would not feed all the mouths already in the house and one more was too much. She told me to go out and find a job.

Anderson (1999) contended that street culture in poor urban communities can exert a stronger influence on adolescent and young African American males' paternal identity and role performance than parental expectations expressed or modeled by their parents and family of origin. Such differences in research findings raise important questions about the circumstances under which family relationships and atmosphere facilitate or buffer paternal involvement among young African American fathers.

Mother's Family of Origin Influence on Paternal Involvement

Equally important are the experiences and observations of young unwed mothers within their families of origin in their maternal development. Young African American mothers' identification with their own fathers and male family figures potentially shapes their perception of appropriate paternal involvement for their own children. The young unwed mother's family of procreation's dependence on her family of origin potentially affects the procreative family's stability.

When unemancipated adolescent and young adult women have children out of wedlock, their families of origin are generally viewed as gatekeepers who limit the young fathers' involvement with their partners and children. Yet, even fewer studies have examined the influence of the maternal family-of-origin influence on paternal involvement among young unwed fathers (Sullivan, 1986; Danziger & Radin, 1990; Cervera, 1991). These examinations are unidirectional and describe or assess the mother's family of origin as a barrier to paternal involvement. Empirical studies that examine how the maternal family of origin facilitates paternal involvement are lacking and could be informative in developing strategies to improve paternal involvement among these young fathers. John's girlfriend's parents, for example, recognized his potential long-range contributions to his child's well-being. He reported that the baby's maternal grandparents supported his involvement with the baby and did not demand that he provide financial support as a condition of his involvement with his child.

> Her parents were really cool about the baby. It made me feel better because my family was "sweating" [reprimanding] me about the being irresponsible and getting a job. They [the maternal grandparents] encouraged me to visit the baby and to bring the baby to my house to see my family. They said that they did not expect me to support [provide child support or financial assistance] the baby right now because I am still in school. I promised to find a job and help out when I can. I think we are going to work everything out.

John's disclosure minimally suggests that the range of responses to adolescent and young adult paternity by maternal and paternal families of origin do not reflect conventional wisdom.

Father's Ability to Provide Financial Support

Fathers often cite the provision of financial support to their children as the most important paternal obligation (Cazenave, 1979). Fathers, young and old alike, strongly identify with the instrumental obligation of fatherhood. Societal expectations also herald this shared paternal value as tantamount to father's other parental responsibilities. Young unwed fathers, however, are generally unprepared to provide sustaining financial support due to incomplete formal education and limited or no work experience and subsequently less involved with their children than older fathers (Sorenson & Mincy, 1994; Johnson, 1999a, 1999b).

Work preparation and experience are important credentials for gaining entry and sustaining oneself in the labor market (Johnson, in press), and the lack of these credentials by young unwed fathers tends to stymy their entry into the labor market and subsequently limit their earning potential. As a result, the kind and degree of financial support necessary for young unwed fathers to gain and sustain paternal involvement is often elusive. Challenged by a failure to provide consistent, substantive financial support and the absence of a legal bond to their children, it is unclear whether young unwed mothers mandate financial support as a condition for paternal involvement. If so, what level of support is considered minimum? Does it evolve over time? Can financial support provided by his family of origin replace or supplement direct support provided by the young unwed father? In-depth interviews with poor African American mothers and nonresident fathers revealed that the vast majority of parents believe that nonresident fathers should provide financial support to their children, that fathers' time is not a substitute for money, and that fathers have a right to see their child, even if they do not pay child support (McLanahan, 1999). A preceding disclosure by John confirmed this contention. In this scenario, the maternal grandparents valued John's involvement with his son more strongly than the meager financial support than he could possibly provide. Todd, a twenty-one-year-old father, expressed embarrassment that he has only twice earned money for his newborn son: "I have to depend on my mother to give me money for my son. I would like to earn the money myself but I am still searching for a job. But the baby needs things every day." If financial support from the father is not a condition for paternal involvement, what is minimally required? Does this minimal expectation evolve over time? These questions heavily impinge on determining a father's ability to provide financial support.

Father's Financial Contributions

Given the strong paternal identification with the "breadwinner" role shared by fathers in general, many fathers view their identity and self-respect as integrally tied to their work (Gaylin, 1992). Financial support for children is most assured when children are born into intact marriages where the father resides with the child. Formal break-ups of marriages generally provide a legal mechanism by which financial support is sustained until the child reaches the age of consent. Ideally, changes in the parents' relationship status do not negatively affect the economic well-being of the child (Cherlin, 1992).

Fathers' financial contributions to children born out of wedlock are indeed different. These contributions often serve as the link to paternal visitation and involvement. The status of the parents' relationship often affects paternal provision of financial support. As stated earlier, unlike child custody and visitation guidelines resulting from parents' legal separation or divorce, young unwed nonresident fathers are expected to provide financial support but are not guaranteed visitation by law. Personal circumstances may affect fathers' financial contributions to their children. Maintaining residence independent of his children or having to provide financial support to other children and/or households could minimize the financial contributions a father might otherwise make to his children. The young unwed African American fathers examined in this chapter are challenged by many of these issues. They do not reside with their children, and only one father is employed full time. Although John's girlfriend (and mother of his child) and her parents do not expect him to provide the primary financial support for his child, he does feel that he should provide some support.

> It's really like part of the agreement. If she [the mother] has to take care of the baby every day, I can see how she believes that I should help out. That's the way it's always been. My mother agrees and she told me that I should help out with the baby's expenses. She says that's what a real man do.

John's evolving commitment to his son was subsequent to his son's birth. The following disclosure affirms the contention that many young unwed fathers feel strongly that they should provide some financial support to their children, even if they have no visible means of doing so.

> I did not visit my son in the hospital because I did not have anything to take [him]. I wanted to give my girlfriend some money but I didn't have none. I

asked my mother to help me out but she started sweating [reprimanding] me. She finally gave me some money but not before she let me have it [gave him a lecture].

Research on adolescent and young unwed fathers has examined the importance of young unwed fathers' financial support to their children in their construction of paternal identity (Rivara, Sweeney, & Henderson, 1986; Christmon, 1990b; Danziger & Radin, 1990; McAdoo, 1990; Miller, 1994; Kiselica, 1995; Johnson, 1993; 1998; in press). Some research findings document that many young unwed fathers provide financial and other material support to their children (Sullivan, 1986; Danziger & Radin, 1990; Miller, 1994). Several of these studies also suggest that many young unwed fathers sustain paternal involvement in spite of their failure to provide financial support to their children.

Father's Age

Conventional wisdom suggests that the age of the father is a good predictor of his involvement with his child. Adults are presumed to be better equipped to respond to both the emotional and instrumental needs of their children. While these developmental transitions are not entirely chronologically bound, age is indeed indicative of the approximate point for transition into adulthood. Age is a prime factor in assessing not only a father's commitment but also his capacity to undertake his paternal obligations. Developmental transitions from adolescence to adulthood occur over time and are crucial in the formation of parenting skills that enable fathers to successfully undertake instrumental and noninstrumental parenting obligations (Elster & Lamb, 1982). The large number of young unwed fathers and the problems they encounter sustain interest in father's age and its explanatory power. Findings from baseline surveys administered to unwed African American and Latino fathers in the Oakland, California, and Austin, Texas, samples of the Fragile Families Study suggest that when fathers' visits to see the baby in the hospital were examined as a measure of paternal involvement, younger fathers (less than age 20) were no less likely to visit the hospital than older fathers (ages 21 to 30) (Johnson, 1999a). Of the young unwed African American fathers interviewed in the Chicago pilot immediately following their child's birth, John expressed far more anxiety about his desire to provide some financial support for his son. He was also the youngest of the unwed fathers at age fifteen.

Age and developmental readiness for assuming paternal obligations is not only problematic for adolescent and young adult fathers. Keith, a thirty-four-year-old father (who had become a first-time father in his twenties) was also unprepared to assume paternal responsibilities, although he recognized that he should have been:

> I am older and I want to be a better father to my daughter than I have been to my son but I can hardly make ends meet. I was laid off my job two months ago and I have very little money saved. I didn't know I would be laid off otherwise I would have moved out of my grandmother's house. I probably would not have had this new baby either. I am looking for another job right now. I know that I must get some money coming in and in a hurry. With all the things that I got to do and people to take care of, I got to get myself a job.

Intergenerational poverty is a common thread in the lives of each young unwed African American father examined. It is possible that becoming fathers at a young age exacerbated their ability to fully assume fatherhood due to their impoverished statuses.

The Education and Young Unwed African American Fathers

High school completion is a time-honored goal among African American families. This commitment to personal progress and racial uplift has been strongly espoused for more than a century by numerous civil rights leaders, including W.E.B. Dubois and Revs. Martin L. King, Jr. and Jesse L. Jackson. African Americans who migrated to the Midwest and Northeast during the Great Migration and subsequent migrations not only sought immediate, improved work opportunities in the booming factories but also quality primary, secondary, and postsecondary educational opportunities for their children and families. There is a substantial reduction in black–white inequality in the basic amount of schooling received. Education attainment is associated with improved socioeconomic status for all groups (Jaynes & Williams, 1989) and viewed as an equalizer for African Americans.

African Americans and Latinos are disproportionately poorer than whites in American society, and a number of factors contribute to this dilemma, including premature parenthood and poor work preparation. Failure to complete high school limits their employment options and earning potential. As fathers who share societal expectations for providing financial support for their children, young unwed African American fathers and mothers who do not complete high school are at risk of forming persistently poor families. This is reflected in the circumstances of the young unwed African American fathers under examination. Only two young fathers graduated from high school, and only one young father is employed full time. John, the fifteen-year-old father, personifies the dilemma that many of his male peers face in terms of the perceived value of a high school education for gaining employment:

> I don't feel that I will be any better off to get a job when I graduate from high school than I am now. I am staying in school because people say you need a high school diploma to get a job. I know folks in my neighborhood with high school diplomas and they can't find jobs.

John's commitment to completing high school is rather weak. His experiences with others suggested that the supposedly long-range benefits of a high school education have not materialized for those like himself. Todd, a twenty-one-year-old father, also had little confidence that completing high school would land him a job so he dropped out:

> When I was going to school, we were not learning the skills I needed to get a job. I had a part-time job and I was learning more in that job about work than I was in school. So I quit school because I had to help out my parents and younger sisters. My mother wanted me to stay in school but I could not see how it would help me.

The young fathers' failure to complete high school as a pathway to future employment and their higher reservation wage are examples of their personal responses to a dynamic labor force for which the requirements for entry continue to evolve. These young fathers are also hampered by the disappearance of work training opportunities like the Comprehensive Employment and Training Act (C.E.T.A.) and the mayor's summer work programs, which served as way station jobs in earlier years in preparation for young workers' subsequent full-time employment. Collectively, these factors impact their likelihood of acquiring employment, earning potential, and subsequently their paternal involvement (Johnson, under review).

Paternal Values about Fatherhood

Pleck and Pleck (1997) suggest that fatherhood ideals have varied by race and ethnicity historically in American society. In contrast to the conventional notion that the stern patriarch of colonial America represented the original American paternal ideal, Native Americans and the genteel-like southern planters were more permissive. Southern planters were known to leave corporate punishment to tutors and servants. Some authors contend that Native American fathers were unconcerned with maintaining authority or commanding obedience of children:

Many were not patriarchs at all, since they belonged to tribes that traced lineage through the female line. Families in such tribes might dwell in long houses or hogans that contained related kin members on the mother's side. Fathers did not live with their children. The mother's brother, rather than her husband, often took the father's role in childrearing. Even Indian men in patrilineal tribes did not expect children to be obedient out of fear. They believed that the community, rather than an individual parent, was responsible for the proper behavior of children. (Mintz & Kellogg, 1988)

The latter description of paternal identity in association with a fatherhood ideal more closely resonates with the demographic profile of contemporary young unwed fathers. African American fathers not only comprise the largest proportion of these young unwed fathers, they also evolve from a familial context historically in which childrearing is conceptualized as a community responsibility.

How African American men view their family experiences, what they are able or willing to do as family members, and even when they decide to do it are often directly affected by ethnicity. It is assumed that any discussion of fatherhood and generative fathering must be embedded in an ethnocultural context. This requires a basic knowledge of the history, culture, and philosophy of both the United States and the nations of Western Africa. This discussion must also address the balance between the differences from and similarities with other ethnic groups. African American men operate from a unique historical and sociopolitical context, yet they share aspects of their past and present with men in other ethnic groups. Maintaining this balance when discussing the adaptations that African American men have made interpreting their family roles is essential if we are to avoid erroneous conclusions and inappropriate comparisons. (Allen & Connor, 1997)

Given that many young unwed fathers do not reside primarily with their children, their development of a fatherhood ideal is potentially minimized. In the absence of their own fathers and a consistent male presence during their own formative years, the young unwed fathers in the Chicago pilot turned to other sources in constructing their paternal identities. Russell, a twenty-five-year-old father, offered the following disclosure:

I have been reading about how a father's presence in his child's early development can make a difference in a child's later development. I don't think that this is anything new. A father can give a lot to his child, not just money but that is important. I hope to always be able to meet my daughter's basic needs but I also hope to guide her in other ways. I'm not trying to be religious on you but this is where I'm at right now.

The value of fatherhood is closely associated with ongoing connection that fathers share with their children. Qualitative findings from the

Fathers' Fair Share, a national demonstration project designed to increase low-income noncustodial parents' employment, earnings, and ability to pay child support and possibly to help them establish or reestablish contact with their children, suggest that many of the noncustodial fathers in the study shared a strong paternal identity and often sought ways to undertake paternity against tremendous odds (Johnson, Levine, & Doolittle, 1999).

Baseline findings from the Oakland, California and Austin, Texas samples of the Fragile Families and Child Well-Being Study suggest that unwed fathers closely identified with fatherhood. When asked to respond the following contention, "Being a father is the one of the most fulfilling experiences a man can have," 67 percent of the unwed fathers reported that they "strongly agreed" and 31 percent "agreed." Similarly, 71 percent strongly agreed and 28 percent agreed with the contention, "Losing the chance to be a part of the child's life is one of the worst things that could happen" (Johnson, 1999a). These preliminary findings encourage a better understanding about unwed fathers' value of paternity. Identification with fatherhood represents an important step in undertaking paternity among young unwed fathers. Their chronological, employment, and psychological statuses often truncate their desired behavioral responses to paternity. Involvement with their children is often sustained only as a result of their strong values about fatherhood, enabling them to overcome financial and interpersonal barriers to their involvement.

Spirituality and Young Unwed African American Fathers

The common depiction of young unwed fathers is devoid of any spiritual embodiment. Unlike the spiritual yearning espoused by Bly (1990) that supposedly guides men in connecting themselves with their inner selves in order to better assume their multiple roles of responsibility, young unwed fathers are depicted as existing solely for the purpose of advancing their own needs and proclivities. Abramovitch (1997) contended that fatherhood is undergirded by mythological, biblical and contemporary images that are affected by historical changes in the image of masculinity and the father. This spiritual aspect of fatherhood, according to Abramovitch, is innate.

Early qualitative examinations of adolescent and young adult African American paternity suggest that some young fathers view fatherhood from a spiritual perspective (Johnson, 1993, in press). Referencing an Old Testament biblical scripture in which Adam and Eve were told "to be fruitful and multiply," several young unwed African American fathers discussed their paternity in terms of a divinely ordained phenomenon. When queried about the timing and their preparation for these divine events, some young fathers stated that their own imminent mortality (resulting from residence in violent, urban communities) engendered a sense of procreative urgency in order to leave a legacy (Johnson, 1993). These uncanny disclosures are difficult to reconcile given the unsecured legacy that these young fathers pass on to their offsprings given their socioeconomic statuses.

Equally surprising, findings from the Fragile Families baseline data suggest that church attendance (used as a proxy for spirituality) was negatively correlated with paternal involvement. Fathers who regularly attended religious services (once a week or more) were less likely to visit their children in the hospital immediately following birth. Clearly, the dimensions of spirituality are far more complicated than attendance at religious activities, in that attendance at religious activities may be an inadequate proxy.

Parenting Support Services for Young Unwed African American Fathers

American fathers are so heavily identified with the provider role that until recent research studies examining the importance of paternal nurturance and other noninstrumental contributions to child development, societal perceptions suggested that a father's ability to "bring home the bacon" essentially defined his paternal role and involvement (Lamb, 1997). The recognition that fathers also make important noninstrumental contributions to child development and well-being is reshaping paternal expectations and obligations. It is also identifying areas where parenting support services may be needed. As evolving social and demographic changes in society challenge the most prepared fathers in sustaining their provider-role status, fathers less prepared to assume provider and/or noninstrumental roles will face greater difficulty in sustaining paternal support to their children.

The availability of social services for young unwed fathers has been examined and cited as a factor affecting paternal involvement (Leashore, 1981; Allen-Meares, 1984; Barth, Claycoomb, & Loomis, 1988; Anderson-Smith, 1988; McAdoo, 1990; Johnson, 1998). While many of these studies explored access to parental support services in the context of traditional maternal and child services, these examinations include a mixed bag of programs with varying service qualifications and provisions.

Fatherhood programs are among the chief agents designed to assist young fathers in their paternal development (Johnson, 1998). Although an emerging literature describes these programs as crucial to supporting paternal involvement among young unwed fathers, their effects are mixed at best. The fatherhood programs chronicled or assessed to date tend to be either small, community-based programs with a broad range of foci and services or large demonstration projects which provide a range of support services but seldom survive beyond the pilot phase (Klinman, Sander, Rosen, & Longo, 1986; Achatz & MacAllum, 1994; McLaughlin, 1995; Salter, 1997; Johnson, Levine, & Doolittle, 1999). In addition, fatherhood programs are extremely limited in number, therefore raising concern about their capacity to serve the escalating number of fathers in need.

Current gaps in research reflect a need to better understand how fatherhood programs are implemented, their successes, their shortcomings, and how to improve them. Do fatherhood programs help to foster parenting relationships between the young couples? Do they recognize and respond to the families of origin as potential factors in fostering paternal involvement? How do they relate to the workforce and the young father regarding his labor force activities? How do they impact on child well-being?

FATHER'S INFLUENCE ON CHILD WELL-BEING

As suggested by Perloff and Buckner (1996), if the financial aspects of low-income fatherhood are unclear in terms of their impact on paternal involvement, even more ambiguity surrounds the nature and quality of interaction between low-income fathers and their children. Research on how fathers of varying socioeconomic levels influence their children's development has produced inconsistent findings across studies. Some studies have shown that father contact is positively associated with cognitive test scores in children (Radin, 1981), while father absence is linked to poorer behavioral functioning and lower cognitive performance (Dornbush et al., 1985; Gringlas & Weinraub, 1995). Other findings suggest that the fathers' involvement has little effect on their children's functioning after controlling for other explanatory variables such as child and maternal characteristics (Crockett, Eggebeen, & Hawkins, 1993; Furstenberg & Harris, 1993).

The case for improving paternal outcomes is based largely on the benefits of such involvement for their children. For young unwed fathers barely out of childhood, the case takes on other dimensions including concern about social and developmental trajectories of the young unwed father. Father contact seems to improve a child's cognitive well-being (Johnson, 1996). This finding builds a case for father contact, but how much and what quality of contact? Is father contact synonymous with residential status? If so, most young unwed fathers will experience difficulty in sustaining that level of contact because they do not reside with their children. Yet, studies document that young unwed fathers are often more involved with their children than their nonresident status suggests (Danziger & Radin, 1990; Perloff & Buckner, 1996), raising questions about how paternal presence and absence are measured and assessed.

Early childhood outcomes include preschool African American and white children who show more cognitive competence, more internal locus of control, more empathy, and less gender-role stereotyping as a result of father involvement (Lamb, 1987). How does paternal involvement affect child well-being among older children? Does it remain constant or does it impact other dimensions of child well-being? Are there indirect effects? In the previously mentioned studies, it is unclear whether paternal involvement is facilitated by residential status or merely physical presence. Given that young unwed African American fathers are presumed to be absent and less involved with their children, these issues are extremely important. Even fewer studies examine the consequences of paternal involvement on child well-being among young unwed fathers (Rangarajan & Gleason, 1998).

AN INTEGRATIVE PERSPECTIVE FOR EXAMINING PATERNAL INVOLVEMENT AMONG YOUNG UNWED AFRICAN AMERICAN FATHERS

Becoming a father prematurely and out of wedlock means that many of the ways in which fathers become involved in their children's lives are truncated. Given their usual impoverished status, young unwed fathers, like young unwed mothers, are in need of formal and informal social supports to lessen their otherwise difficult transitions into parenthood (Kiselica, 1995). The young unwed parents' relationship and their respective families of origin are among the most important of informal social supports that impact paternal involvement among young unwed fathers. These informal supports also influence their values about fatherhood and potentially their spiritual connection to paternity. The young unwed fathers' financial contributions are also influenced by the status of the couples' relationships and his relationship with the families of origin but impacted by his age, his racial–ethnic identity, and educational status. The latter demographic factors are associated with his ability to provide financial support.

Fathers in general often face difficulty in gaining access to formal parenting support services. Because parenting support services are tied to child custody, young unwed fathers who have not established legal paternity are at risk of being ignored and unserved (Allen-Meares, 1984; Anderson-Smith, 1988; Barth, Claycoomb, & Loomis, 1988). These young unwed African American fathers are the neediest of young parents in terms of access to formal social supports like parenting support services. In response, fatherhood and paternal components of traditional maternal and children services designed for noncustodial parents (who are generally fathers) have emerged. Parenting support for noncustodial parents or fatherhood programs, in theory, are poised to tackle many of the needs of this population (which is largely overlapping), but the family support field has not given sufficient attention to the needs of fathers as parents (Johnson & Pouncy, 1998). Among these programs, however, there is little consistency in organization and service provision. Efforts to identify paternal role issues and best practices for addressing issues confronting noncustodial parents remain at the infant stages of development. Development of the family support field is further complicated by the scarcity of fatherhood and noncustodial parent programs nationally and their geographical concentration in midwestern and eastern urban centers.

The Ford Foundation Strengthening Fragile Families Initiative includes basic research on the relationships between young low-skilled unwed couples before, during, and shortly after their children are born; development of policies and family support practices that encourage low-skilled fathers to become involved in the lives of their children, establish legal paternity, and increase employment, earnings, and child support payments; and outreach efforts to policy makers, researchers, grant makers, and the broader public to promote the idea of reconnecting fathers and families and discussions between men and women at the local and national level about the advantages and risks associated with reconnecting fathers to families. This initiative also supports the development of the field of community-based programs working to strengthen fragile families and family support practices that help unwed parents resolve conflicts and cooperate to provide for their children's needs (Ford Foundation, 1996). Collectively, these issues raise legitimate concern about the focus and the effectiveness of these programs in promoting paternal involvement among all young unwed fathers and sustaining family development for unwed parents and their children.

Young unwed African American fathers are disproportionately represented among those poor fathers in fragile families who, because of their weak labor force attachment, nonmarital, and nonresident statuses, are unlikely to provide sustaining financial support to their children (Landry & Forrest, 1995). Although race may appear to shape these paternal patterns, it is an intervening variable in the larger context of socioeconomic status, paternal identity, and involvement in out-of-wedlock childbearing. Young unwed African American fatherhood among urban poor males often reflects this description. Their chronological and developmental statuses as trained and experienced laborers limit their abilities to achieve provider role success.

Among older African American fathers, failure to provide financial support to their children and families results in episodic participation in family life. Because their worth as contributing members of these families and of society is assessed largely in terms of their provider role success, their failure as fathers has been attributed to the rise in alternative family structures aided by public institutions which offer poverty-level support to their children. Young unwed African American fathers also experience marginalized involvement with their children when they are unable to support them financially. In contrast to older fathers, their marginalization or uninvolvement is much more likely to be chronic. Young unwed African American fathers are less likely to have established households with their families of procreation, and their nonresident status with their children truncates their involvement. They are generally reliant upon their families of origin not only for their own economic support but also for the financial support of their children.

CONCLUSION

Rising concern regarding the involvement of young unwed fathers in the lives of their children continues to mount. Increasingly, the intimate relationships between unwed expectant young mothers and fathers often dissolve before the pregnancies come to full term. As a result, the young unwed father often becomes distant and uninvolved during the pregnancy and following the birth. The unborn child becomes at risk of growing up without the economic and social well-being that is provided by the paternal parent.

Social science research on young unwed African American fathers conducted during the last decade has yielded a limited body of knowledge about their paternal involvement. This is due in part to the preoccupation with the effects of adolescent maternal parenting outcomes and the failure to draw survey samples which include these young men. In addition, conceptual frameworks that examine paternity and paternal role functioning among adult men, single, married, and divorced, formed the basis of investigations of paternity among young unwed African American fathers. Finally, the link between race and poverty status has not been fully embraced as a contextual factor in examining the disproportionality of young parenthood among African Americans and other racial and ethnic groups of color.

Identification of indicators of paternal involvement among young unwed African American fathers and the role they play in promoting positive paternal role functioning and child well-being will guide researchers and policy and intervention practitioners in developing better efforts designed to increase such involvement. The benefits of these improved efforts will enhance paternal role functioning and identity, family formation and functioning, father–child relationships, and subsequently, better child well-being outcomes.

REFERENCES

Abramovitch, H. (1997). Images of the "father" in psychology and religion. In M. Lamb (Ed.), *The role of the father in child development* (pp. 19–32). New York: John Wiley and Sons.

Achatz, M., & MacAllum, C. (1994). *The young unwed fathers demonstration project: A status report*. Philadelphia: Public–Private Ventures.

Adams, G., and Pittman, K. (1988). *Adolescent and young adult fathers: Problems and solutions*. Washington, DC: Adolescent Pregnancy Prevention Clearinghouse Report, Children's Defense Fund.

Allen, W., & Connor, M. (1997). An African American perspective on generative fathering. In A. Hawkins & D. Dollahite (Eds.), *Generative fathering: Beyond deficits perspectives* (pp. 52–70). Thousand Oaks, CA: Sage.

Allen-Meares, P. (1984). Adolescent pregnancy and parenting: The forgotten adolescent father and his parents. *Journal of Social Work and Human Sexuality, 3* (1), 27–38.

Anderson, E. (1999). *Code of the street: Decency, violence and moral life of the inner city*. New York: W. W. Norton.

Anderson-Smith, L. (1988). Black adolescent fathers: Issues for service provision. *Social Work, 33*, 269–271.

Barrett, R., & Robinson, B. (1982). A descriptive study of teenage expectant fathers. *Family Relations, 31*, 349–352.

Barth, R., Claycoomb, M., & Loomis, A. (1988). Services to adolescent fathers. *Health and Social Work, 13*, 277–286.

Bly, R. (1990). *Iron John: A book about men*. Reading, MA: Addison-Wesley.

Card, J., & Wise, L. (1978). Teenage mothers and teenage fathers: The impact of early childbearing on their personal and professional lives. *Family Planning Perspectives, 10*, 199–205.

Cazenave, N. (1979). Middle income black fathers: An analysis of the provider role. *Family Coordinator, 28* (4), 583–593.

Cervera, N. (1991). Unwed teenage pregnancy: Family relationships with the father of the baby. *Families in Society: A Journal of Contemporary Human Services, 71*, 29–37.

Cherlin, A. (1992). *Marriage, divorce and remarriage*. Cambridge: Harvard University Press.

Christmon, K. (1990a). Parental responsibility of African American unwed adolescent fathers. *Adolescence, 25*, 645–653.

Christmon, K. (1990b). Parental responsibility and self-image of African American fathers. *Families in Society: A Journal of Contemporary Human Services, 71*, 563–567.

Cochran, D. (1997). African American fathers: A decade review of the literature. *Families in Society: The Journal of Contemporary Human Services*, 340–350.

Crockett, L., Eggebeen, D., & Hawkins, A. (1993). Father's presence and young children's behavioral and cognitive adjustment. *Journal of Family Issues, 14*, 355–377.

Danziger, S., & Radin, N. (1990). Absent does not equal uninvolved: Predictors of fathering in teen mother families. *Journal of Marriage and the Family, 52*, 636–642.

Dornbush, S., Carlsmith, J., Bushwall, S., Ritter, P., Leiderman, H., Hastorf, A., & Gross, R. (1985). Single parents, extended households and the controls of adolescents. *Child Development, 56*, 326–341.

Elster, A., & Lamb, M. (1982). Adolescent fathers: A group potentially at risk of parenting failure. *Infant Mental Health Journal, 3* (3), 148–155.

Elster, A., & Lamb, M. (Eds.) (1996). *Adolescent fatherhood*. Hillsdale, NJ: Erlbaum.

Elster, A., & Panzarine, S. (1981). The adolescent father. *Seminars in Perinatology, 5* (1), 39–51.

Florsheim, P., Moore, D., & Suth, A. (1997, November). *He says, she says: Factors related to the quality of partnerships between expectant adolescent mothers and fathers*. Unpublished paper presented at the National Council on Family Relations annual conference in Arlington, VA.

Ford Foundation. (1996). *Strengthening fragile families initiative*. New York: The Ford Foundation.

Fry, P., & Trifiletti, R. (1983). Teenage fathers: An exploration of their developmental needs and anxieties and the implications for clinical–social intervention services. *Journal of Psychiatric Treatment and Evaluation, 5*, 219–227.

Furstenberg, F., & Harris, K. (1993). When and why fathers matter: Impacts of father involvement on the children of adolescent mothers. In R. Lerman and T. Ooms (Eds.), *Young unwed fathers: Changing roles and emerging policies* (pp. 117–138). Philadelphia: Temple University Press.

Gaylin, W. (1992). *The male ego*. New York: Viking.

Gringlas, M., & Weinraub, M. (1995). The more things change . . . : Single parenting revisited. *Journal of Family Issues, 16*, 29–52.

Hendricks, L. (1982). Unmarried black adolescent fathers' attitudes toward abortion, contraception and sexuality: A preliminary report. *Journal of Adolescent Healthcare, 2*, 199–203.

Hendricks, L., Howard, C., & Caesar, P. (1981). Black unwed adolescent fathers: A comparative study of their problems and help-seeking behavior. *Journal of the National Medical Association, 73* (9), 863–868.

Hendricks, L., & Montgomery, T. (1983). A limited population of unmarried adolescent fathers: A preliminary report of their views on fatherhood and the relationship with the mothers of their children. *Adolescence, 18*, 201–210.

Jaynes, G., & Williams, R. (1989). *A common destiny: Blacks and American society*. Washington, DC: National Academy Press.

Johnson, D. (1996). *Father presence matters: A review of the literature*. Commissioned paper for the National Center on Fathers and Families. Philadelphia: University of Pennsylvania.

Johnson, E., Levine, A., & Doolittle, F. (1999). The only game in town: Walking through the doorway of Parents' Fair Share. In *Parents' Fair Share: Helping poor men manage child support and fatherhood* (pp. 104–127). New York: Russell Sage Foundation.

Johnson, J., & Pouncy, H. (1998). Developing creative ways to address the needs of fathers and fragile families. *Harvard Journal of African-American Public Policy, 5*, 5–22.

Johnson, W. (1993). *Perceptions and patterns of paternal role functioning among urban, lower socioeconomic status adolescent and young adult African American males: A social choice–social norms perspective*. Ph.D. diss., University of Chicago.

Johnson, W. (1995). Paternal identity among urban, adolescent males. *African-American Research Perspectives, 2* (1), 82–86.

Johnson, W. (1998). Paternal involvement in fragile African American families: Implications for clinical social work practice. *Smith College Studies in Social Work, 68* (2), 215–232.

Johnson, W. (1999a). *The determinants of paternal involvement among unwed fathers*. Paper presented at the Fragile Families and Welfare Reform Workshop, Institute for Research on Poverty, University of Wisconsin at Madison, August.

Johnson, W. (1999b). *Increasing paternal involvement among children in substitute care*. Preliminary report to the director of the Illinois Department of Children and Family Services, Springfield, IL.

Johnson, W. (2000). Work preparation and labor market experiences among urban, poor nonresident fathers. In S. Danziger and A. Lin (Eds.), *Coping with poverty: The social contexts of neighborhood, work and family in the African American family* (pp. 224–261). Ann Arbor: University of Michigan Press.

Johnson, W. (in press). Time out of bound: High school completion and work preparation among urban, poor, unwed African American fathers. In W. Allen, C. O'Connor, & M. Spencer (Eds.), *New perspectives on African American education: Race, achievement and social inequality*. Greenwich, CT: JAI Press.

Kiselica, M. (1995). *Multicultural counseling with teenage fathers: A practical guide*. Newbury Park, CA: Sage.

Klinman, D., Sander, J., Rosen, J., & Longo, K. (1986). The teen father collaboration: A demonstration and research model. In M. Lamb and A. Elster (Eds.), *Adolescent fatherhood* (pp. 155–170). Hillsdale, NJ: Erlbaum.

Lamb, M. (1987). *The father's role: Cross-cultural perspectives*. Hilllsdale, NJ: Erlbaum.

Lamb, M. (1997). Father and child development: An introductory overview. In M. Lamb (Ed.), *The role of the father in child development* (pp. 1–18). New York: John Wiley and Sons.

Landry, D., & Forrest, J. (1995). How old are U.S. fathers? *Family Planning Perspectives, 27*, 159–161, 165.

Lawson, A., & Rhodes, D. (1993). *The politics of pregnancy: Adolescent sexuality and public policy*. New Haven, CT: Yale University Press.

Leashore, B. (1979). Human services and the unwed father: The forgotten half. *The Family Coordinator, 28* (4), 487–534.

Lee, C. (1994). Adolescent development. In R. Mincy (Ed.), *Nurturing young black males: Challenges to agencies, programs and social policy* (pp. 33–44). Washington, DC: Urban Institute Press.

Lerman, R. (1993). A national profile of young unwed fathers. In R. Lerman and T. Ooms (Eds.), *Young unwed fathers: Changing roles and emerging policies* (pp. 27–51). Philadelphia: Temple University Press.

Luker, K. (1996). *Dubious conceptions: The politics of teen pregnancy*. Cambridge: Harvard University Press.

Males, M., & Chew, K. (1996). The ages of fathers in California adolescent births. *American Journal of Public Health, 86* (4), 565–568.

Marsiglio, W. (1987). Adolescent fathers in the United States: Their initial living arrangements, marital experience and educational outcomes. *Family Planning Perspectives, 19*, 240–251.

Marsiglio, W. (1988). Commitment to social fatherhood: Predicting adolescent males' intentions to live with their child and partner. *Journal of Marriage and the Family, 50*, 427–441.

Marsiglio, W. (1989). Adolescent males' pregnancy resolution preferences and family formation intentions: Does family background make a difference for blacks and whites? *Journal of Adolescent Research, 4*, 214–237.

Marsiglio, W., & Cohan, M. (1997). Young fathers and child development. In M. Lamb (Ed.), *The role of the father in child development* (pp. 227–244). New York: John Wiley and Sons.

Marsiglio, W., & Day, R. (1997). *Social fatherhood and paternal involvement: Conceptual, data and policy issues*. Presentation at the NICHD-sponsored conference on Fathering and Male Fertility: Improving Data and Research. Bethesda, MD: National Institutes of Health, National Institute of Child Health and Development.

McAdoo, J. (1990). Understanding African-American teen fathers. In P. Leone (Ed.), *Understanding troubled and troubling youth: Multi disciplinary perspectives* (pp. 229–245). Newbury Park, CA: Sage.

McAdoo, J. (1993). The roles of African American fathers: An ecological perspective. *Journal of Contemporary Human Services, 74*, 28–35.

McLanahan, S. (1999, September). *Time, love, cash and children in Chicago: An interim report to the MacArthur Foundation Research Network on the family and the economy*. Albuquerque, NM.

McLaughlin, W. (1995). *The Fathers' Resource Center: Executive summary*. Indianapolis, IN: Wishard Memorial Hospital.

Miller, D. (1994). Influences on parental involvement of African-American adolescent fathers. *Child and Adolescent Social Work, 2*, (5), 363–378.

Miller, D. (1997). Adolescent fathers: What we know and what we need to know. *Child and Adolescent Social Work Journal, 14* (1), 55–69.

Mintz, S., & Kellogg, S. (1988). *Domestic revolutions: A social history of American family life*. New York: Free Press.

Montemayor, R. (1986). Family variation in parent–adolescent storm and stress. *Journal of Adolescent Research, 1*, 15–31.

Perloff, J., & Buckner, J. (1996). Fathers of children on welfare: Their impact on child well-being. *American Journal of Orthopsychiatry, 66* (4), 557–571.

Pleck, E., & Pleck, J. (1997). Fatherhood ideals in the United States. In M. Lamb (Ed.), *The role of the father in child development* (pp. 33–48). New York: John Wiley and Sons.

Pleck, J. (1997). Paternal involvement: Levels, sources, and consequences. In M. Lamb (Ed.), *The role of the father in child development* (pp. 66–103). New York: John Wiley and Sons.

Radin, N. (1981). The role of the father in cognitive, academic and intellectual development. In M. Lamb (Ed.), *The role of the father in child development* (2d ed.). New York: John Wiley and Sons.

Rangarajan, A., & Gleason, P. (1998). Young unwed fathers of AFDC children: Do they provide support? *Demography, 35* (2), 175–186.

Rivara, F., Sweeney, P., & Henderson, B. (1986). Black teenage fathers: What happens when the child is born? *Pediatrics, 78*, 151–158.

Rivara, F., Sweeney, P., & Henderson, B. (1987). Risk of fatherhood among black teenage males. *American Journal of Public Health, 77*, 203–205.

Robinson, B. (1988). *Teenage fathers*. Lexington, MA: Lexington Books.

Salter, W. (1997). *The Paternal Involvement Project: Annual report to the board of advisors*, Chicago: The Chicago Commons.

Sorenson, E., & Mincy, R. (1994, November). *Deadbeats and turnips in welfare reform*. Paper presented at the 1994 annual meeting of the Association for Public Policy and Management, Chicago.

Sullivan, M. (1985). *Teen fathers in the inner city: An exploratory ethnographic study*. Ford Foundation Report, Urban Poverty Programs, New York.

Sullivan, M. (1986). *Ethnographic research on young black fathers and parenting: Implications for public policy*. New York: Vera Institute for Justice.

Waller, M. (1997). *Redefining fatherhood: Paternal involvement, masculinity and responsibility in the "other America."* Ph.D. diss., Princeton University, Princeton, NJ.

Westney, O., Cole, O., & Munford, T. (1986). Adolescent unwed prospective fathers: Readiness for fatherhood and behaviors toward the mother and the expected infant. *Adolescence, 21* (84), 901–911.

9

Reflections of the Forum: Graduate Students on the Inside Track

Anita C. Heard, Madinah Ikhlas, and
Michelle D. Mitchell

The 1999 Kent State Psychology Forum brought together researchers and community service providers whose emphasis was on improving the mental health of African American children.[1] We are African American clinical psychology students in the Kent State University doctoral program who were offered the opportunity to attend the 1999 Forum. Madinah is in her fourth year of graduate study and her area of interest is children and families. Michelle is in her third year of graduate study and her area of interest is anxiety as it relates to African Americans. Anita is in her second year of graduate study and her area of research is psychological testing.

At this time only one of us has chosen to focus specifically on research with African Americans. Nevertheless each of our respective areas of research will enable us to better serve African American populations in the future, demonstrating that there are a variety of research topics graduate students of color can pursue which will allow them to meet the needs of their ethnic–cultural group. Many graduate students of color have chosen areas of research that do not specifically focus on their ethnic–cultural group; however, this does not mean they are not concerned with psychological issues pertaining to their group. Despite our varied areas of research, our common interest in African American children brought the three of us together to participate in the conference.

Therefore, it was only appropriate that we collaborate to share our collective experiences at the conference with you, the reader.

EXPECTATIONS

When we heard that we were invited to the forum we were excited. Free food, free room, community experts, and scholars all under one roof; what could be better? We didn't know what to expect from this gathering or what our role as graduate students would be. Would it be an opportunity to network with people in the field? We hoped that we would enter a supportive environment where we would be encouraged to grow in our roles as scientists and practitioners. Many of our questions about African American children were answered, and we were inspired about future research projects and about our careers and the contributions we could make in research and practice. We were motivated to pursue future research projects examining issues relevant to African American children, and the discussions gave us ideas about contributions that we could make in research and practice. We also received insight about the direction in which research about African American children is moving.

Although our department attempts to expose us to ethnic-minority research, it is not the primary focus of the department. Therefore the breadth of research that is being conducted on African American children was not something with which we were intimately familiar. Our anticipation peaked as the forum time drew near because we looked forward to being encouraged in our respective research areas. As we expected, Dr. Neal-Barnett brought in scholars who were conducting cutting edge research in the field of African American children. We looked forward to meeting the African American scholars and community leaders from around the country.

FIRST IMPRESSIONS

The opportunity to take a break from our grueling lives as graduate students was a welcome change. As we traveled to the Inn at Honey Run we were pleasantly surprised by the rolling green hills and the horse-drawn carriages. The serene beauty of the pristine countryside created a calming atmosphere, which was the perfect place for a think tank. As everyone gathered and began to settle in, Kent State University's Gospel Choir uplifted us with song. This manner of starting a conference was different from what we had previously experienced. Since this was a group of African American scholars, the use of a gospel choir seemed a natural choice.

THE PRESENTATIONS

On the first night, Robert M. Sellers presented his model of racial identity. His emphasis on the idiographic nature of racial identity can have a great impact on psychological research and practice because it challenges the unidimensional approach behind the categorization of African American children. Ronald D. Taylor presented a useful paradigm to understand psychological adjustment among inner-city African American adolescents. Taylor's presentation demonstrated the influence of kinship ties to enhance successful parenting in adverse environments. However, he also discussed the need for families to access community resources (e.g., schools, churches, police departments) as an additional source of social support. Deborah J. Johnson presented a model that may help explain how parents racially socialize their children. She also discussed how self-esteem and personal stress could affect parents' ability to effectively communicate strategies of racial coping to their children.

Angela M. Neal-Barnett addressed the issue of social anxiety in African American young women and adolescents. She suggested that the social anxiety these young women experienced could result from their peers' perception that they are "acting white." Dr. Neal-Barnett suggested that being accused of acting white may be a threat to ethnic identity and possibly result in social anxiety. The next topic of discussion was unwed African American fathers. Waldo E. Johnson, Jr. suggested that unwed African American fathers' paternal involvement in their children's lives is not a simple matter, but rather a very complex and multifaceted social dilemma.

Robert E. Stadulis, Gary Waters, and Angela M. Neal-Barnett collaborated on the investigation of the values and aspirations of young African American males involved in sport. Stadulis and Waters presented differing viewpoints regarding the role of sport in social development examining both the positive and negative influences.

Esther J. Jenkins presented an informative session on community violence. She highlighted research examining African American children's exposure to violence and its connection to the type of pathology expressed by them. Michael C. Lambert described the inadequacies of many assessment tools currently being used with African American children. He underscored the importance of investing time in the development of assessment tools specific to this group. Lambert described the development of an assessment tool specifically geared toward measuring psychopathology among African Americans. Jessica Henderson-Daniel talked about the importance of spirituality in the success of African American women. She also emphasized the importance of studying success in African Americans versus looking at them from a deficit viewpoint.

Many of the ideas that we gathered while listening to each speaker carried a great impact. Through discussions that we shared during and after the forum, we have also been able to gain many practical ideas concerning various approaches to research and mental health services with children in African American communities. In the following paragraphs we would like to share with you some of the ideas that came from our discussions.

Overall, the talks focused on various aspects of African American children. The consistent underlying theme, however, was the heterogeneity observed within this group. An issue that exemplifies this point is the definition of race itself. Race means different things to different individuals, and research should reflect that. When researchers use race as a generic construct, it erroneously allows them to assume that race is homogeneous. The extended family is an additional area of research that should be considered when conducting research with African American children. Many issues can not be addressed when the family is not included. Researchers should recognize that children must be placed within their family context. Parents are not the only caregivers that contribute to the child's environment. When working with African American families, the extended family must be considered to avoid excluding significant caregivers.

Another issue that was addressed was assessment. Once issues such as the family and the complexity of race are considered, making sure that measures are valid and standardized on African Americans is essential. The inclusion of a few African Americans in the normative sample is not sufficient to guarantee the applicability of the research to African Americans. One obvious solution is to have a separate standardization for African American children. Another is to develop separate measures specifically for African American children. The measures should reflect the culture, history, and experiences of African American children. Sometimes this requires extra work, such as running focus groups. Researchers should go beyond demonstrating face validity and strive to attain the same high empirical standards as research done with European American children.

An additional consideration when conducting research in the community is the utilization of community service providers. For example, churches and neighborhood community centers are an invaluable resource for enhancing involvement of the members of the target community. In order to facilitate this relationship, it is necessary to become familiar with, build relationships with, and gain the trust of the community. Researchers should look at the available resources of each community to assess its current needs. This assessment should be done in conjunction with the members of the community. Once the needs of the community have been assessed, researchers can not only design their studies to gather their data but also make a concerted effort to make a positive contribution to the community. It is inappropriate to take from people and not give anything in return; therefore, it is necessary, in the research planning stage, to factor in the time necessary to establish a familiar presence. This will help to build the aforementioned rapport and trust necessary to work within an African American community.

As we close this section, there is one last idea that we believe is important for researchers to consider. There are various perspectives that can be utilized when conceptualizing studies. We would like to see researchers approach research with African American children and African Americans as a whole from the perspective of examining their strengths. Approaching a group from a deficit perspective is not only unfair, but also negligent. The strengths of African American children are just as valid and interesting as their apparent weaknesses and clearly merit the attention of researchers.

FIRESIDE CHAT

The fireside chat was an opportunity for us to ask direct questions of a captive audience of leading scholars and community service providers. We were the only graduate students present and this was our chance to ask them anything we wanted, so we put a great deal of thought into our preparation of the questions. Dead silence followed the first question; it seemed like an eternity. Then Esther J. Jenkins broke the silence, and the chat began. We received advice on issues such as ethnic matching in therapy, client–therapist relationships, multicultural training from the American Psychological Association, spirituality, socioeconomic status, and child assessment. In addition, we talked about issues of class, wealth, and other environmental factors, which should be considered when doing research. What we took away from the fireside chat was threefold: first, that we should get all that we can from graduate school so that we would be prepared for anything; second, that gathering data from the African American community can be challenging, yet rewarding; and last, that the area of research with African American children and the community is wide open, and opportunities are freely available.

BRINGING IT BACK TO THE COMMUNITY

Dr. Neal-Barnett brought the culminating event of the forum back to the community. She chose a setting where African American people have gathered across the centuries: the church. The purpose of the venue was to make an earnest attempt to share research findings with the community. By going to the community, the intention was to try to open lines of communication and increase the chances that community members could benefit from the research. Jessica Henderson-Daniel talked about the five essential needs for success, which she called "The 5 Ms": memories, monitoring, mastering, mentoring, and mantras. These factors are found throughout the child psychopathology literature and are commonly suggested as tools needed for successful parenting.

Dr. Henderson-Daniel took these parenting skills and expanded on them in a way that was relevant to the African American community. She presented her ideas about African American parenting in a way that made sense to anyone who was not an African American psychologist. The community eagerly accepted her presentation, which was evidenced by the many questions that were asked at the close of her talk. The audience was interested and found the information extremely useful. This response challenged the idea that "lay people" are unable to consume psychological research due to lack of understanding and interest. This means that it is up to us, the researchers, to make our work readily accessible to the community by using language that can be easily understood and finding creative ways to disseminate the information.

THE END OF THE CONFERENCE

Being involved in a think tank with African American researchers and community leaders was a unique experience. These researchers have moved beyond comparative research between African American and European American children and are looking at African American children as the focus of their research. We believe that this is the direction that African American research should be headed. Instead of looking at African American children from the singular view of low socioeconomic status, these researchers acknowledged and were interested in looking at African American children from middle-class backgrounds and were making no apologies for that. These children deserve to be the focus of research in their own right and not just included as an afterthought. We believe that it is important that faculty and community leaders recognize that this is the direction future research needs to head in if we hope to understand the unique characteristics of this group.

WORDS TO GRADUATE STUDENTS OF COLOR

We have a few suggestions that graduate students of color may benefit from. We understand that it is very easy to become isolated in the sea of your department. It can be hard when people think that you are the representative for all of the people that look like you, and you may feel that you have to defend yourself from stereotypes. Classmates may behave in ways that can cause you to be defensive, but you have to keep the larger goal in mind and not put up a wall and close down your potential for inclusion in future projects.

It is extremely important to get to know your professors and make them aware of your interests, whether you work in their lab or not. Professors are not going to approach you unless they know that you are open and available to be approached. This process is important because when you appear accessible, professors will think of you when relevant opportunities arise. It is also important to be actively involved in departmental activities. Networking with professors and graduate students will help you keep up with what is going on. This is vital to your success because it is through these rich interactions that we broaden our learning experiences. In addition to professors in your department, one can network through attendance at conferences which present culturally relevant topics and are attended by colleagues from your culture. Being in a place where you can be surrounded by people who talk, think, and act like you is refreshing and can be a validating and affirming experience.

Aside from networking and accepting assignments, publishing is particularly important. The adage "publish or perish" is applicable to graduate students, particularly if considering a career in academia. Sometimes students of color make the mistake of attending and presenting at conferences exclusively, feeling that this experience will be enough. While networking with faculty and attending conferences is vital, one should try to expand these contacts into collaborations on projects that lead to publications. This places you in a position to complete graduate studies with the necessary credentials to compete in the job market.

Collectively, we have found that building strong relationships within the department not only helps professionally, but makes the journey more pleasant. If afforded the opportunity to participate in activities that may place more demands on your already tight schedule, do it anyway. This will be something that will be well worth it in the long run. Use discretion, however, and don't spread yourself too thin.

WORDS TO THE FACULTY

While we realize that graduate students must make themselves available to professors, we also believe that this is a two-way street. The relationships between graduate students and faculty are vital. These relationships should be cultivated, shaped, and built upon a firm foundation of trust, mutual respect, and professionalism. Sharing information is one way of strengthening these relationships and reaching out to graduate students. It is vital that you, the faculty, keep your ears and eyes open to look out for various opportunities (e.g., workshops, conferences) you can offer to graduate students to grow as professionals, even to students that do not work in your lab. It is likely that they may be unaware of this opportunity and you may be their only connection to the information. As our mentors, you are a very valuable source of information. Because graduate students' time is limited, their chance to seek out opportunities can become thwarted because of the multiple responsibilities that are a part of the graduate experience. Without the faculty's guidance, many graduate students can become lost.

There are ways to prevent this potential disengagement. For example, faculty members can make themselves more approachable. They should be culturally sensitive and open to discussing cultural topics inside and outside of class. This can come in the form of informal conversations, course content, or even simply being receptive to a differing opinion. They may also attempt to be receptive to exploring ethnic-minority topics in their research. This posture will help create a supportive environment in which your students of color are more likely to feel that their interests and concerns are worthy of attention as they proceed through the graduate process.

CLOSING THOUGHTS

Through attending this conference and writing this chapter, we have been able to reflect on the many things that we learned during this process. We received inspiration and validation for ourselves as future researchers. This experience is proof that one can handle the demands of graduate studies and still publish. On a personal note, we would like to say that we really enjoyed writing this chapter. We have had fun and it has brought us closer together. It was time consuming, but well worth the energy and effort. We are now published authors!

NOTE

We would like to thank Dr. Angela Neal-Barnett for showing interest in our professional development as future African American psychologists and affording us this unique experience.

10

The 1999 Kent State Forum: Take Home Messages and Future Challenges for the Field of Developmental Psychology

Kathryn A. Kerns

The 1999 Kent State Psychology Forum and accompanying book are timely with their focus on the development of African American children. Many developmental psychologists would say that sustained and in-depth study of ethnic-minority children is long overdue. The field has often viewed minority samples as providing an opportunity to test the universality of developmental theories (Coll, Crnic, Lamberty, Wasik, Jenkins, Garcia, & McAdoo, 1996; Zahn-Waxler, 1998). More recently, developmental psychologists are acknowledging the need to study ethnic-minority children in their own right, rather than in comparison to white children (Coll et al., 1996). There has been some progress in the study of minority children in the 1990s. For example, the premier journal in the field, *Child Development*, published a special section on the development of minority children (1990), and there has been an improvement in the representation of cultural and ethnic diversity in samples (Zahn-Waxler, 1998). There is also a recognition that new models incorporating variables unique to minority children, such as ethnic identity development, are needed to move toward a better understanding of the unique developmental pathways for ethnic-minority children (Coll et al., 1996). The 1999 Kent State Psychology Forum and the present book illustrate contemporary approaches to understanding the development of African American children.

In this chapter, I argue that the research presented at the forum and in this book illustrates approaches that, if adopted more widely, would benefit the larger field of developmental psychology. Thus, the purpose of this chapter is to highlight conceptual approaches and methodologies discussed in this book that would enhance the study of children from either majority or minority backgrounds. I begin with several themes which are clearly illustrated in the book and then consider future directions where additional work is still needed.

TAKE-HOME MESSAGES FOR THE FIELD OF DEVELOPMENTAL PSYCHOLOGY

The Need for a Wider Perspective on Family Influence

Developmental psychology has emphasized the family's role in socialization since the time of Freud. Most often, family influence is conceptualized solely in terms of the role played by parents, and even then often only mothers are studied. In his chapter, Waldo E. Johnson, Jr. focuses on the role of fathers, which in and of itself represents a relatively new direction of research. The new twist here is that he considers the role of African American, noncustodial fathers living away from their children, a group that has rarely been studied (McLoyd, 1990). It is estimated that approximately half of the children in the United States will spend some time living in a single parent household due to divorce or to parents never marrying (Hetherington, Bridges, & Insabella, 1998). The role of noncustodial parents deserves much more attention given the large number of children in all ethnic groups who live in single parent households. Waldo Johnson's chapter points to several factors that predict paternal involvement by noncustodial fathers.

Similarly, the influence of siblings and extended family has largely been ignored in the literature. Some of the authors in the present book adopt a wider perspective. Although relatively little attention is given to siblings, the extended family is considered. For example, Waldo Johnson reviews evidence on the ways in which the family of origin influences the paternal involvement of young unwed African American fathers.

The role of the extended family has been examined in earlier studies of African Americans, with special attention to the contributions of grandmothers. As Coley and Chase-Lansdale (1998) note, young African American mothers are often found to benefit psychologically when receiving support from their own mothers, especially when the mother and grandmother reside in different households. Less attention has been paid to the contributions of grandparents and other extended family members in white samples, perhaps because white children are less likely than African American children to be living with a grandparent (Uhlenberg & Hammill, 1998). Nevertheless, ignoring extended kin appears to be an oversight given that Caucasian children also frequently have kin living in close proximity. For example, over 40 percent of both Caucasian and African American grandparents not living with grandchildren report seeing grandchildren at least once a week (Uhlenberg & Hammill, 1998). Therefore, understanding family influence requires looking beyond the nuclear family.

Placing Family Influence in a Broader Context

A commonly studied question when examining family socialization is to ask how the family affects the child's social, emotional, or cognitive development. The family is often viewed as an autonomous influence, despite ecological models pointing out that the family is embedded in and influenced by the larger context (Bronfonbrenner, 1986). Coll and colleagues (1996) have recently proposed a multifactor model of the development of ethnic-minority children that includes multiple levels of influence (e.g., exposure to racism and effects of schools and neighborhoods as well as family influences). Of course, nonminority children are exposed to many of the influences they identify, and socialization effects emanating from outside the family need to be incorporated in studies of children from a variety of ethnic backgrounds.

A strength of some of the research presented in this book is that it incorporates multiple levels of influence on children's development and therefore illustrates how factors outside the family can be included in models of child development. To cite some examples, Taylor discusses socioeconomic conditions as a setting variable that in turn influences family processes and child development outcomes. Stadilus, Waters, and Neal-Barnett consider how sports participation can affect African American children's values and goals. Deborah J. Johnson explores how parents' experience of racial stress influences children's racial coping.

The Power of Qualitative Data

In developmental psychology, there has been a move toward increasingly larger samples and correspondingly an emphasis and reliance on quantitative rather than qualitative methods. By contrast, many of the investigators in the present book incorporate qualitative methods into their studies. The book thus provides several examples of how qualitative data can be used. The data are useful to identify new directions for research and to provide a richer description of the phenomena under study. For example, Neal-Barnett used interviews to study how anxiety can influence identity development. In addition, qualitative approaches such as focus groups can be used to determine whether a construct has been operationalized in a meaningful way for a particular group, as illustrated in the chapters by Sellers, Morgan, and Brown, and Lambert, Markle, and Bellas. The field of developmental psychology would benefit by once again incorporating qualitative methodologies into research designs.

A FOCUS ON PROCESS

The overriding theme across all of the chapters is on how development in African American children can be *explained*. This work provides a clear antidote to earlier studies whose primary aim was description of ethnic group similarities and differences. The process focus also highlights the need to consider within-group ethnic differences. A focus on process is also critical for efforts to intervene in the lives of African American (and other) children.

A Clear Concern with the Application of Research Findings to Current Real-World Problems

Almost all research in developmental psychology has applications to applied problems, although the link is often not an immediate one. The children studied often represent a relatively advantaged group (middle-class children in two-parent families), who may rarely experience some of the most serious social problems such as exposure to violence at schools. By contrast, many of the investigators in the present book are testing theoretical processes as they operate in higher risk environments. For example, Jenkins is studying exposure to violence in an inner-city sample in which children report frequently seeing violent acts, and Taylor examines family processes and child mental health outcomes in a low-income, inner-city sample. Consequently, the intervention and policy implications of the research discussed in this book are more direct than in many studies of child development (see Jenkins's and W. Johnson's chapters for discussion of how their research findings can inform intervention and prevention efforts). Studies of children growing up in higher risk environments serve as a reminder that the ultimate goal of studies of child development is to improve the lives of children.

The Difficulties in Studying Minority Populations Can Be Overcome

One reason for the lack of research on minority populations may be the perceived difficulty in recruiting minority families. When studying minorities, it is important to identify a relatively homogeneous group (e.g., African American children from similar socioeconomic levels; distinguishing between Puerto Rican American and Mexican American children). Their smaller numbers, especially for identified subgroups, means that the base from which to recruit is smaller. This problem may be especially acute in some regions of the country that lack large communities of any one minority group. Minority families who are also low income may be difficult to recruit due to lack of telephones or lack of an established connection to, and trust of, university researchers.

The diverse research presented in this book shows that the difficulties in studying minority families can be overcome. In some cases, large samples of minority children and families were recruited. Taylor (in a personal communication) indicated that his research team did not experience great difficulty recruiting a relatively large low-income, African American sample. Of course, adequate resources (e.g., money to hire project personnel) are needed when recruiting large-scale samples from any ethnic group. Community outreach and trust building are also necessary in the recruitment process, especially when approaching minority families. All the forum participants have active research programs on the development of African American children, and along with other investigators of minority children, possess a wealth of knowledge concerning how to recruit minority families. The "how to" of participant recruitment and retention is rarely discussed in journal articles (for exceptions, see Capaldi & Patterson, 1987; Miranda, Azocar, Organista, Munoz, & Lieberman, 1996; Thompson, Neighbors, Munday, & Jackson, 1996). Dissemination of knowledge regarding successful recruitment strategies would facilitate the study of minority children (by both minority and majority researchers).

FUTURE DIRECTIONS FOR THE FIELD OF DEVELOPMENTAL PSYCHOLOGY

The Importance of Developing Assessments That Are Appropriate for Minority Children

A thorny problem when studying minority children is identifying appropriate measures (i.e., measures that are reliable and valid for a given group). This problem has been recognized in cross-cultural research. For example, Western cultures tend to define cognitive competence in terms of reasoning abilities and intelligence, whereas many non-Western cultures also include in the definition behavioral traits such as being obedient and reliable (Kagitcibasi, 1996). The same problem applies when studying minority groups residing within the United

States. It is therefore critical that measures tap the way a construct is defined in a particular context.

This point is illustrated in some detail in Lambert's chapter on assessing behavior problems and competencies in African American children. Lambert and colleagues argue that some measures frequently used, such as the Achenbach checklist, ignore competencies and problems found in minority groups. For example, they report that problems identified by African American parents bringing their children to clinics were often not found on the Achenbach checklist. Their approach was to use focus groups to identify areas that have been neglected on traditional child behavior instruments. A similar approach could be taken to develop new measures in other areas (e.g., relevant family process variables, parents' desired child outcomes).

The Need to Disentangle the Effects of Minority Culture and Economic Circumstances

Many of the samples studied by investigators in this book were low income. One forum participant, D. Johnson, noted at the conference the need to disentangle the effects of poverty and culture. However, none of the authors explicitly addresses this issue. It will be important to address this issue in future research. Some of the challenges and developmental processes identified as key for understanding the development of low-income, African American children may more generally account for the development of children growing up in poverty. The systematic study of different minority groups, carefully selected on socioeconomic status, will be needed to disentangle poverty and cultural effects.

It is also important to recognize the wide variability in cultural practices within particular racial, ethnic, or geographic groups. For example, Latinos vary widely in the degree to which they have been acculturated into American society. The southern United States is a different cultural context than New York City in many respects. An emphasis on racial groups per se may lead investigators to inadvertently ignore within-group differences. To understand the role of culture, measures will also be needed that can capture within-group cultural variation.

Facilitating the Study of Minority Children

A final challenge concerns how to develop further research on minority children. Earlier I discussed the potential difficulties in recruiting minority samples. There are other barriers, such as the lack of research instruments validated for minority groups, the relatively small number of minority scientists (see Lambert's chapter), and difficulties working with families for whom English is a second language. Material resources and sustained effort are needed to address some of these difficulties. McLoyd (1990) also notes that collaboration between minority and majority scholars would be beneficial, given that the two have often received different training and bring a different perspective to research questions. McLoyd's view is consistent with the main theme of this essay, namely that research on African American children can inform research conducted with other ethnic groups.

CONCLUSIONS

The field of developmental psychology has much to learn from a close examination of recent research on African American children. An understanding of (all) children's development would be facilitated by considering development in a broader context, using both qualitative and quantitative approaches. It is also important to recognize that there are likely to be some differences in the constellation of developmental processes that account for the development of minority and majority children (as well as some differences among different ethnic-minority groups). Thus, adopting the same constructs and methods across different groups will not necessarily provide confirming evidence for the universality of development hypothesis.

NOTE

This essay is based on papers presented at the 1999 Kent State Psychology Forum and chapters in this book. The conference support provided by the Kent State University Applied Psychology Center is gratefully acknowledged. I also thank Angela Neal-Barnett and Josefina Contreras for their comments on an earlier draft of this chapter.

REFERENCES

Bronfonbrenner, U. (1986). Ecology of the family as a context for human development: Research perspectives. *Developmental Psychology, 22,* 723–742.

Capaldi, D., & Patterson, G. R. (1987). An approach to the problem of recruitment and retention rates for longitudinal research. *Behavioral Assessment, 99,* 169–177.

Coley, R. L., & Chase-Lansdale, P. L. (1998). Adolescent pregnancy and parenthood: Recent evidence and future directions. *American Psychologist, 53,* 152–166.

Coll, C. G., Crnic, K., Lamberty, G., Wasik, B. H., Jenkins, R., Garcia, H. V., & McAdoo, H. P. (1996). An integrative model for the study of developmental competencies in minority children. *Child Development, 67,* 1891–1914.

Hetherington, E. M., Bridges, M., & Insabella, G. M. (1998). What matters? What does not? Five perspectives on the association between marital transitions and children's adjustment. *American Psychologist, 53,* 167–184.

Kagitcibasi, C. (1996). *Family and human development across cultures.* Mahwah, NJ: Erlbaum.

McLoyd, V. C. (1990). Minority children: Introduction to the special issue. *Child Development, 61,* 263–266.

Miranda, J., Azocar, F., Organista, K. C., Munoz, P. F., & Lieberman, A. (1996). Recruiting and retaining low-income Latinos in psychotherapy research. *Journal of Consulting and Clinical Psychology, 64,* 868–874.

Thompson, E. E., Neighbors, H. W., Munday, C., & Jackson, J. S. (1996). Recruitment and retention of African American patents for clinical research: An exploration of response rates in an urban psychiatric hospital. *Journal of Consulting and Clinical Psychology, 64,* 861–867.

Uhlenberg, P., & Hammill, B. G. (1998). Frequency of grandparent contact with grandchildren sets: Six factors that make a difference. *Gerontologist, 38,* 276–285.

Zahn-Waxler, C. (1998). Editorial: A time of transition. *Developmental Psychology, 34,* 1157–1158.

Index

About the Editors and Contributors

Valerie François Bellas is a doctoral candidate in the college of human ecology at Michigan State University. Her research interest is in the African diaspora, including intellectual development and academic achievement in very low birth weight children of African descent. She also studies resource management by single parents in relationship to their stress level. This research has been conducted with three different ethnic groups on the island of Trinidad in the Caribbean.

Tony N. Brown is currently a research investigator with the Program for Research on Black Americans (PRBA) in the Institute for Social Research (ISR) at the University of Michigan. He is currently involved in research that investigates the epidemiology of psychiatric disorder, race-related predictors of young adults' well-being, and risk factors for licit and illicit substance use. Dr. Brown's Ph.D. dissertation examined the psychological costs of racism for African Americans and assessed the mental health benefits that some white Americans receive as a consequence of racism.

Josefina M. Contreras is an Assistant Professor at Kent State University. She is a clinical-developmental psychologist whose research interests include parent–child relationships and the development of social-emotional competence in children. Her research focuses on normative aspects of parent–child relationships, as well as on other factors influencing parenting in at-risk and minority populations, with special emphasis on Latino families.

Anita C. Heard is a second-year graduate student at Kent State University. Her research interest focuses on assessment and testing.

Madinah Ikhlas is a fourth-year graduate student in clinical psychology at Kent State University. Her research interest focus on racial identity and on children of color.

Esther J. Jenkins is former chairperson and professor of psychology at Chicago State University and research director at the Community Mental Health Council, Inc., a comprehensive community mental health center on the south side of Chicago. Dr. Jenkins is a member of the steering committee of the Institute on Domestic Violence in the African American Community and the Association of Black Psychologists, among other organizations.

Deborah J. Johnson is professor of family and child ecology and faculty at the Institute for Children, Youth, and Families at Michigan State University. As a developmental psychologist, her interests focus on race and status-related development, parental socialization, and parent–child relations in early and middle childhood. Much of her work has been in the area of racial–ethnic identity development principally among African American and cross-culturally among Zimbabwean children, but also among Korean American and EuroAmerican children. This work is soon to be extended to the indigenous peoples of Australia. This work is being further explored through her associations with the MacArthur Network on Pathways through middle childhood and the role of race–ethnicity in development, the National Center on Fathers and Families, and the NIMH Family Consortium III's study group on race, culture and family processes. She is working at the forefront of the burgeoning area of racial–ethnic socialization among children of color. For her contributions to this area, she received an award from the American Psychological Association's Minority Fellowship Program in 1997. On the NICHD study of early child care and youth development project, she has worked closely with a team of minority investigators to understand the nuances of minority status, ethnicity, and culture interacting within and through various child care experience and family contexts.

Waldo E. Johnson, Jr., is assistant professor at the School of Social Service Administration at the University of Chicago. Dr. Johnson's research interests include male involvement in adolescent pregnancy, noncustodial fathers in fragile families, the mental health status of African American males, and the use of qualitative research methods in policy research. He is coprincipal investigator for Time, Love, Cash, Care and Children (TLC3), which examines the norms and expectations about the rights and obligations of unmarried parents, especially fathers in Chicago, Milwaukee, and New York City; coprincipal investigator for the Fathers and Child Welfare Study, which examines paternal participation among unwed, noncustodial fathers in case planning and service provision in child welfare activities undertaken by the Illinois Department of Children and Family Services; and investigator for the Fragile Families and Child Well-Being Study, a longitudinal study of the circumstances of unmarried parenthood among African Americans, whites, and Hispanics in twenty-one U.S. cities.

Kathryn A. Kerns is a developmental psychologist with research interests in the areas of parent–child and peer relationships. Some of her studies have examined how parent–child attachment is related to the quality of children's peer relationships. In addition, she has investigated age-related changes in friendships and peer groups. Dr. Kerns is an associate professor at Kent State University.

Michael Canute Lambert is associate professor, Department of Psychology, and adjunct professor, David Walker Research Institute, College of Human Medicine, at Michigan State University. He is also associate lecturer in the Departments of Psychiatry and honorary lecturer in the Department of Child Health at the University of the West Indies, Mona, Jamaica, West Indies. His research interests include taxonomy and measurement of psychopathology in children and families of the African diaspora, cross-national research on child and adolescent psychopathology, and adult attitudes and behavior regarding child behavior and emotional problems.

Faith Markle is a graduate student in developmental psychology at Cornell University. She is studying young children's social and cognitive development, especially in regard to children's interactions with authority.

Michelle D. Mitchell is a third-year graduate student in clinical psychology at Kent State University. Her research interests focus on anxiety disorders in African Americans.

Laura M. Morgan is a doctoral candidate in organizational psychology at the University of Michigan. Her primary research interests address the intersections of racial identity, professional identity, work experiences and mental health.

Angela M. Neal-Barnett is a nationally recognized expert in the area of anxiety disorders among African Americans. She is the author of numerous articles and book chapters on the topic and the recipient of several grants. Her most recent research focuses on the acting white phenomenon in African American adolescents and the relationship between panic disorder and hypertension in African American women. Dr. Neal-Barnett is coeditor of *Family and Peers: Linking Two Social Worlds* (Praeger, 2000).

Robert M. Sellers is an associate professor in the Department of Psychology at the University of Michigan and research associate at the Institute for Social Research. A native of Cincinnati, Ohio, his primary research activities center around the development of a conceptual model of the processes associated with the way that African Americans attribute significance and meaning to race as a way in which they define themselves (i.e., racial identity). In addition to this research, Dr. Sellers has published several research articles and book chapters examining the life experiences of student athletes.

Robert E. Stadulis has practiced his scholarship at Kent State University for the past twenty-seven years and is graduate coordinator of the Sport Studies Program in the School of Exercise, Leisure and Sport. His instructional responsibilities include psychological dimensions of motor behavior, psychology of coaching, and sport in society, as well as serving as the primary instructor for undergraduate and graduate level instruction in measurement and evaluation, research methods, and statistics. Two areas have dominated his scholarship of discovery efforts: competitive anxiety in children and the perception (and interception) of moving objects.

Ronald D. Taylor is an associate professor in the Department of Psychology and assistant director of the Center for Research in Human Development and Education at Temple University. Dr. Taylor has produced numerous articles and chapters on the social and emotional development of ethnic-minority children and is coeditor of the recently published books, *Social and Emotional Adjustment and Family Relations in Ethnic Minority Families* and *Resilience across Contexts: Family, Work, Culture and Community*. Dr. Taylor also serves on the editorial board of several journals.

Gary Waters is the head men's basketball coach at Kent State University. A two-time Mid American Conference coach of the year, Waters has led his teams to NCAA and NIT tournament appearances. For ten years, Waters served as an associate professor of student development and psychology at Ferris State University. Prior to coming to Kent State, Waters served as associate head coach at Eastern Michigan University. He is the creator of the nationally acclaimed Gary Waters basketball camps, which emphasize interpersonal values along with athletic skills. Currently, his research interests focus on black male adolescents and sports.